The Science of the Kabbalah

by Lazare Lenain

Published in 1823

Including the Preface by
Papus to the 1909 edition
& new Appendices giving
usable sigils and seals

Translated by
Piers A. Vaughan

June 2020

Library of Congress Control Number: 2020909687

© Piers A. Vaughan 2020
All rights reserved. No part of this publication may be reproduced, distributed, or transmitted in any form or by any means, including photocopying, recording, or other electronic or mechanical methods, without the prior written permission of the publisher, except in the case of brief quotations embodied in critical reviews and certain other noncommercial uses permitted by copyright law. For permission requests, write to the publisher at the address below.

ISBN 978-1-947907-09-6

Rose Circle Publications
P.O. Box 854
Bayonne, NJ 07002, U.S.A.
www.rosecirclebooks.com

Contents

Contents 3
Introduction... 5
    Preface by Papus 13
    Preface.. 15
    1. On the Name of God and His Attributes 17
    2. On the Origin of the Divine Names 22
    3. Explanation of the 72 Attributes of God 33
    4. Kabbalistic Tables 37
    5. Explanation of the Sacred Calendar 51
    6. Influences of the 72 Geniuses 55
    7. The Geniuses of the Third Class.................................... 99
    8. Kabbalistic Astrology with Favorable Influences 109
    9. Favorable Influences 132
    10. The Etymology of the Name Jehovah 138
    Appendix A: Creation of Names of Geniuses................ 143
    Appendix B: 28 Houses of the Moon................................ 145
    Appendix C: The Mysterious Seal of the Sun 147
    Appendix D: Sigils of the 72 Geniuses............................ 149
    Appendix E: Rosicrucian Sigils 157
    Appendix F: Lévi's Seals of the 72 Geniuses.................... 171
    Appendix G: Lévi's Notes.. 187

Acknowledgements

The translator would like to thank Mathieu Ravignat, Chic and Tabby Cicero, Stewart Clelland, Aaron Leitch, Barry Eastham, Patrick O'Sullivan and Derek Dunivan for their continuing support and encouragement, and in helping to answer important questions during the translation of this book.

The day we think we know everything is the day we die from a surfeit of arrogance! The most insightful comments can sometimes come from the newest student…

Note: *The Sigils and Seals in Appendices E and F are small since there are six to a page. This means they're difficult to read. However, the purpose was to see them together rather one at a time. Files of the **full-size seals** can be obtained free at* **www.rosecirclebooks.com** *under the Blogs concerning Lenain.*

It's recommended that you bookmark and visit the site regularly for updates, notifications of new books, and other information –
PV.

Introduction

Those who have purchased this book are unlikely to have picked it up at an airport bookstore as something fun to read on a flight. I have to assume that those who have decided to obtain it have a working knowledge of the subject matter in advance.

This book represents the first translation of Lazare Lenain's seminal book on the Shemhamephorash into English. Since its first appearance in 1823, it was been a key source for both the Martinist and Golden Dawn traditions. Many books written since have referenced it, notably R. Ambelain's *La Kabbale Pratique*, which quoted extensively from it. This makes it important in its own right.

It is regrettable that although Lenain had intended to write a sequel to it if it received suitable acclaim, as he mentions in his book, apparently he didn't; since the most mysterious omission is the actual seals or sigils themselves (for the purposes of this book a 'sigil' is a glyph or name of an angel or genius – what it or we would call the entity – while a seal is a composite image, usually contained within a circle drawn on parchment or other appropriate material, by which we would perform a ceremony of invocation or evocation in order to invite it to be present or to accomplish a given task). Indeed, I included a frontispiece to his original book, on page 11, in which he states "We are now engraving the Kabbalistic Sphere, representing the mysterious Talismans of the 72 Geniuses ruling over the Sphere and over the Elements with their division into the 12 Signs of the Zodiac; and this will be sold separately with an explanation for 3 Francs, or 2 Frances for subscribers." Whether this supplement was ever produced and whether there were subscribers who received it is a matter of conjecture: to date no such supplement has come into the public domain.

No doubt he was inspired in this by the monumental *Origine des Cultes ou Religion Universelle* by Charles-François Dupuis, whose three-volume masterpiece was accompanied by a fourth book containing the Plates for the volumes, and which he quotes extensively.

Another challenge has been the errors which crept into both the original publication and subsequent editions. For example, a number of the Latin biblical quotations accompanying the descriptions of the 72 Geniuses used in the Rituals and Seals give incorrect Psalm and Verse numbers; while the subsequent editions of Papus and more recent ones in French have managed to miscopy the quotations themselves, leading to the translator having to spend significant time comparing them to the original Latin Vulgate Bible in order to correct them, both in the text and some of the Seals.

Which brings us to the question of the Seals. In Lenain's book, he uses an example from Dupuis' book *Origine des Cultes ou Religion Universelle* and the other frequently quoted book by Kircher, *Œdipus Egyptiacus* to give an example in Chapter 9 of the 'Mysterious Seal of the Sun', without giving an image of the seal. This Seal is now included in Appendix C.

When Lenain didn't produce a list of the Seals he intended to accompany this volume, the vacuum was – of course – filled by others. Both McGregor Mathers of the Hermetic Order of the Golden Dawn towards the end of the 19th Century, and Robert Ambelain in the late 1940s gravitated towards the extensive esoteric archives in the Librairie de l'Arsenal in Paris, and homed in on Manuscript 2495 in search of the absent seals, each including them in their respective systems for the invocation of the Shemhamephorash, or 72 angels. However, since then controversy has arisen over their use, and therefore the translator has included two more systems for practitioners to use: a variation based on the Rosicrucian Rose used by the Golden Dawn and other currents to generate Angelic Sigils; and a recreation of the system provided by Eliphas Lévi in some of his private (now public!) teachings to his followers. In the latter the images are sometimes lacking, and the translator has had to interpret some Seals from descriptions which can be less than a few words long. However, the application of consistent formulae has, he believes, made these workable.

In all this it is worth mentioning that Mathieu Ravignat was the first to draw my attention to the Lévi seals and to their relevance to the present work, and whose realization now forms the contents of Appendix F. In the future he plans to dig deeper in order to trace their origins and use in the French Esoteric Tradition.

As ever, while doing my best to translate this seminal work, to correct errors and to add usable Sigils and Seals to bring the work to life, all errors are mine alone, and I apologize in advance if any mistakes are detected or if anyone disagrees with my interpretations. Nevertheless, I have always maintained that the good Angels are tolerant of our human errors, and that any errors committed through human frailty will be forgiven!

Piers A. Vaughan
Spring 2020

THE SCIENCE
OF THE KABBALAH

or

THE ART OF KNOWING THE GOOD GENIUSES

That affect the destiny of men; with an explanation of their talismans and mysterious characters, and the true manner of composing them; following the doctrine of the ancient Egyptian, Arab and Chaldean Mages, collected from the most famous Authors who have written about the High Sciences.

DEDICATED TO LOVERS OF TRUTH,
BY LENAIN

Descend from highest heaven, wise Truth,
Spread upon my words thy strength and clarity.
VOLTAIRE, *Henriade*, 1st Canto.

IN AMIENS,

Chez L'AUTEUR, in the Reading Room, Pl. Saint-Firmin S, N.I.

1823

A PARIS,

Chez { A. EYMERY, libraire, rue Mazarine, N. 30;
DELAUNAY, libraire, au Palais-Royal, galeries de bois,
E. BABEUF, rue Saint-Honoré, N. 72, hôtel d'Aligre.

ET A BRUXELLES,

Chez E. BABEUF, libraire, rue de la Montagne, N. 307, section 7, quartier du Parc.

Les exemplaires de cet Ouvrage ont été déposés à la Bibliothèque royale. Je déclare que je poursuivrai, selon la rigueur des lois, tout contrefacteur ou débitant du présent Ouvrage qui ne sera point signé de ma main. J'assure à celui qui me fera connaître le contrefacteur ou débitant, la moitié du dédommagement que la loi m'accorde.

Lenain.

Nota. L'on grave en ce moment la *Sphère Cabalistique*, représentant les Talismans mystérieux des 72 GÉNIES dominant sur la sphère et sur les éléments, avec leur division dans les 12 Signes du Zodiaque; elle se vendra séparément avec l'analyse, 3 francs, et 2 francs pour les souscripteurs. *Les lettres doivent être affranchies.*

Preface by Papus

ORDRE KABBALISTIQUE DE LA ROSE†CROIX

No publication could benefit the progress of Kabbalistic studies more than the reissue of Lenain's very rare tract.

Like all truly initiatory work, this small volume is the starting point for fruitful meditations.

Indeed, the Kabbalah can only be studied following a dual method. Books and manuscripts serve only as a starting point, and meditation aided by the assistance of the Invisible Plane alone can accomplish the rest.

I hope that reading Lenain's work will tempt many people to further their studies by reading Stanislas de Guaita and Saint-Yves d'Alveydre, then Lacuria and Fabre d'Olivet. The reader will then be able to address original works such as the Zohar, *reissued by Lajuma, and the* Sepher Yetzirah *to which I've devoted a few studies.*

But I cannot repeat too much that without the assistance of the Invisible Plane, no real progress can be made in these studies.

The editors of this publication therefore deserve to be seriously encouraged, and I extend our congratulations to them in the name of the Ordre Kabbalistique de la Rose†Croix.

For the Chambre de Direction of the Order,
D^R. PAPUS,
Grand Master of the Ordre Kabbalistique de la Rose†Croix.

Preface

The purpose of this Work is to make the Public aware of what Magic is, so that each may obtain a correct notion of it, for ignorance demonizes everything it doesn't understand. It shouldn't be confused with the LITTLE ALBERT, THE RED DRAGON, and so many other rhapsodies that don't deserve to be mentioned.

It's the result of a work on which I have long meditated to rediscover a *Science*[1] that was lost in the night of time. For the little that remains from the ancients is found only in fragments in a few rare works, most of which are not printed. In general, the authors who were concerned with this subject wrote in such an obscure, abstract way that it's impossible to understand them unless one has the key.

So, I limited myself to writing as clearly and simply as possible, so that all readers will understand it; it's even classical in its approach, if perhaps I may use that expression.

I've noticed, moreover, that all those who've written about the *Occult Sciences* have all veiled their writings, some through the use of enigmas, others by symbols and emblems; others have used the fables of Mythology[2], in order to hide their mysteries from the profane: so that their secrets were known only to their Adepts.

I won't promise to do the impossible; I only intend to talk about the Science of the Ancient Egyptians, Chaldeans, Arabs, etc.

Finally, the results of my research and my vigils have led me to a knowledge of the GOOD GENIUSES. I was particularly interested in learning about their influences, their Elemental qualities, the various parts of the globe over which they preside with their revolutions through the days and hours; and finally, their mysterious talismans which I collected with the utmost care from the rarest manuscripts, as well as their explanation and how to create them, so that they may be favorable to those who invoke

---

[1] As previously explained, *la science* in French can mean 'science' or 'knowledge' – PV.
[2] Those who wish to know the mystical explanation of the fables of the Ancients and the mysteries of all Religions should read *l'Origine des Cults*, by Dupuis. If you apply yourself to the reading of this book, you will easily discover all the secret mysteries of the Occult Sciences, although I do not share other aspects of Dupuis' system.

them. To that end, I have set them out in order in the Kabbalistic sphere.

With the help of those tables you will see the days and the hours which the GENIUSES rule; so that to know a person's GENIUS, it's enough to have the day and time of their birth. Then, if you look for the day and time in those same tables, you will find the name of the person's GENIUS, and the influence it has over their good and negative destiny.

This, dear Reader, is the product of my research; I hope you find it useful.

LAZARE LENAIN

THE SCIENCE
OF THE KABBALAH

1. *On the Name of God and His Attributes*

The Kabbalists express the name of God by a single letter named *yod*, written thus ׳ ; it forms the tenth Hebrew letter, and also corresponds to the number 10.

The unity of this number represents the first principle, the zero and a hieroglyphic character that forms the emblem of the world.[3]

The first proportion of the compass, that is, the first geometric figure, results in the number 10. It's necessary to rely on a point, without which one cannot act; if you extend that point, you make it into a line; by extending that line, you make it into a surface, and by going through that surface, you make it into body that has the same shape as the zero. The point at the center forms the unity that gives the number 1; the value of these two figures gives 10, symbol of God and the Universe.[4]

From one point to the number 1, etc., everything exists; and beyond the number 1, and the form of a point, infinity begins... But before infinity, before the number 1, and before the form of a point, there is nothing.

Consequently, *nothing* is the principle of all things with which God created all that exists in the Universe.

---

[3] The first Egyptians worshipped the Supreme Being represented by an imperceptible point in the center of a circle.

Adepts divide all Sacerdotal and Masonic knowledge into ten grades, that is, it's necessary to go through ten different works before entering the Sanctuary of Nature.

It's only after acquiring these ten degrees of knowledge that one arrives at the perfection of the Great Work.

[4] It's for this reason that sages always say '*Q* God', etc., in their prayers; the 'O' must be uttered before anything else while aspiring.

The Mages represent the three principal attributes of Deity by the letter yod, repeated three times, in the form of a triangle enclosed in a circle.[5]

The first attribute is Time, symbol of eternity. It is the emblem of the Eternal Father which is divided into three parts: the past, the present and the future.

The second is Space, which represents infinity, which is divided into longitude and latitude; it is the symbol of the Cross and of Christ.

The third is Matter, which is divided and subdivided to infinity by the perpetual and universal movement, symbol of the Eternal Spirit, which is the World Soul, or the Holy Spirit.

All that exists in Nature passes through this mystical triangle, that is to say, everything grows, is destroyed and reproduces itself.[6]

The Great Name of God, worshipped by all the wise philosophers of the Universe, is called Jehovah (יהוה): this Sacred Name is known to all scholars; it is composed of four Hebrew letters.

The ancient sages and the first founders of the Nations of the world wrote this name, each in their own language, with four letters[7], and all these Divine Names refer to the different attributes of the Divinity; they correspond to the great Quaternary Name which presides over the Earth[8], to the four cardinal points, the four Elements and the four seasons that present us with the Cross.

The first initial letter *yod* of the name Jehovah יהוה, expresses the Father or the First Person, the two *heh* הה symbolize the two natures

---

[5] These three letters have much to do with the Masonic dots placed in the form of a square (∴); Father Kircher speaks of them knowledgeably in his book *Œdipus Egyptiacus*, Vol. 2, pp. 24, 106 and 287.

[6] Holy History presents us with three major events which should be fixed in the mind of the Wise: first, the Creation from which came the generation of beings, then the Flood which was their destruction, and then Redemption by Christ, Regenerator of the human race.

[7] This phrase was taken up by Papus when he crafted the Rituals of the Ordre Martiniste, and a lecture refers to the interesting fact that, in many languages, the name of Deity is composed of four letters, the greatest exception, of course, being contemporary English! They are listed in Chapter 4 – PV.

[8] The celestial Divinities are invoked by the number three, and those which preside over the Earth by the number four.

of the Son, both agent and patient, and the letter *vav* ו which unites them represents the Holy Spirit, the Ruach Elohim, that is, the Spirit of God which unraveled chaos.

Voltaire[9], speaking about this name, says that "it's only in France that one pronounces this as 'Jehovah', and that one should pronounce (*ieve*); this is how it is written in Sanchuniathon.[10] It's from the name of the four vowels i, e, o, u, that this sacred name was formed in the East; some pronounced *ieoh*, in aspiring *ieova*, the others *yeaou*, it always took four letters, although here we're rendered it in five, for lack of ability to express these four characters."

He adds, according to the comment of Clement of Alexandria, "that by grasping the true pronunciation of that Name, one could cause death to a man; Clement gives an example of this." And in another place that "the Jews haven't pronounced this name for a long time; it was common to the Phoenicians and the Egyptians. It signified 'that which is', and from that probably comes the inscription of Isis: *I am all that is.*"

The Hebrew Kabbalists say that God communicated to Moses the true pronunciation of His Ineffable Name on Mount Sinai, together with all the principal mysteries of the Law: it was then that this Name was carefully hidden by Moses in the folds of the lining of the priestly regalia.

According to Kircher[11], the High Priest alone had the right and the secret to pronounce it by these characters, once in a week.[12] Others say "that the High Priest uttered it in the Temple only once a year, on the 10th of the month of Tishri (September)[13], a day of fasting and atonement; it was then that Jehovah was called Shemhamephorash שמהמפורש, that is, a name well pronounced and well explained; but it was recommended that the people make a loud noise during this ceremony, so that this Sacred Name would

---

[9] Voltaire, *Dictionnaire philosophique*, see the word Jehovah.
[10] An ancient Phoenician writer – PV.
[11] Kircher, *Œdpius Egyptiacus*, Vol. 2, Ch. 2.
[12] See *Thuileur des 33 degrés de l'Écossisme*, p. 92, 1813 edition. Paris, Delaunay, bookseller, Palais-Royal.
[13] According to others, it's the month of March.

be heard only by those entitled to hear it, for any other, say the Jews, would have been immediately struck by death."

According to modern philosophers, the name Jehovah refers to the Universal Word[14], or *I Am That I Am*.

Others call him the Triple and Generative God, because all the other Divine Names derive from it, and the essence of Divinity is contained within it.

The Adepts and Kabbalists represent the tetragram Jehovah thus[15]:

They enclose these sacred characters in a triangle or delta, and the decomposition of this Name results in three other Names that are given to the three Persons of the Holy Trinity (see the talisman in the frontispiece.)

Here are the explanations of these mystical and symbolic characters.

The first letter of the triangle is called *yod* י ; it's the Name of the God of Abraham, which expresses the Living God; this letter is attributed to God the Father, Who is the First Person and the First Cause which produces and is not produced, that is, that the other Persons emanate from Him, because He is the First Principle of all that exists and He has no principle other than Himself.

The second Name is composed of two letters יה, which means *Yah* (God); it is the name of the God of Isaac, that is, the True God, and is attributed to the Son, the Second Person, Who was produced and engendered, and whose ability is to produce.[16]

---

[14] *Observations sur la parole universelle, ou Jehovah*, printed in Paris, in 1804; Widow Nyon, rue du Jardinet.
[15] See the great magic calendar of Tycho Brahé. (It's also found in *le Thuileur écossais*).
[16] The prophet Isaiah (ch. 7, v. 4), wished to express the dual nature of the Son of God, and the hypostatic union of the Word to human nature, that is to say to the Son of Mary, by the name Emmanuel (*nobiscum Deus*), which means God with us.

The third Name is composed of three letters יהו, which means *Iao*, which is the Name of the God of Jacob, that is, the Holy God, attributed to the Holy Spirit.

These three Persons form the triple triangle[17], the symbol of hypostatic union which constitutes the unity and the identity of the Divine Essence, which is communicated to each Person or Nature without division, that is, the Holy Ghost is produced by the Father and the Son, and produces nothing of Itself; but it proceeds in all things from the two Persons.

The fourth Name is made of four letters יהוה; it contains in it all the mysteries of wisdom; that is why the Kabbalists call this mystical triangle the seal of the Living God; and note that the number of letters in the decomposition of that Name amounts to the number 10.

St. Matthew also gives this name to Jesus (ch. 1, v. 23).

Theologians explain this *nobiscum Deus* by the Man-God, or the Theandric composite.

[17] This triple triangle corresponds to the number 9; the unity at the center is 1, which forms the number 10. It contains several mysteries... Major reasons prevent me from saying more... I open the door to the Sanctuary, it's up to you to enter it... Holy Scripture itself teaches us to learn these words: *Seek, and ye shall find; ask, and it shall be given you; knock, and it shall be opened unto you.* [The attentive reader will note the similarity between this and what Saint-Martin says about the numbers 1, 9 and 10 in *Of Errors & Truth*. While it's not possible for Lenain and Saint-Martin to have met, there is every indication that Lenain was familiar with the latter's works. The close fit may be another reason why Papus not only republished this book but used parts of it in his Rituals – PV.]

2. On the Origin of the Divine Names their Attributes and Their Influences on the Universe

God created all things by weight, number and measure; it is for that reason that Magi and wise philosophers claim that all beings have received an attribute from Him.

From this they state in principle that every number contains a mystery and an attribute which is connected to some Divinity or Intelligence.

Then they draw this conclusion, that everything that exists in Nature forms a chain of causes and effects that multiply infinitely, and that each of these causes always relates to a certain number.

It's up to God alone to know its relationship and infinity.

The ancient Rabbis, Philosophers and Kabbalists, each according to their systems, explained the order, harmony and influences of the heavens upon the world by the twenty-two Hebrew letters that make up the mystical alphabet of the Hebrews.[18]

Here is the explanation of the mysteries contained in this alphabet.

From *aleph* א to the letter *yod* י, it indicates the Invisible World, that is, the Angelic World, which are the Sovereign Intelligences receiving the influences of the first eternal Light, attributed to the Father, from Whom everything emanates.

From the letter *kaph* כ to the one called *tzaddi* צ there, are designated the various Orders of Angels who inhabit the Visible World, that is, the Astrological World, attributed to God the Son, which refers to the Divine Wisdom which created this infinity of globes circulating in the vastness of space, each of which is under the safe-keeping of an Intelligence specifically charged by the Creator to preserve them and maintain them in their orbits, so that no star can disturb the order and harmony He has established.

---

[18] Kircher, *Œdpius Egyptiacus*, Vol. 2, p. 125.
  See also the book entitled *l'Ombre Idéale de la Sagesse universelle* ('The Ideal Shadow of Universal Wisdom'), by Fr. François Marie; 6th image, 1679 edition.

2. On the Origin of the Divine Names 23

From the letter *tzaddi* צ to the last letter *tav* ת, the Elemental World, attributed by the philosophers to the Holy Ghost, is distinguished. It is the sovereign Being of beings Who gives soul and life to all creatures.

It's in the sphere of the Elements that the Order of Angels reigns, influencing the destiny of men. They rule over all living beings; they are also responsible for supporting the generations and multiplying the different species of creatures to infinity.

I will now explain the twenty-two Hebrew letters individually, with the attributes of the Divine Names and Intelligences corresponding to each of those letters. According to the Kabbalistic system *aleph* א, the first letter of all alphabets, corresponds to the first name of God, *Eheieh* אהיה, which is interpreted as Divine Essence. The Kabbalists call it 'He whom the eye has not seen', because it rises to the most sublime elevation, even higher than the Seraphim; it sits in the world called *Ain Soph* אין סוף, which means infinity.

Its attribute is called *Kether* כתר, which is interpreted as Crown or Diadem; it rules over the angels, called by the Hebrews Chayoth ha-kodesch חיות הקדש, which is to say, the Animals of Holiness; it forms the first chorus of angels called the Seraphim שרפים.[19]

The second letter is called *beth*, represented thus ב; the second Divine Name[20] corresponding to this letter, is called *bachour* בחור (*electus juvenis*). It refers to the Angels of the Second Order, called by the Hebrews Auphanim אופנים, that is, Forms or Wheels, which the Orthodox call the Cherubim כרובים: it is by their ministry that Jehovah יהוה unraveled chaos; its number is called *Chokmah* חכמה, that is, Wisdom.

The third letter is called *gimel* ג; it corresponds to the name *gadol* גדול (*magnus*), which means Great; it also refers to the Angels of the Third Order, whom the Hebrews call Aralim ארלים, that is, the

---

[19] Agrippa gives the explanation of the nine choirs of Angels, but he doesn't explain the three worlds; see on this subject the third book of his *Occult Philosophy*.
[20] The twenty-two names of God, corresponding to the twenty-two Hebrew letters, are found in *Thuileur des 33 degrés de l'Écossisme*, pp. 94 and 95.

Great and Strong Angels, names by the Kabbalists as Thrones, the Third Choir of Angels; it's through their ministry that God, Tetragrammaton-Elohim, maintains the form of fluid matter. Its attribute is called *Binah* בונה, which means Providence and Intelligence.

Daleth, the fourth letter ד, represents the name *dagoul* דגול (*insignis*); it also corresponds to the Angels of the Fourth Order, which the Hebrews call Chashmalim חשמלים, that is, the Dominations which make up the Fourth Choir of Angels; it is through their ministry that God, El אל, represents the effigies of bodies and all the various forms of matter. Its attribute is called *Chesed* חסד, which means Mercy and Kindness.

The fifth is named *heh* ה, from which comes the name *hadour* הדור (*formosus, majestosus*), which means the Majesty of God; it indicates the Fifth Order, named by the Hebrews the Seraphim שרפים, and according to the Kabbalists the Chorus of Powers. It's through their ministry that God, Elohim Gibor אלהים גיבור produces the Elements; its number is called *pechad* פחד, which means Fear and Judgment, which the Kabbalists attribute to the left side of God; its attribute is *Geburah* גבורה, which means Strength and Power.

Vav, the sixth letter is written thus ו, from which is formed the name *vezio* וזיו (*cum splendore*), this letter refers to the Sixth Order of Angels, called by the Hebrews Melekim מלכים, that is to say, Choir of Virtues; it's by their ministry that God, Eloah-Vedaath אלוה ודעת, produces the metals and all that exists in the Mineral Kingdom. Its attribute is *Tiphereth* תיפארת, which is interpreted as Beauty, Sun, Splendor.

Zayin ז, the seventh letter, from which comes the name *zakai* זכי (*purus, mundus*), corresponds to the Angels of the Seventh Order, named by the Kabbalists the Children of Elohim, and according to the Orthodox, Principalities; it is through their ministry that God, Tetragrammaton-Tzabaoth, produces the plants, and all that exists in the Vegetable Kingdom. Its attribute is called *Netzach* נצח, which is interpreted as Triumph and Justice.

The eighth letter is called *heth* ח; it refers to the name Hasid חסיד (*misericors*); it also corresponds to the Angels of the Eighth Order, called by the Hebrews Beni-Elohim בני אלהים, that is, Sons of the Gods[21], and according to the Orthodox, the Choir of Archangels; it's by their ministry that God, Elohim-Tzabaoth, produces the animals, and all that exists in the Animal Kingdom. Its attribute is called *Hod* הוד, which means Praise.

The ninth letter is called *teth* ט, which thus drawn, corresponds to the name *tehor* תהור (*mundus, purus*) and to the Angels of the Ninth Order, that is, the Ninth Choir of Angels; they preside over the birth of men; and inspire in them all the illumination necessary to lead them to life eternal. It's through their ministry that Shaddai and El Chaï שדי אלחי send the Guardian Angels to men; it refers to Almighty God who satisfies everything. Its attribute is called Yesod יסוד, which means Foundation.

The tenth letter is named *yod* י, from which comes the name Yah יה (*Deus*), which means God; it refers to the tenth numeration, named by the Hebrews Adonaï-Melech אדני מלך, which means the God-King. Its attributes are Kingdom, Empire and Temple of God; it influences the Anismatic Order of Blessed Souls, called by the Hebrews Ischim אישים, that is to say Heroes, Strong and Blessed Men; they are below the other hierarchies. It's through their ministry that men receive intelligence, industry, and knowledge of Divine things. Here ends the Angelic World.

The eleventh letter is called *kaph* כ, written thus, from which comes the name *kabir* כביר (*potens*), that is to say powerful; it refers to the First Heaven, which is the *primum mobile*, named by the Hebrews El Shaddaï; the *primum mobile* corresponds to the name

---

[21] This name corresponds to Mercury, who is the messenger of the gods.

of God Yod, expressed by a single letter, that is, the First Cause, which puts everything that is mobile in motion.

The first Sovereign Intelligence, which governs the *primum mobile*, that is, the First Heaven of the Astrological World, attributed to the Second Person of the Trinity, is called Metatron מתתרון. His name means Prince of Faces; his mission is to introduce all those who must appear before the Face of the Great God; he has under him Prince Orphiel, with an infinite number of subordinate Intelligences; the Kabbalists say that it was through the ministry of Metatron that God spoke to Moses; it is also through him that all the lower powers of the sensual world receive the virtues of God.[22]

Kaph as a final letter, written thus ך, corresponds to the two Great Names of God, each composed of two Hebrew letters, El אל, Yah יה; they reign over the Intelligences of the Second Order, which govern the heaven of fixed stars, including the twelve Signs of the Zodiac, which the Hebrews call galgol-hamnaziloth גלגל המנזילות. The Intelligence of the Second Heaven is named Raziel רציאל. Its attribute means vision of God, and messenger of God; he has several Princes under him; they are called Magriel, Tsaphiel and Matmoniel.

The Kabbalists[23] say that Raziel was the governor of Adam, and that he receives the influences of God through Metatron, to transmit them to the Powers of the Third Order.

---

[22] Wise philosophers say that the Light of the Word is received by the highest and first Intelligences, and transmitted by them to the lower hierarchies, and from Order to Order, Degree to Degree. See *la Science du Christ et de l'Homme*, Vol. 1, p. 42, 1810 edition.

[23] Rabbi Abraham Ben Diot claims that the first Patriarchs, Prophets and Sage Philosophers all had Angels which were familiar to them. According to him Raziel was the Angel of Adam, the Angel Peliel communicated with Isaac and Jacob; Gabriel with Joseph, Joshua and Daniel; Metatron with Moses; Maltiel with Elijah; Raphaël with the young Tobiah; Cerniel with David; Phadaël with Aximander; Cerael with Avicenna; Hashmaël with Ezekiel; Uriel with Ezdras; Mikaël with Samuel; and Radiel with Solomon.

The same Rabbi adds that each of these Angels gave his disciple, either in writing or in person, the Kabbalah, meaning the Tradition, and that by this means it has always been kept among the Sages.

Thus, it's said that Raziel, who was the master of Adam, brought him a book from God which contained the secrets of very high wisdom, and of which the book called the Zohar speaks.

2. On the Origin of the Divine Names

Lamed ל, the twelfth letter, from which comes the name *limmud* למד (*doctus*), also corresponds to the name Saday שדי, or Shaddaï (*omnipotens*), the name of God in three letters, called the emblem of the Delta; it rules over the Third Heaven, and over the Intelligences of the Third Order which govern the sphere of Saturn; it is the first planet called the errant star, named by the Hebrews Shabbatai שבתאי.[24] Its particular Intelligence is called Shabbatiel שבתיאל; its attribute means contemplation of God; others call it truth of God, or hidden God; he has under him several Princes, who are named Tzaphkiel, Uriel, Cassiel and Agiel: the Kabbalists say that Tzaphkiel was Noah's governor, and Uriel that of Esdras.

According to Kircher[25], Shabbatiel receives God's influences through Raziel, and transmits them to the inferior powers.

The thirteenth letter is called *mem* מ so drawn, where the name *meborak* מברך comes from (*benedictus*), that is, Blessed God; it corresponds to the Fourth Heaven, and the Fourth Name Jehovah יהוה dominates the sphere of Jupiter, named by the Hebrews Tzedek צדק. The Sovereign Intelligence that governs Jupiter's star is called Tzadkiel צדקיאל, who was the governor of Abraham, and Jophiel that of Shem; Tzadkiel receives God's influences through Shebatiel, to transmit them to the Intelligences of the Fifth Order.

Mem as a final letter ם, corresponds to the Fifth Heaven and the Fifth Name of God, Yeheshuah יהשוה composed of five letters; it is the Holy Name of Jesus in Hebrew; it rules over the sphere of Mars, named by the Hebrews Madim מאדים.

The Sovereign Intelligence that governs the Star of Mars is called Kamaël כמאל. He was the governor of Samson; the Kabbalists give him various attributes, such as God's fire, God's punishment, God's help and God's strength; he has under him several Princes, the principals of which are named Samael and Graphiel: Kamaël is responsible for receiving God's influences through Tzadkiel, to transmit them to the Intelligences of the Sixth Order.

---

[24] Dupuis gives the table of the names of the stars according to the Hebrews and the Arabs, Vol. 7, p. 151, *de l'Origine des Cultes*.

[25] Kircher, *Œdipus Egyptiacus*, Vol. 2, pp. 225 and 226.

Nun נ, the fourteenth letter, so drawn, from which comes the name *nora* נורא (*formidabilis*), that is to say Great God; this letter equally corresponds to the name Emmanuel עמנואל (*nobiscum Deus*), and to the Sixth Name of God El-Gibor אלגבור, each composed of six letters, which signifies Strong God; they reign over the Sixth Heaven, which is that of the Sun, named by the Hebrews Shemesh שמש. The first Sovereign Intelligence that governs the sun is named Raphaël רפאל.[26] His attribute means House of God; he has under him several Princes, being; Peliel, Nachiel, Eaphuel and Tardiel. The Kabbalists say that Raphaël was the governor of Isaac and the young Tobiah, and the angel Peliel that of Jacob. Raphaël receives the influences and virtues of God through Kamaël, and then transmits them to the Intelligences of the Ninth Order.

Nun as a final letter ן, so drawn, refers to the Seventh Name of God, Ararita אראריתא composed of seven letters. Its interpretation means (Immutable God[27]); it rules over the Seventh Heaven and over the Intelligences of the Seventh Order that govern the sphere of Venus, named by the Hebrews Nogah נוגה.[28] The first Sovereign Intelligence, which governs the star of Venus, is called Haniel האניאל: the Kabbalists give him various attributes, knowledge of God, love of God, justice of God, and grace of God; he has under him several Princes, who are named Cerviel and Hagiel; the wise Philosophers say that Cerviel was the governor of David. Haniel receives the influences of God through Raphaël, to transmit them to the Intelligences of the Eighth Order.

The fifteenth letter is named *samekh* ס, so drawn, from which comes the name *somek* סומך (*fulciens, firmans*), it also corresponds to the Eighth Name of God, named Shemhamphorash שמהמפורש, composed of eight letters: the Kabbalists call him Holy God, Just

---

[26] The Kabbalists do not agree with one another on the Sun's Intelligence; some say that Raphaël governs the sphere of Mercury and that Mikaël rules the Sun; however the most famous authors name Raphaël as the Intelligence of the Sun.

[27] No Hebrew or Latin epithet is given for this name, which appears in the original in parentheses – PV.

[28] See *l'Origine des cultes*, by Dupuis, p. 161, t. 7.

2. On the Origin of the Divine Names   29

and Terrible; he reigns over the Eighth Heaven, named by the Hebrews *kokab* כוכב, that is to say the star of Mercury. The Intelligence that governs it is called Mikaël מיכאל; he was the governor of Solomon and Samuel; he has Prince Tiriel under him; he receives the power of God through Raphaël, to pass them on to the Angels of the Ninth Order.

The sixteenth letter is called *ayin* ע, thus drawn, where the name *hazaz* עזז (*fortis*) comes from, which means Strong God; it corresponds to the names Jehovah-Tzabaoth יהוה צבאות; it governs the Ninth Heaven, named by the Hebrews Iareach ירח[29] and according to the Arabs Ianeah, that is, the Moon. The Intelligence that governs it is called Gabriel; he was the governor of Joseph, Joshua and Daniel (see footnote 23 above).

Gabriel receives the power of God through Mikaël, to transmit it to the lower Orders that govern the Earth and the Elements. Here the Astrological World ends: then we see the Third World, that is, the Elemental World attributed to the Holy Ghost.

The seventeenth letter is called *peh* פ, so drawn; the Seventeenth[30] Name corresponds to this letter, and is called *phodeh* פודה (*redemptor*), which means Redeemer: the letter *peh* refers to fire, the First Element where the Salamanders live.[31] The Sovereign Intelligence that governs Fire is called by the Hebrews[32], Seraphim שרפים. He has several Princes under him, being: Meneaelop and Arathon; their principal ministers, or chief subalterns are thus named: Casmaran, Gargatel, Tabiel, Gaviel and Festativi. Each religion has its own names because, according to the Magi, the Intelligence of Fire is called Milaïm; the Adepts call him Ptah or

---

[29] Or, more usually Levanah לבנה - PV.
[30] In the original book this is incorrectly called 'Eighteenth' – PV.
[31] See *le comte de Gabalis; ou les Entretiens sur les sciences secrètes et mystérieuses, suivant les principes des anciens mages ou sages cabalistes; ornés de figures cabalistiques* ('the Comte de Gabalis; or the Secret and Mysterious Science Interviews, following the principles of the ancient Magi or wise Kabbalists; decorated with Kabbalistic images'). The best edition is that of Amsterdam, 1700: the author of this book is the Abbé de Villars.
[32] Magic Calendar of Tycho Brahé, 4th series; and Agrippa.

Ardarel[33]; according to the Egyptians it is Naomiphtah[34]; the Arabs call him Phelmanim[35]; the Persians call him Tascheter.[36] The Intelligences of Fire preside in the South in Summer.

Peh as a final letter is drawn thus ף; this letter denotes the Air where the Sylphs live; the Sovereign Intelligence that governs this Element is named by the Hebrews Cherubim כרובמ; it has under it the Princes Amadieh and Agiathon. The principal leaders of the sub-order are called Talvi, Caracasa, Amatiel, Comisoros, Spugliguel and Amadaï. The Intelligences of the Air rule in the Spring season, to the East[37].

The eighteenth letter is called tzaddi צ, so drawn, where the name *tzedek* צדק (*justus*) comes from, which means Righteous God; this letter refers to Water where the Nymphs live. The first Intelligence that governs this Element is called by the Hebrews *tharshish* תרשיש, she has under her the Princes Emachiel and Begud; they have several chiefs in command, namely: Farlas, Amabael, Ctarari, Altarib, Gerenia; in the season of Autumn they rule in the West.[38]

The nineteenth letter is called *koph* ק, so drawn, from which comes the name *kadosh* קדש (*sanctus*), which means Holy God; this letter corresponds to the Earth where the Gnomes live. The Intelligence of Earth is called Ariel; he has under him the Princes Damalech, Taynor and Sayanon, and other subordinate chiefs,

---

[33] According to the *Thuileur Écossais*, p. 201, the four Angels of the Elements are named as follows: Ardarel, Casmaran, Talliud and Furlac: the last plate in this book indicates that the reign of Ptah is eternal. [In English the four Elemental Angels are most commonly spelled: Arel (Fire), Chassan (Air), Taliahad (Water), and Phorlach (Earth) – PV].

[34] The four Angels of the Egyptians, according to Kircher (*Œdipus Egyptiacus*, Vol. 3, p. 55), are named thus: Nemiphtah, Phrisphtah, Neimhisphtah, Niephtah.

[35] The Arabs call them Phelmanim, Phakmin, Liali and Beniac (Kircher, *Œdipus Egyptiacus*, Vol. 2, p. 385.)

[36] According to the Persians, the four Angels who preside over the four corners of the world and the heavens are established as sentinels for the surveillance of the fixed stars. Here are their names: Tascheter, Sarevis, Venant, Haflorang (see *Zoroastre ou le Zend-Avesta*, Vol. 2, and Dupuis, *l'Origine des Cultes*, Vol. 2, p. 93.)

[37] The original book had both the Angels of Air and Water ruling in the West, which is clearly an error. Using the accepted formula, the translator has situated Air in the East and Water in the West – PV.

[38] Curiously, the end of word form of Tzaddi (ץ) is omitted here – PV.

whose names are Ardarael, Tarquam, Guabarel, Torquaret and Rabianira. The Intelligences of Earth preside, in Winter, in the North.

Resh ר, the twentieth letter, so drawn, from whence comes the name *rodeh* רדה (*imperans*), that is, God Who Commands: this letter is attributed to the first principle of God, which applies to the Animal Kingdom, and to Man, the first of all animals, and the only one closest to the Creator by his intelligence and spirit. God created him in his image.

Shin ש, the twenty-first letter, so drawn, whence comes the name Shaddaï שדי (*omnipotens*), which means Omnipotent God; this letter is attributed to the second principle of God, which gives the seed to all vegetable substances.

The twenty-second and final Hebrew letter is called *tav* ת, thus drawn, whence comes the name *tekinah* תחנה (*gratiosus*), which means Gracious God; this letter refers to the third principal of God, who gives the seed to all that exists in the Mineral Kingdom.
The Kabbalists say that this letter is the symbol of man, because it designates the end of all that exists, just as man is the end and perfection of all creatures.

This is what comprises the mystical alphabet of the Hebrews. I am giving a summary of then here with their numbers, because the Israelites have no other form of numbers. That's why every letter has its own numerical value.

Firstly, they divide their alphabet into three sets, as follows:

First series

9.	8.	7.	6.	5.	4.	3.	2.	1.
ט	ח	ז	ו	ה	ד	ג	ב	א

Second series

90.	80.	70.	60.	50.	40.	30.	20.	10.
צ	פ	ע	ס	נ	מ	ל	כ	י

Third series

900.	800.	700.	600.	500.	400.	300.	200.	100.
ץ	ף	ן	ם	ך	ת	ש	ר	ק

In this table, the first series shows units; the second, the tens; and the third the hundreds. These three series also refer to the three worlds shown above; here is that mystical triad, symbol of the Holy Trinity, which the ancient Egyptians and Chaldeans carefully concealed from the profane.

3. Explanation of the 72 Attributes of God and the 72 Angels Who Govern the Universe, and Who Surround the Throne of the Great Jehovah

God being the First Cause of all that exists, it's clear that all our actions must tend towards him, just as the celestial bodies are all drawn towards the center of their vortex, and this infinity of vortexes all tend equally towards a common center.[39]

Thus, man should always strive towards God, without ever deviating from Him, for without Him all is confused and falls into chaos; with Him everything is in order and participates in His Light. The ancient sages were all imbued with these great truths; it was by following these precepts that they became enlightened by the Divine Spirit.

It's for that reason that I said previously, in Chapter One, that His Holy Name contains within it all the mysteries of wisdom. It's by means of its mystical triangle that the Kabbalists have revealed its attributes and mysteries.

The tetragram Jehovah, drawn thus, is composed of ten letters, the first of which is Yod.	י	10
	י ה	15
	י ה ו	21
	י ה ו ה	26
		72

Its numeric value is...	10
The next two letters of the name Iah יה, give…..................	15
Then the three letters of the name IAO יהו give...................	21
And the four letters of the name Jehovah, יהוה, give..........	26
All these numbers added together form........................	72

From this comes the number of 72 attributes of God, and of the 72 Angels that surround His throne.

---

[39] This is what has led some Philosophers say that God is the center of centers.
 One of two things, either you believe it, or you don't believe it: if you admit its existence, you enter into all the consequences of faith... if you don't believe it, my book is useless to you.

According to the testimony of the Zohar, this is the ladder which Jacob saw in a dream, formed of 72 rungs, whose summit, placed on the rays of the sun and moon, was lost in the vastness of the dwellings of Divinity.[40]

It is by means of this ladder that God's influences descend and communicate with all the Orders of the heavenly hierarchies and to all the creatures of the Universe...

(1) The 72 angels preside over the 72 quinaries of heaven, 72 Nations, and the 72 parts of the human body.[41]

(2) Holy Scripture teaches us that, in addition to the twelve Apostles, Jesus Christ chose 72 Disciples who were sent to all parts of the world to proclaim God's word to the Nations.[42]

There were also 72 Elders in the synagogue, and the same number of interpreters of the Old Testament.

The reader should note that the Scriptures contain a mystical and hidden meaning in them; for most of the Divine Names were extracted from the main verses of Scripture by the Magi and Kabbalists.

Thus, the names of the 72 Angels are formed from the three mysterious verses of Chapter 14 of Exodus, namely, the 19th, 20th and 21st, which verses, according to the Hebrew text, each consists of 72 Hebrew letters. The first word of the 19th verse begins with *vaisa* ויכע, the 20th with *vaibo* ויבא, and the 21st with *vaiet* ויט. The way to extract the 72 names from these three verses is as follows:

First write these verses separately, forming three beginning on the left, then take the first letter of the 20th verse, which is the middle one, beginning with the right; these three first letters form the attribute of the Genius; following the same order to the end, you have the 72 attributes of Divine virtues. If you add to each of these

---

[40] This curious reference clearly confirms that Lenain was a Freemason. Anyone who has seen the Tracing Board of the First Degree will recognize this unusual description immediately. For those unfamiliar with the image, this link was working as of May 14, 2020: https://www.masonslibrary.org/item/13-explanation-of-the-first-degree-tracing-board - PV.

[41] Agrippa.

[42] St. Luke, ch. 10, vss. 1 and 17.

3. Explanation of the 72 Attributes of God 35

names one of these two great Divine Names, Yah יה or El אל[43], then you will have the 72 names of the Angels, composed of three syllables, each of which contains in it the name of God, following this verse of Scripture. (*My angel will walk before you; observe him, for he bears my name in him.*)[44]

This is how Kabbalists create their names; there are others who take the first letter of each word which that composes a verse; for example, the name of Jesus in Hebrew, ישו, is formed from the first three letters of the three words of this verse יבא שילה ולי, that is, in Latin, *quo usque veniat Messia*; in English, until the coming of the Messiah. It also appears in the following verse יגוך שמו וית, *permanet nomen ejus*, that is, His Name endures forever; ...similarly, the name Amen אמן is taken from this verse אדני מלך נאמן, *dominus rex fidelis*, which means faithful Lord King.

There are even several other mysterious names which were extracted in this way; we will talk about it in another Chapter.

I think the reader is sufficiently enlightened about the formation of Divine Names and their origin; I will now talk about the names, influences and attributes of the 72 Geniuses, and go into the

---

[43] All Kabbalistic names end with a Divine Name, because there is nothing in the world which isn't sustained by the virtue of God; the Hebrew names end with one of these four names, namely: Iah, El, Ael and Iel. God commanded it from our first father Adam, who gave names to all ariel and earthly creatures.

The Philosopher Jean Belot, curé of Milmont, says positively in his works, page 438, 1704 edition, that the names of the Intelligences that inhabit the East and the West end with these names, El, Iel or Iael, and that those which inhabit the Southern and Northern parts end in Iah and Ael.

Voltaire, in his *Philosophie générale*, and in his *Metaphysique*, Ch. 21, when speaking of the Arabs and Persians, says that all the names of the Persian Angels end in El, which name has as an attribute messenger of God, soldier of God, friend of God.

The Jews also added this name El to the name Iaho, which is a Phoenician name, from which they formed the name Jehovah.

Voltaire adds that the names Eloï, Eloah are also formed from the Persian name El.

[44] These instructions are so mangled in the original it's hard to know if Lenain had decided to obscure the method after all: for a writer usually so clear it seems out of character. For readers who don't know the technique, it's as follows: write the 72 letters comprising verse 19 from right to left (the normal way to write Hebrew). Then write the 72 letters comprising the 20th verse from left to right; then the 72 letters of the 21st verse from left to right again. You will end up with 72 columns of 3 letters, reading downwards. Then add -el, -iel, -iah or -ael after each set of three letters to 'charge' it with a name of God. For example, if you got the letters 'Han', by adding '-ael' you obtain the Angelic name Hanael – PV.

greatest details on their mysteries. To begin with, the following Chapters contain my Kabbalistic Tables which lists the 72 Geniuses; the first contains their names with their attributes; the second, the 72 parts of the globe which are under the influence of these Geniuses[45]; the third indicates the days they rule; and the fourth indicates the days over which they preside.

---

[45] Perhaps a comparison of this Table with the *Steganographia* of Trimethius, or John Dee's experiments to secure spiritual communication with the Geniuses of various Nations would be interesting, while being outside the limits of this translation – PV.

4. Kabbalistic Tables

FIRST KABBALISTIC TABLE

Which lists the names of the 72 Geniuses with their attributes, the first 72 peoples of the earth who were under their influences, and the names that these Peoples give to God; which are all of four letters.

Numerical Order of the 72 Geniuses	Their Names	Names of the 72 first Nations who were under the influence of the 72 Geniuses	The 72 Names of GOD composed of 4 letters according to the languages of the 72 first Nations of the world, corresponding to the 72 Geniuses.
1	Vehuiah	Hebrews	JEHOVAH
2	Jeliel	Turks	AYDI
3	Sitael	Arabs	ALLA
4	Elemiah	Chaldeans	(ANNU)[46]
5	Mahasiah	Egyptians	TEUT
6	Lelahel	Ethiopians	ABGD
7	Achaiah	Armenians	(MAZD)[47]
8	Cahetel	Georgians	MOTI
9	Haziel	Abyssinians	AGZI
10	Aladiah	Persians	EIPI
11	Lauviah	Latins	DEUS
12	Hahaiah	Greeks	TEOS
13	Iezalel	Illyrians	BOOG

---

[46] This was blank, and in a foreign script in the original drawing of Kircher. The earliest God of the Chaldeans is listed at ANU, so ANNU has been inserted for completion – PV.
[47] Similarly, this was blank in the book and in a corrupted script in the Kircher diagram. To preserve the 4-letter theme the name MAZD for Ahura Mazda or Armazd has been inserted – PV.

14	Mebahel	Spanish	DIOS
15	Hariel	Italians	IDIO or IDDIO
16	Hakamiah	French	DIEU
17	Lauviah	Germans	GOTH (GOTT?)
18	Caliel	Polish	BOOG
19	Leuviah	Hungarians	BOGI
20	Pahaliah	Muscovites	TIOS
21	Nelchael	Bohemians	BUEG
22	Ieiaiel	English	GOOD[48]
23	Melahel	Hibernians	DIEH
24	Hahiuiah	Etruscans	ESAR
25	Nith-Haiah	Mages	ORSY
26	Haaiah	Saracens	AGDY or ABDI
27	Ierathel	Copts	TEOS
28	Seehiah	Assyrians	ADED
29	Retiel	Peruvians	SIMI
30	Ormael	Indians	TURA
31	Lecabel	Chinese	TELI
32	Vasariah	Tartars	ANOT
33	Iehuiah	Hesperides	AGAD
34	Lehahiah	Congoese	ANEB
35	Chavakiah	Angolans	ANUP
36	Menadel	Moors	ALLA
37	Aniel	Philosophers	ABDA
38	Haamiah	Kabbalists	AGLA
39	Rehael	Scottish	GOOT
40	Ieiazel	Belgians	GOED
41	Hahahel	Irish	GUDI
42	Mikael	Canadians	BIUD
43	Veualiah	Californians	SOLU

---

[48] To give a sense of just how 'stretched' this was, note that the English 'God' has been rendered as 'Good' in order to fit the pattern!) – PV.

4. Kabbalistic Tables

44	Ielahiah	Mexicans	BOSA
45	Sealiah	People of Quito	HOBO
46	Ariel	Paraguayans	PINO
47	Asaliah	Chilians	HANA
48	Mihael	Japanese	ZACA
49	Vehual	Filipinos	MARA
50	Daniel	Samaritans	POLA
51	Hahasiah	(Barsians)[49]	BILA
52	Imamiah	(Melindais)	ABAG
53	Nanael	Maltese	OBRA
54	Nithael	(Zaflanians)	BORA
55	Mebaiah	Those from Ormus	ALAI
56	Poiel	Those from Aden	ILLI
57	Nemamiah	Cyrenians	POPA
58	Ieialel	(Celamoites)	PARA
59	Harahel	Mesopotamians	ELLA
60	Mitzruel	Tibetans	GENA
61	Umabel	(Bethuians)	SILA
62	Iahhel	(Carmanians)	SUNA
63	Anauel	Cambodians	MIRI
64	Mehiel	Mongols	ALLI
65	Damabiah	Gymnosophists	TARA
66	Manakiel	Brahmans	PORA
67	Eiael	Albanians	BOGO
68	Habuiah	Peloponnesians	DEPOS
69	Rochel	Cretans	DEOS
70	Jabamiah	Beotians	ARIS
71	Haiaiel	Phrygians	ZEUT
72	Mumiah	Thracians	KALO

---

[49] A number of Nations' names are unrecognizable. An exhaustive study of source books has not shed any light on these. Similarly, since Lenain has tinkered with Kircher's original diagram it's impossible to work out what these were originally. Those in doubt have been indicated by parentheses – PV.

Note that this table is the most exact, in comparison to those which may be found in other works, imprints and manuscripts, since the greater part of their names are disfigured and the numerical order confused. Fr. Kircher gives their names and attributes according to the Hebrew text (see *Œedipus Egyptiacus*, Vol. 2, pp. 273 and 287). I have made extensive use of his Table, which I consider to be the most exact. Agrippa also gives it in his *Occult Philosophy*, Book 3, pp. 109 and 110; in the la Haye edition of 1727. It agrees perfectly with Kircher's, in the Hebrew text and the numerical order of names; but it doesn't mention their attributes and gives no details. The three tables which follow are of my invention.

According to Kabbalistic tradition, the confusion at the Tower of Babel gave birth to 72 languages according to the number of families which were there, and they then separated and spread over the face of the Earth to live there. In the course of time, all these families peopled the various countries of the world, and then became the Nations.

All these peoples always revered the eldest among them as their chief. As a result, he was obliged to maintain order and discipline among those he governed; he imposed upon them the obligation for them to respect one another, and to lend mutual aid; thus, he was at the same time the head of the priesthood, the law and the country he inhabited.

This is how the descendants of Noah were the founders of the 72 first Nations of the world. As they all worshipped the God of Abraham, Isaac and Jacob, Who is the first and the Greatest Name, composed of four letters, Jehovah יהוה, they all wrote, in their own languages, the same name with four letters; which signifies that God is worshipped by all the peoples of the world, in all languages, and in all religions. Wherever the same intent exists; it's always the same God Who is worshipped, because all are connected to Him.

As the number four is the symbol of the Cross which rules over the Earth, it tells us that, as a result the Cross will extend over all the globe and Christ will reign over all the Universe. That is how everything will be accomplished…

SECOND KABBALISTIC TABLE

Which lists the influences of the 72 Geniuses which govern the 72 parts of the Earth[50], the sphere and the whole Universe. It serves to know the Genius which rules over man's physical constitution.

The 1st Genius rules from March 20 to March 24
The 2nd Genius from March 25 to April 3
The 3rd Genius from April 4 to April 8
The 4th Genius from April 9 to April 13
The 5th Genius from April 14 to Apri 18
The 6th Genius from April 19 to April 23
The 7th Genius from April 24 to April 28
The 9th Genius from April 29 to May 3
The 10th Genius from May 4 to May 8
The 11th Genius from May 9 to May 13
The 12th Genius from May 14 to May 18
The 13th Genius from May 19 to May 23
The 14th Genius from May 24 to May 28
The 15th Genius from May 29 to June 2
The 16th Genius from June 3 to June 7
The 17th Genius from June 8 to June 12
The 18th Genius from June 13 to June 17
The 19th Genius from June 18 to June 22
The 20th Genius from June 23 to June 27
The 21st Genius from June 28 to July 2
The 22nd Genius from July 3 to July 7
The 23rd Genius from July 8 to July 12
The 24th Genius from July 13 to July 17
The 25th Genius from July 18 to July 22

---

[50] In the preceding Table we saw that Kircher had a Genius for each Nation, which is an error; the names are subject to change in the same way the greatness of Kingdoms, which sometimes include several different Nations under the same denomination.
The world has had frequent revolutions; new peoples have taken the place of older ones. By following Kircher's system one can therefore be in error, by giving two or three Geniuses to a single people due to the different names they've been called.
I've corrected this error by dividing the sphere into 72 equal parts, as may be seen in the Table above; so that those who inhabit the part of the globe corresponding to the first five degrees of the sphere are truly under the influence of the first Genius, and those who are born between March 20 to 24 inclusive are under the same influence.

The 26th Genius from July 23 to July 27
The 27th Genius from July 28 to August 1
The 28th Genius from August 2 to August 6
The 29th Genius from August 7 to August 11
The 30th Genius from August 12 to August 16
The 31st Genius from August 17 to August 21
The 32nd Genius from August 22 to August 26
The 33rd Genius from August 27 to August 31
The 34th Genius from September 1 to September 5
The 35th Genius from September 6 to September 10
The 36th Genius from September 11 to September 15
The 37th Genius from September 16 to September 20
The 38th Genius from September 21 to September 25
The 39th Genius from September 26 to September 30
The 40th Genius from October 1 to October 5
The 41st Genius from October 6 to October 10
The 42nd Genius from October 11 to October 15
The 43rd Genius from October 16 to October 20
The 44th Genius from October 21 to October 25
The 45th Genius from October 26 to October 30
The 46th Genius from October 31 to November 4
The 47th Genius from November 5 to November 9
The 48th Genius from November 10 to November 14
The 49th Genius from November 15 to November 19
The 50sth Genius from November 20 to November 24
The 51st Genius from November 25 to November 29
The 52nd Genius from November 30 to December 4
The 53rd Genius from December 5 to December 9
The 54th Genius from December 10 to December 14
The 55th Genius from December 16 to December 19
The 56th Genius from December 20 to December 24
The 57th Genius from December 25 to December 29
The 58th Genius from December 30 to January 3
The 59th Genius from January 4 to January 8
The 60th Genius from January 9 to January 13
The 61st Genius from January 14 to January 18
The 62nd Genius from January 19 to January 23
The 63rd Genius from January 24 to January 28
The 64th Genius from January 29 to February 2
The 65th Genius from February 3 to February 7
The 66th Genius from February 8 to February 12

The 67th Genius from February 13 to February 17
The 68th Genius from February 18 to February 22
The 69th Genius from February 23 to February 27
The 70th Genius from February 28 to March 4
The 71st Genius from March 5 to March 9
The 72nd Genius from March 10 to March 14

From the Table above one can determine the names of the Genius which rules over man's material body. These 72 names are each composed of 5 Hebrew letters, which make 72 times 5 letters or 5 x 72; these numbers when added give 360, which is the number of the 360 degrees of the sphere.

These 72 Geniuses govern the 72 rays of Heaven, and the 72 parts of the circle which contains a space of 5 degrees, or 5 days over which each of them presides.

The Mages and Kabbalists begin the year on the first degree of Aries, that is, March 20.

The Second Table above shows that the first Genius rules from March 20 to 24 inclusive, and so forth. By following this order, you will come to the 72nd Genius, who rules from March 10 to 14. Five days therefore remain, which are consecrated by the Egyptians and Persians to five divinities, named the Epagomenes, which they call the *Sacred Pentad*.[51]

Modern Kabbalists attribute these five last days to the Intelligences which govern the four Elements (according to the ancients), the four Cardinal Points, the Equinoxes and the Solstices and the four Seasons: one day remains, which is dedicated to the Great Principle (God); when the year is bissextile, two days remain: the number attributed to the Genius of man.

Orpheus, in his theology, admitted 360 days or Geniuses, seeing that there are that number of degrees in a circle and in the year, of which five days are deducted and dedicated to five divinities, namely: Osiris, Apollo, Isis, Typhon and Venus.

There were 360 urns used by the priests of Egypt, to make libations in honor of Osiris; from this comes the origin of the 260 divisions of the circle which decorate the tomb of Ozymandias; the

---

[51] See *l'Origine des Cultes*, by Dupuis, Vol. 1, Year 3 edition, pp. 233, 328 and 565.

Egyptian priests made the libations in the town of Achante, beyond the Nile towards Libya, 20 stadiums[52] from Memphis: there was there a bored cask into which the priest poured 365 cups of water from the Nile, representing the year, that is, one for each day.

THIRD KABBALISTIC TABLE

Which lists the five revolutions of the 72 Geniuses over the days. It serves to know the Genius which rules over a man's morals.

The 1st Genius rules Mar. 20, May 31, Aug. 11, Oct. 22, Jan. 2
The 2nd rules Mar. 21, Jun. 1, Aug. 12, Oct. 23, Jan. 3
The 3rd rules Mar. 22, Jun. 2, Aug. 13, Oct. 24, Jan. 4
The 4th rules Mar. 23, Jun.3, Aug. 14, Oct. 25, Jan. 5
The 5th rules Mar. 24, Jun. 4, Aug. 15, Oct.26, Jan. 6
The 6th rules Mar. 25, Jun. 5, Aug. 16, Oct. 27, Jan.7
The 7th rules Mar. 26, Jun. 6, Aug. 17, Oct. 28, Jan. 8
The 8th rules Mar. 27, Jun. 7, Aug. 18, Oct. 29, Jan. 9
The 9th rules Mar. 28, Jun. 8, Aug. 19, Oct. 30, Jan. 10
The 10th rules Mar. 29, Jun. 9, Aug. 20, Oct. 31, Jan. 11
The 11th rules Mar. 30, Jun. 10, Aug. 21, Nov. 1, Jan. 12
The 12th rules Mar. 31, Jun. 11, Aug. 22, Nov. 2, Jan. 13
The 13th rules Apr. 1, Jun. 12, Aug. 23, Nov. 3, Jan. 14
The 14th rules Apr. 2, Jun. 13, Aug. 24, Nov. 4, Jan. 15
The 15th rules Apr. 3, Jun. 14, Aug. 25, Nov. 5, Jan. 16
The 16th rules Apr. 4, Jun. 15, Aug. 26, Nov. 6, Jan. 17
The 17th rules Apr. 5, Jun. 16, Aug. 27, Nov. 7, Jan. 18
The 18th rules Apr. 6, Jun. 17, Aug. 28, Nov. 8, Jan. 19
The 19th rules Apr. 7, Jun. 18, Aug. 29, Nov. 9, Jan. 20
The 20th rules Apr. 8, Jun. 19, Aug. 30, Nov. 10, Jan. 21
The 21st rules Apr. 9, Jun. 20, Aug. 31, Nov. 11, Jan. 22
The 22nd rules Apr. 10, Jun. 21, Sept. 1, Nov. 12, Jan. 23
The 23rd rules Apr. 11, Jun. 22, Sept. 2, Nov. 13, Jan. 24
The 24th rules Apr. 12, Jun. 23, Sept. 3, Nov. 14, Jan. 25
The 25th rules Apr. 13, Jun. 24, Sept. 4, Nov. 15, Jan. 26
The 26th rules Apr. 14, Jun. 25, Sept. 5, Nov. 16, Jan. 27
The 27th rules Apr. 15, Jun. 26, Sept. 6, Nov. 17, Jan. 28
The 28th rules Apr. 16, Jun. 27, Sept. 7, Nov. 18, Jan. 29

---

[52] A *stade* or 'stadium' was about 202 yards – PV.

4. Kabbalistic Tables

The 29th rules Apr. 17, Jun. 28, Sept. 8, Nov. 19, Jan. 30
The 30th rules Apr. 18, Jun. 29, Sept. 9, Nov. 20, Jan. 31
The 31st rules Apr. 19, Jun. 30, Sept. 10, Nov. 21, Feb. 1
The 32nd rules Apr. 20, July 1, Sept. 11, Nov. 22, Feb. 2
The 33rd rules Apr. 21, July 2, Sept. 12, Nov. 23, Feb. 3
The 34th rules Apr. 22, July 3, Sept. 13, Nov. 24, Feb. 4
The 35th rules Apr. 23, July 4, Sept. 14, Nov. 25, Feb. 5
The 36th rules Apr. 24, July 5, Sept. 15, Nov. 26, Feb. 6
The 37th rules Apr. 25, July 6, Sept. 16, Nov. 27, Feb. 7
The 38th rules Apr. 26, July 7, Sept. 17, Nov. 28, Feb. 8
The 39th rules Apr. 27, July 8, Sept. 18, Nov. 29, Feb. 9
The 40th rules Apr. 28, July 9, Sept. 19, Nov. 30, Feb. 10
The 41st rules Apr.29, July 10, Sept. 20, Dec. 1, Feb. 11
The 42nd rules Apr 30, July 11, Sept. 21, Dec. 2, Feb. 12
The 43rd rules May 1, July 12, Sept. 22, Dec. 3, Feb. 13
The 44th rules May 2, July 13, Sept. 23, Dec. 4, Feb. 14
The 45th rules May 3, July 14, Sept. 24, Dec. 5, Feb. 15
The 46th rules May 4, July 15, Sept. 25, Dec. 6, Feb. 16
The 47th rules May 5, July 16, Sept. 26, Dec. 7, Feb. 17
The 48th rules May 6, July 17, Sept. 27, Dec. 8, Feb. 18
The 49th rules May 7, July 18, Sept. 28, Dec. 9, Feb. 19
The 50th rules May 8, July 19, Sept. 29, Dec. 10, Feb. 20
The 51st rules May 9, July 20, Sept. 30, Dec. 11, Feb. 21
The 52nd rules May 10, July 21, Oct. 1, Dec. 12, Feb. 22
The 53rd rules May 11, July 22, Oct. 2, Dec. 13, Feb. 23
The 54th rules May 12, July 23, Oct. 3, Dec. 14, Feb. 24
The 55th rules May 13, July 24, Oct. 4, Dec. 15, Feb. 25
The 56th rules May 14, July 25, Oct. 5, Dec. 16, Feb. 26
The 57th rules May 15, July 26, Oct. 6, Dec. 17, Feb. 27
The 58th rules May 16, July 27, Oct. 7, Dec. 18, Feb. 28
The 59th rules May 17, July 28, Oct. 8, Dec. 19, Mar. 1
The 60th rules May 18, July 29, Oct. 9, Dec. 20, Mar. 2
The 61st rules May 19, July 30, Oct. 10, Dec. 21, Mar. 3
The 62nd rules May 20, July 31, Oct. 11, Dec. 22, Mar. 4
The 63rd rules May 21, Aug. 1, Oct. 12, Dec. 23, Mar. 5
The 64th rules May 22, Aug. 2, Oct. 13, Dec. 24, Mar. 6
The 65th rules May 23, Aug. 3, Oct. 14, Dec. 25, Mar. 7
The 66th rules May 24, Aug. 4, Oct 15, Dec. 26, Mar. 8
The 67th rules May 25, Aug. 5, Oct. 16, Dec. 27, Mar. 9
The 68th rules May 26, Aug. 6, Oct. 17, Dec. 28, Mar. 10
The 69th rules May 27, Aug. 7, Oct. 18, Dec. 29, Mar. 11

The 70th rules May 28, Aug. 8, Oct. 19, Dec. 30, Mar. 12
The 71st rules May 29, Aug. 9, Oct. 20, Dec. 31, Mar. 13
The 72nd rules May 30, Aug. 10, Oct. 21, Jan. 1, Mar. 14

In his work entitled *la Science des signes*, third part, page 65, M. d'Odoucet, successor to Eteilla, says categorically "that the revolution of the Geniuses over the years, months weeks days and hours, has been 72 days each 72 days since the Creation."[53]

This follows the principle I had conceived in the two preceding Tables and the one which follows; the subject of the First Table is taken from Fr. Kircher and Agrippa; the Table above includes the five revolutions of the 72 Geniuses for the 360 days; the five days remaining are attributed to the four Intelligences of the four Elements, and the last day is attributed to God, the same as the first day of the year, that is to say, March 20 is also attributed to Divinity, because God is the Beginning, the End and the Principle of all things.

This is the Alpha and Omega[54] of the Sages of Greece, adored by all the wise philosophers in the Universe. That mystery was revealed to St. John, as he tells us himself in his Apocalypse, Ch. 21, v. 6, and Ch. 22, v. 13: "*I am Alpha and Omega, the First and the Last, the Beginning and the End.*" It's during the night of March 19 to 20, at precisely midnight, that the Mages and Kabbalists create the mysterious seal of Divinity together with that of the Sun; we will talk about this at the end of this work.

From the calculation of the previous Table, the first revolution of the 72 Geniuses begins during March 20 at midnight to May 31; the second from May 31 to August 11; the third from August 11 to October 22; the fourth from October 22 to January 2; and so forth. See the Third Table.

The revolution of the 72 Geniuses, over the hours of the day and night, is made in 24 hours; beginning with the first hour of the day, that is, midnight, the sun follows the 360 degrees of the sphere in space during these 24 hours.

We say that in 72 there is 3 times 24; in an hour there are 3 times 20 minutes, and in 24 hours there are 24 times 60 minutes, which gives 1,440

---

[53] See Eteilla, in his *Philosophie des Hautes-Sciences*, p. 66; 1785 edition. [That is, that there are 72 days between each of the 5 dates, and 72 x 5 = 360, the number of days in the year or degrees in the sphere – PV.]

[54] Voltaire, speaking about Angels, Indians and Persians, said: "God presides over the day where the sun enters Aries, and that day is a Sabbath day; which proves that the Sabbath Festival was observed among the Persians in the most ancient times." See Voltaire, *Dictionnaire philosophique*, in his article on Angels, Indians and Persians.

minutes; in this number there are 72 times 20 minutes, which are for the 72 Geniuses; as a result, 3 Geniuses consecutively rule every 20 minutes of every hour of the day and night, as is shown in the following Table.

FOURTH KABBALISTIC TABLE

Containing the revolution of the 72 Geniuses operating each 24 hours. It serves to know the Genius which rules over man's mind and soul.

The 1st Genius rules from midnight exactly till 20 minutes after midnight.
The 2nd from midnight 20 minutes to midnight 40 minutes.
The 3rd from midnight 40 minutes to 1 o'clock exactly.
The 4th from 1:00 am to 1:20 am.
The 5th from 1:20 am to 1:40 am.
The 6th from 1:40 am to 2:00 am.
The 7th from 2:00 am to 2:20 am.
The 8th from 2:20 am to 2:40 am.
The 9th from 2:40 am to 3:00 am.
The 10th from 3:00 am to 3:20 am.
The 11th from 3:20 am to 3:40 am.
The 12th from 3:40 am to 4:0 am.
The 13th from 4:00 am to 4:20 am.
The 14th from 4:20 am to 4:40 am.
The 15th from 4:40 am to 5:00 am.
The 16th from 5:00 am to 5:20 am.
The 17th from 5:20 am to 5:40 am.
The 18th from 540 am to 6:00 am.
The 19th from 6:00 am to 6:20 am.
The 20th from 6:20 am to 6:40 am.
The 21st from 6:40 am to 7:00 am.
The 22nd from 7:00 am to 7:20 am.
The 23rd from 7:20 am to 7:40 am.
The 24th from 7:40 am to 8:00 am.
The 25th from 8:00 am to 8:20 am.
The 26th from 8:30 am to 8:40 am.
The 27th from 8:40 am to 9:00 am.

The 28th from 9:00 am to 9:20 am.
The 29th from 9:20 am to 9:40 am.
The 30th from 9:40 am to 10:00 am.
The 31st from 10:00 am to 10:20 am.
The 32nd from 10:20 am to 10:40 am.
The 33rd from 10:40 am to 11:00 am.
The 34th from 11:00 am to 11:20 am.
The 35th from 11:20 am to 11:40 am.
The 36th from 11:40 am to midday.
The 37th from midday to midday 20 minutes.
The 38th from midday 20 minutes to midday 40 minutes.
The 39th from midday 40 minutes to 1:00 pm.
The 40th from 1:00 pm to 1:20 pm.
The 41st from 1:20 pm to 1:40 pm.
The 42nd from 1:40 pm to 2:00 pm.
The 43rd from 2:00 pm to 2:20 pm.
The 44th from 2:20 pm to 2:40 pm.
The 45th from 2:40 pm to 3:00 pm.
The 46th from 3:00 pm to 3:20 pm.
The 47th from 3:20 pm to 3:40 pm.
The 48th from 3:40 pm to 4:00 pm.
The 49th from 4:00 pm to 4:20 pm.
The 50th from 4:20 pm to 4:40 pm.
The 51st from 4:40 pm to 5:00 pm.
The 52nd from 5:00 pm to 5:20 pm.
The 53rd from 5:20 pm to 5:40 pm.
The 54th from 5:40 pm to 6:00 pm.
The 55th from 6:00 pm to 6:20 pm.
The 56th from 6:20 pm to 6:40 pm.
The 57th from 6:40 pm to 7:00 pm
The 58th from 7:00 pm to 7:20 pm.
The 59th from 7:20 pm to 7:40 pm.
The 60th from 7:40 pm to 8:00 pm.
The 61st from 8:00 pm to 8:20 pm.
The 62nd from 8:20 pm to 8:40 pm.
The 63rd from 8:40 pm to 9:00 pm.
The 64th from 9:00 pm to 9:20 pm.

The 65th from 9:20 pm to 9:40 pm.
The 66th from 9:40 pm to 10:00 pm.
The 67th from 10:00 pm to 10:20 pm.
The 68th from 10:20 pm to 10:40 pm.
The 69th from 10:40 pm to 11:00 pm.
The 70th from 11:00 pm to 11:20 pm.
The 71st from 11:20 pm to 11:40 pm.
The 72nd from 11:40 pm to midnight.

PROCEDURE

To know one's Genius or that of the person who made the request.

According to the doctrine of Agrippa[55], all men have three Guardian Angels or Geniuses. The first is sacred: he doesn't emanate from the power of the stars, but he comes from God as soon as the soul is created. That spirit is Universal and above Nature; he is the director of life; he communicates the Divine Light, that is, *the Light of the Word which lighteth all men that cometh into the world*[56], and he exalts the soul towards the Creator: he is known by means of the Table of Hours.

The second Genius emanates from the Astrological World, that is, from the power of the stars; bring brings man to virtue; he influences the moral side and speech: he is known by means of the Table of Days.

The third Genius emanates from the Elemental World; he rules over mans' physical body; he influences health, movement and actions: he is known by means of the Table of Quinaries.

EXAMPLE

Suppose a person wishes to know their Geniuses. She says she was born on November 17 at 10:15 in the morning. First, I look in the Table of Quinaries (see the Second Table) and I see that the 49th

---

[55] *Occult Philosophy*, Book 3, Ch. 22.
[56] Gospel according to St. John, Ch. 1, v. 9.

Genius is rules from November 15th to 19th inclusive, which influences the person's physical body. Then I look in the Table of Days (see the Third Table), and I see that the 27th Genius corresponds to November 17th, which governs the morality of the person. In last place I look in the Table of Hours (see the Fourth Table) and I see that the 31st Genius rules from 10:00 am to 10:20 am inclusive; which influences the mind and soul of the person.

As only a few know the exact hour and minute of their birth, it then becomes difficult to know the Genius which rules the soul.

Here's the means which I use to avoid this inconvenience: we can see from the 4th Table that 3 Geniuses rule each hour; that is, every 20 minutes. It is enough only to know the hour of birth, and then look at the Chapter of Geniuses to determine their influences; the one of the three which is most closely connected with the character and temperament of the person is the one which will be their Genius.

5. *Explanation of the Sacred Calendar*

The ancient people all knew the sacred year. We have proofs of that in the monument the Egyptians, the Persians, the Greeks, the Mexicans and through knowledge of Astrology. They divided the months of the year into three decades, which in total made 36, and we can see this by the division of the 36 Constellations which divide the sky after the twelve Signs of the Zodiac.

Each decade contained a space of six days and corresponded to the influence of a planet or a Genius. That division was very similar to the Republican calendar: It's probable that this was its origin.[57]

***TABLE** of the influences of the planets on the sphere, containing the division of the Zodiac into 36 equal parts, with the names of the Geniuses corresponding with each decade, according to the system of the Greeks.*

The two first Geniuses are called Chontaré and Asican (Senator)[58]; they rule from March 20 at midnight until March 29 inclusive, under the influence of Mars, and so on for the others, and following the same order.

---

[57] The Republican or Revolutionary calendar was adopted during the French Revolution between 1793 and 1805. It stripped the traditional calendar of all Saints days and Royalist holidays and was an attempt at decimalization. It had twelve months each divided into three ten-day periods called 'decades'. Every tenth day was a day of rest, and the 'missing' five or six days were tacked onto the end of each year. Each month was given a new name. For example, Winter had three months: Nivôse, Pluviôse and Ventôse, meaning Snowy, Rainy and Windy respectively – PV.

[58] The names which belong to the first series come from the Greeks, and those belonging to the second are found in the Tables of Firmicus.

2. Chontacre[59] and Senacher (Senacher[60]), from March 30 to April 8, under the influence of the Sun.
3. Seket and Asentacer (Sentacher), from April 9 to 18, under the influence of Venus.
4. Chous and Asicat (Suo), from April 19 to 28, under the influence of Mercury.
5. Ero and Viroaso (Aryo), from April 29 to May 8, under the influence of the Moon.
6. Rombomarè and Atarph (Romanae), from May 9 to 18, under the influence of Saturn.
7. Théosolk and Thésogar (Thesogar), from May 19 to 28, under the influence of Jupiter.
8. Ouêré and Verasua (Ver), from May 29 to June 7, under the influence of Mars.
9. Phuor and Tepisatosoa (Tepis), from June 8 to 17, under the influence of the Sun.
10. Sothis and Sothis (Sothis), from June 18 to 27, under the influence of Venus.
11. Sith and Syth (Sith), from June 28 to July 7, under the influence of Mercury.
12. Chumis and Thiumis (Thiumis), from July 8 to 17, under the influence of the Moon.
13. Charchumis and Aphruimis (Craumonis), from July 18 to 27, under the influence of Saturn.
14. Hépê and Sithacer (Sic), from July 28 to August 6, under the influence of Jupiter.
15. Phupê and Phuonisié (Futile), from August 7 to 16 under the influence of Mars.

---

[59] With regard to the Greek decans, each of which referred to a bright star (e.g. Sirius or Sothis – see 10.) or constellation, there is no definitive list to draw from, since there were many Greek calendars in use. However, a good one for comparison purposes with the French names listed by Lenain can be found (as of May 15, 2020) at https://en.wikipedia.org/wiki/Decan - PV.

[60] Since the names were in French, the Translator consulted a contemporary translation of the *Matheseos* written by Firmicus Maternus, by Jean Rhys Bran of Hunter College, NY,1975, Book Four, Chapter XXII, pp. 148 – 150. In most cases the names are identical or similar, but there were extreme variants on occasion. Because of this the names from the English translation have been added in parentheses after the names listed in Lenain's book – PV.

5. Explanation of the Sacred Calendar

16. Tomi and Thumis (Thumis), from August 17 to 26, under the influence of the Sun.
17. Ouestucati and Thopitus (Thopicus), from August 27 to September 5, under the influence of Venus.
18. Aphoso and Aphut (Afut), from September 6 to 15, under the influence of Mercury.
19. Souchoë and Serucuth (Seuichut), from September 16 to 25, under the influence of the Moon.
20. Ptêchut and Aterchinis (Sepisent), from September 26 to October 5, under the influence of Saturn.
21. Chonaté and Arpien (Senta), from October 6 to 15, under the influence of Jupiter.
22. Stoch-Nêné and Sentacer (Sentacer), from October 16 to 25, under the influence of Mars.
23. Sesmê and Tépiseuth (Tepisen), from October 26 to November 4, under the influence of the Sun.
24. Siemê and Senciner (Sentineu), from November 5 to 14, under the influence of Venus.
25. Rêuo and Eregbuo (Eregbuo), from November 15 to 24, under the influence of Mercury.
26. Sesmê[61] and Sagen (Sagon), from November 25 to December 4, under the influence of the Moon.
27. Chomé and Chénen (Chenene), from December 5 to 14, under the influence of Saturn.
28. Smat and Thémeso (Themes), from December 15 to 24, under the influence of Jupiter.
29. Srô and Epima (Epiemu), from December 25 to January 3, under the influence of Mars.
30. Isrô and Homoth (Omot), from January 4 to 13, under the influence of the Sun.
31. Ptiau and Oroasoër (Oro), from January 14 to 23, under the influence of Venus.
32. Aseu and Astiro (Catero), from January 24 to February 2, under the influence of Mercury.
33. Ptêbiou and Tépisatras (Tepis), from February 3 to 12, under the influence of the Moon.

---

[61] This appear to repeat the Genius from 23 – PV.

34. Abiou and Archatapias (Acha), from February 13 to 22, under the influence of Saturn.
35. Chontaré and Thopibui (Tepibui), from February 23 to March 4, under the influence of Jupiter.
36. Ptibou and Atembui (Uiu), from March 5 to 14, under the influence of Mars.

6. Influences of the 72 Geniuses with their Attributes and Mysteries

I'm going to explain the influences of the Geniuses on the Universe, on Nature and on Man in great detail; their Elements, the Signs over which they rule; the planets which rule them, how to make them favorable in order to distance the influence of evil Geniuses with an explanation of the 72 mysterious verses which are written around their talismans in the Hebrew language, and which were extracts of the Psalms by the ancient Rabbis and Kabbalists.[62] Each of these verse contains the Great Name of four letters (Jehovah), with the names of three letters and the attributes of the 72 Geniuses (see the Kabbalistic sphere).[63]

Thus, the ancient sages of the First Nations of the world admitted the existence of the intermediate beings between God and man, who were named differently according to time and place. They claimed that the superior beings influenced the inferior beings, and that there was a connection between spiritual beings and material beings.[64]

1st – Vehuiah והויה. His attribute is interpreted as "God elevated and exalted above all things". He rules over the Hebrews. The Name of God in that language is Jehovah. He governs the first ray from the East in the season of Spring, that is to say the first five degrees of the circle which begins at midnight on 20th March until the 24th inclusively, corresponding to the first decade of the sacred calendar, and to the first Genius, called Chontare[65], under the

---

[62] Kircher gives their text in Hebrew and Latin, with their interpretations and attributes. *Œdipus Egyptiacus*, Vol. 2, p. 275.
See Reuchlin in Book 3, *de Arte cabalistica*, and the Treatise *de Verbo mirifico*.
[63] See Appendix A for a detailed Table showing how the names are derived - PV
[64] See the book entitled *la Thréicié, ou la seule Voie des Sicences divines et humaines*, edition of year 7, page 226. [Note: 'year 7' referred to the French Revolution, when the Republicans reset their history from 'year 1' – PV.]
[65] Chontaré in French. Note, these 'secondary' angelic names are based on Egyptian astrological angelic forces attributed to the decans. The names used in this document appear to be a mixture between those listed by Hephaestion (Greek) and Firmicus (Roman) – PV.

influence of Mars: this Genius, and those which follow up to the 8th one, belong to the First Order of Angels which the Orthodox call the Choir of the Seraphim. He inhabits the realm of Fire: his sign is Aries, and he rules the following five days: March 20th, May 31st, August 11th, October 22nd and January 2nd. His invocation is made towards the East, from midnight exactly until 12:20am, to receive light. It's by virtue of these Divine Names that one may become illuminated by the Spirit of God; one must pronounce them from midnight precisely until 12:20 am, reciting the third verse of Psalm 3: "But thou, O Lord, art a shield for me; my glory, and the lifter up of mine head" (*Et tu Domine susceptor meus et gloria mea et exaltans caput meum*). His talisman should be prepared according to the principles of the Kabbalistic art (see Chapter 8 on this). The person born under the influence of this Genius has a skillful nature; they are blessed with great wisdom, a lover of the Arts and Sciences, capable of undertaking and executing the most difficult things; having a love for military service, due to the influence of Mars; having abundant energy due to the dominance of Fire.

The bad (negative) Genius influences turbulent men; and rules over promptness and anger.

2nd – Jeliel יליאל. His attribute is "Helpful God". He rules over Turkey (these people give God the Name of Aydy). His ray begins from the 6th degree until the 10th inclusive, corresponding to the influence of the Genius called Asican (see the Sacred Calendar) and to the first decade. He rules over the following days: March 21st, June 1st, August 12th, October 23rd and January3rd.

One invokes this Genius to calm popular sedition, and to obtain victory over those who would attack you unjustly. One must pronounce the request with the name of the Genius and recite the 20th verse of Psalm 21[66]: "But be thou not far from me, O Lord: O my strength, haste thee to help me" (*Tu autem Domine ne elongaveris auxilium tuum a me ad defensionem meam conspice*). The favorable period begins at 12:20 am up to 12:40 am. This

---

[66] The quotation actually seems to be verse 19 – PV.

Genius rules over kings and princes and keeps their subjects obedient; he has influence over the generation of all beings which exist in the Animal Kingdom; he reestablishes peace between spouses and maintains conjugal fidelity. Those born under this influence have a cheerful spirit, agreeable and genteel manners; they are passionate in sex.

The bad Genius dominates everything detrimental to animate beings; he delights in sundering spouses by distracting them from their duties; he inspires a taste for celibacy, and bad morals.

3rd – **Sitael** סיטאל. His attribute is "God, the hope of all creatures". His ray begins at the 11th degree of the sphere to the 15th inclusive, corresponding to the second decade and to the Genius called Chontachre, under the influence of the Sun; he presides over the following days: March 22nd, June 2nd, August 13th, October 24th, January 4th. One invokes this Genius against adversity; one makes the request with the Divine Names and the 2nd verse of Psalm 90: "I will say of the Lord, He is my refuge and my fortress: my God; in him will I trust" (*Dicet Domino: susceptor meus es tu et refugium meum: Deus meus, sperabo in eum*). The favorable time begins at 12:40 am and continues to 1:00 am. He rules over nobility, magnanimity and great works; he protects against arms and ferocious beasts. A person born under this influence loves truth, keeps his word and takes pleasure in helping those who need assistance.

The bad Genius rules hypocrisy, ingratitude and perjury.

4th – **Elemiah** עלמיה. His attribute is "Hidden God". He corresponds to the Divine Name of God: Allah in the Arabic language. His ray begins at the 16th degree of the sphere up to the 20th inclusive, corresponding to the second decade and to the Genius called Senacher. He rules over the following days: March 23rd, June 3rd, August 14th, October 25th and January 5th. One invokes this Genius against spiritual torment and to know the names of traitors. One should state the request with the 4th verse of Psalm 6: "Return, O Lord, deliver my soul: O save me for thy mercies' sake" (*Convertere Domine, et eripe animam meam:*

salvum me fac propter misericordiam tuam). The favorable time begins at 1:00 am up to 1:20 am. This Genius rules over travel, maritime expeditions, and over useful discoveries. The person born under this influence will be industrious, happy in his enterprises, and will have a passion for travel.

The bad Genius rules over bad education, discoveries dangerous to society; he brings hindrance to all enterprises.

5th – **Mahasiah** מהשיה. His attribute is "God Savior". He corresponds to the Divine Name of Teut or Theuth[67], after the Egyptian language. His ray begins at the 21st degree up to the 25th degree inclusive, corresponding to the third decade and the Genius called Seket, under the influence of Venus; he rules over the following five days: March 24th, June 4th, August 15th, October 26th and January 6th. His invocation is performed from 1:20 am till 1:40 am. One invokes this Genius to live in peace with the entire world; he must say the divine names and the 4th verse of Psalm 33: "I sought the Lord, and he heard me, and delivered me from all my fears" (*Exquisivi Dominum, et exaudivit me: et ex omnibus tribulationibus meis eripuit me*). He rules over the high sciences, occult philosophy, theology and the liberal arts. The person born under this influence learns all that they desire with ease; has an agreeable physiognomy and character and will be keen on honest pleasures.

The bad Genius rules ignorance, libertinage and all bad qualities of mind and body.

6th – **Lelahel**␣ללהאל. His attribute is "Praiseworthy God". He corresponds to the Divine Name Abgd, from the Ethiopian language. His ray begins from the 26th degree to the 30th inclusive, corresponding to the third decade and to the Genius called Asentacer; he rules over the following days: March 25th, June 5th, August 16th, October 27th, January 7th. One invokes this Genius to acquire knowledge and to cure illnesses; one should recite the 11th

---

[67] This name is written with four letters in Egyptian characters. The 'h' is not a letter, and only marks an aspiration; as the Greek 'theta' is a single letter. [In English this would be 'Thoth' – PV].

verse of Psalm 9: "Sing praises to the Lord, which dwelleth in Zion: declare among the people his doings" (*Psallite Domino, qui habitat in Sion: annuntiate inter gentes studia ejus*). The favorable time begins at 1:40 am till 2:00 am. This Genius rules over love, renown, sciences, arts and fortune. The person born under this influence will love to converse and will acquire fame through his talents and actions.

The bad Genius rules ambition; he brings men to want to elevate themselves above their fellow man; he influences all those who seek to acquire a fortune through illicit means.

7th – Achaiah אכאיה. His attribute is "Good and Patient God". His ray begins at the 31st degree of the sphere up to the 35th inclusive, corresponding to the fourth decade and to the Genius called Chous, under the influence of Mercury. He presides over the following days: March 26th, June 6th, August 17th, October 28th and January 8th. The invocation is made from 2:00 am till 2:20 am. One must recite the 8th verse of Psalm 102: "The Lord is merciful and gracious, slow to anger, and plenteous in mercy" (*Miserator et misericors Dominus: longanimis et multum misericors*). This Genius rules over patience; he reveals the secrets of nature; he influences the propagation of knowledge and industry. The person born under this influence will love to learn about useful subjects; he will glory in executing the most difficult works and will discover many useful practices of the arts.

The bad Genius is the enemy of knowledge; he rules over negligence, laziness and insouciance for study.

8th – Cahethel כהתאל. His attribute is "Adorable God". He corresponds to the Divine Name Moti from the Georgian language. His ray begins at the 36th degree of the sphere up to the 40th degree inclusive, corresponding to the fourth decade and to the Genius called Asicat. He presides over the following days: March 27th, June 7th, August 18th, October 29th and January 9th. The aid of this Genius is invoked from 2:20 am to 2:40 am by reciting the 6th verse of Psalm 94: "O come, let us worship and bow down: let us kneel before the Lord our maker" (*Venite adoremus, et procidamus: et* *ploremus ante Dominum, qui fecit nos*). He serves to obtain God's blessing and to chase away evil spirits. This Genius rules over all agricultural production, and principally those, which are necessary to the existence of men and animals. He inspires man to raise himself towards God, to thank Him for all the goods He sends to the earth. The person born under this influence will love work, agriculture, the countryside and hunting, and will be very active in business.

The bad Genius provokes all that is harmful to agriculture; he incites man to blaspheme against God.

9th – Haziel הזיאל. His attribute is "Merciful God". He corresponds to the Divine Name Agzi, from the language of the Abyssinians. His ray begins at the 41st degree up to the 45th degree inclusive, corresponding to the fifth decade and to the Genius names Ero; under the influence of the Moon. This Genius and those which follow up to the 16th belong to the Second Order of Geniuses, which the Orthodox calls the Choir of the Cherubim. He rules over the following days: March 28th, June 8th, August 19th, October 30th and January 10th. The invocation must be done from 2:40 am to 3:00 am, by reciting the 6th verse of Psalm 24: "Remember, O Lord, thy tender mercies and thy lovingkindnesses; for they have been ever of old" (*Reminiscere miserationum tuarum, Domine, et misericordiarum tuarum quae a saeculo sunt*). He serves to obtain God's mercy, the friendship and favors of the great, and the execution of promises made by a person. He rules over good faith and reconciliation. Those born under this influence will be sincere in their promises and will easily pardon those who commit any offence against them.

The bad Genius dominates hate and hypocrisy; he rules those who seek to deceive by all possible means; he keeps enemies irreconcilable.

10th – Aladiah אלדיה. His attribute is "Propitious God". He corresponds to the Divine names of Siré and Eipi, in the tongue of the Persians. His ray begins at the 46th degree to the 50th inclusive, corresponding to the fifth decade and to the Genius called Viroaso.

He rules the following days: March 29th, June 9th, August 20th, October 31st and January 11th. The invocation is made from 3:00 am till 3:20 am, reciting the 22nd verse of Psalm 32: "Let thy mercy, O Lord, be upon us, according as we hope in thee" (*Fiat misericordia tua Domine super nos: quemadmodum speravimus in te*). He is good for those who have hidden crimes and who fear discovery. This Genius rules against rabies and plague, and influences recovery from illnesses. The person who is born under this influence enjoys good health and will be happy in his enterprises. Esteemed by those who know him, he will frequent the most sophisticated societies.

The bad Genius influences those who neglect their health and business.

11th – Lauviah לאויה. His attribute is "Praised and Exalted God". It corresponds to the Holy Name Deus from the Latin tongue. His ray starts at the 51st degree of the sphere up to the 55th inclusive, corresponding to the sixth decade, and to the Genius named Rombomare, under the influence of Saturn. He rules the following days: March 30th, June 10th, August 21st, November 1st and January 12th. The propitious time begins at 3:20 am till 3:40 am. One says the 50th verse from Psalm 17: "The Lord liveth; and blessed be my rock; and let the God of my salvation be exalted" (*Vivit Dominus et benedictus Deus meus, et exultetur Deus salutis meæ*).

He serves against lightning[68] and to obtain victory. This Genius rules renown; he influences great persons, the wise, and all those who become famous through their talents.

The bad Genius rules pride, ambition, jealousy and slander.

12th – Hahaiah הַהֲעִיה. His attribute is "God of Refuge". He corresponds to the Divine Name "Theos" from the Greek tongue. His ray begins from the 56th degree of the sphere to the 60th inclusive, corresponding to the sixth decade and to the Genius called Atarph; he rules over the following days: March 31st, June 11th, August 22nd, November 2nd, January 13th. One invokes the

---

[68] *Foudre*: this could be taken as meaning 'against sudden emotions, such as love or hatred' – PV.

help of this Genius against adversaries; say the 1st verse of Psalm 10: "Why standest thou afar off, O Lord? Why hidest thou thyself in times of trouble? (*Ut qui Domine recessisti longe, despicis in opportunitatibus, in tribulatione*). The auspicious period begins at 3:40 am and lasts till 4:00 am. He rules over depths and reveals hidden mysteries to mortals. He influences wise, spiritual and discreet persons. A person born under this influence has affable habits, a pleasant physiognomy and agreeable manners.

The bad Genius rules indiscretion and untruth; he rules over all those who abuse peoples' trust.

13th – Iezalel יזלאל. His attribute is "God Glorified In All Things". He corresponds to the Divine Name of the God "Boog" from the Illyrian tongue. His ray begins at the 61st degree and goes to the 65th inclusive, corresponding to the seventh decade and to the Genius called Theosolk, under the influence of Jupiter. He rules over the following days: April 1st, June 12th, August 23rd, November 3rd, January 14th. The propitious time begins at 4:00 am and ends at 4:20 am. One must recite the 4th verse of Psalm 98: "Make a joyful noise unto the Lord, all the earth: make a loud noise, and rejoice, and sing praise" (*Jubilate Deo omnis terra: cantate, et exultate, et psallite*). He rules friendship, reconciliation and conjugal fidelity. A person born under this influence will learn everything he desires with ease; he will have happy memories and will distinguish himself through his speech.

The bad Genius rules over ignorance, error and lies, and influences those limited souls who wish neither to learn nor to do anything.

14th – Mebahel מבהאל. His attribute is "Conservative God". He corresponds to the Divine Name "Dios", from the Spanish tongue. His ray begins at the 66th degree up to the 70th degree inclusive, corresponding to the seventh decade and to the Genius called Thesogar. He rules over the following days: April 2nd, June 13th, August 24th, November 4th, January 15th. One invokes this Genius against those who seek to usurp another's fortune; one must recite the 9th verse of Psalm 9: "The Lord also will be a refuge for the oppressed, a refuge in times of trouble" (*Et factus est Dominus refugium pauperis: adjutor in opportunitatibus, in tribulatione*). The auspicious time begins at 4:20 am till 4:40 am. He rules over justice, truth and liberty; he delivers the oppressed and makes truth to be known. The person born under this influence will love jurisprudence and will distinguish himself at the Bar.

The bad Genius rules over calumny, false witness and proceedings.

15th – **Hariel** הריאל. His attribute is "Creator God". e corresponds to the Divine Names "Idio" or "Iddio", from the Italian tongue. His ray begins at the 71st degree up to the 75th degree inclusive, corresponding to the eighth decade and to the Genius called Ouere. He rules over the following days: April 3rd, Ju 14th, August 25th, November 5th, January 16th. One invokes this Genius against those who blaspheme against religion; one must recite the names with the divine names and the 22nd verse of Psalm 94: "But the Lord is my defence; and my God is the rock of my refuge" (*Et factus est mihi Dominus in refugium: et Deus meus in adjutorium spei meæ*). The auspicious time begins at 4:40 am till 5:00 am. This Genius rules over the arts and sciences; he influences useful discoveries and new methodologies. The person born under this influence will love the company of good people; he will love religious sentiment and will distinguish himself through the purity of his morals.

The bad Genius rules over schisms, and religious wars; he influences the impious and all those who spread dangerous sects and who search for the means to establish them anew.

16th – **Hakamiah** הקמיה. His attribute is "God Who Establishes the Universe". He rules over France and corresponds to the Name of "Dieu" in the language of this Nation. His ray begins at the 76th degree up to the 80th degree inclusive, corresponding to the eighth decade and to the Genius called Verasua. He rules over the following days: April 4th, June 15th, August 26th, November 6th, January 17th. One invokes this Genius against traitors, to obtain victory over the enemy, and to be delivered from those who wish to oppress us; one must recite their names with that which follows: "O God Sabaoth, thou who created the universe and protects the French nation, I invoke thee, in the name of Haramiah, that thou mightest deliver France from its enemies." Then one must pronounce the first mysterious verse of Psalm 88: "O Lord God of my salvation, I have cried day and night before thee:" (*Domine Deus salutis meæ, in die clamavie, et nocte coram te*). One must recite this prayer every day, face turned towards the East, from 5:00 am till 5:20 am. This Genius rules over crowned heads and great captains; he gives victory and warns of sedition; he influences fire, arsenals and all things connected with the genie of war. The man who is born under this influence has a frank, loyal and brave character, susceptible to honor, faithful to his obligation and passionate in love[69].

The bad Genius rules over traitors; he provokes treason, sedition and revolt.

17th – Lauviah לאויה. His attribute is "Admirable God". He corresponds to the Name of "Goth", from the German tongue. His ray begins at the 81st degree up to the 85th degree inclusive, corresponding to the ninth decade and to the Genius called Phuor, under the influence of the Sun. He rules over the following days: April 5th, June 16th, August 27th, November 7th, January 18th. This Genius and those which follow belong to the Third Order of Geniuses called the Choir of Thrones. The invocation is made each day, fasting, from 5:00 am till 5:20 am; one should recite the 1st verse of Psalm 8: "O Lord our Lord, how excellent is thy name in all the earth! Who hast set thy glory above the heavens" (*Dominus Deus noster, quam admirabile est nomen tuum in universa terra*). He serves against spiritual torment, sadness and to sleep well at night. He rules over the high sciences, marvelous discoveries, and gives revelations in dreams. The person who is born under this influence will love music, poetry, literature and philosophy.

The bad Genius dominates atheism, impious philosophers and all those who attack religious dogma.

---

[69] *Passionné pour Vénus* in the original - PV.

6. Influences of the 72 Geniuses 65

18th – Caliel כליאל. His attribute is "God Prompt To Grant". He corresponds to the Name "Boog", from the Polish tongue. His ray begins at the 86th degree of the sphere up to the 90th, corresponding to the ninth decade and to the Genius named Tepistatosoa; he rules the following days: April 6th, June 17th, August 28th, November 8th, January 19th[70]. One invokes this Genius to obtain prompt assistance in the face of some adversity; one must recite the 8th verse of Psalm 7 "Judge me, O Lord, according to my righteousness, and according to mine integrity that is in me[71]" (*Judica me Domine secundum justitiam meam, et secundum innocentiam meam super me*). The auspicious time begins at 5:40 am till 6:00 am. This Genius allows knowledge of truth in proceedings, and allows innocence to triumph, he confounds the guilty and false testimony. The person born under this influence will be just and possess integrity, love truth, and will distinguish himself in magistracy.

The bad Genius rules over scandalous processes and influences, vile, base and rampant men, and those who seek to confound business and enrich themselves at the expense of their clients.

19th – Leuviah לוויה. His attribute is "God Who Forgives Sinners". He corresponds to the Name "Bogy" of the Hungarian language. He governs the first ray of the South, which begins at the 91st degree up to the 95th degree inclusive, corresponding to the tenth decade and to the Genius named Sotis, under the influence of Venus; he presides over the following days: April 7th, June 18th, August 29th, November 9th, January 20th. One invokes the aid of this Genius towards the South, from 6:00 am to 6:20 am, reciting the 1st verse of Psalm 40: "I waited patiently for the Lord, and he inclined unto me[72]" (*Expectans expectavi Dominum, et intendit mihi*). He serves to obtain God's grace. This Genius rules over memory and intelligence in man. The person who is born under this influence will be amiable and jovial, modest in speech and simple

---

[70] Incorrectly listed as January 18th in the original – PV.
[71] The first phrase appears to be missing. The full text of Psalm 7, verse 8 is: "The Lord shall judge the people: judge me, O Lord, according to my righteousness, and according to mine integrity that is in me" – PV.
[72] The last phrase is missing. The full text of Psalm 40, verse 1 is: "I waited patiently for the Lord; and he inclined unto me and heard my cry" – PV.

in manner of being, enduring adversity with resignation and much patience.

The bad Genius rules vexation, losses and mortification; he incites debauchery and despair.

20th – Pahaliah פהליה. His attribute is "Redeemer God". He corresponds to the Divine Name "Tios" in the Muscovite tongue. His ray begins at the 95th degree to the 100th degree inclusive, corresponding to the tenth decade and to the angle called Sothis; he presides over the April 8th, June 19th, August 30th, November 10th, January 21st, which correspond to the influence of Venus (see the Sacred Calendar). The invocation is performed from 6:20 am to 6:40 am; he must recite the 2nd verse of Psalm 120: "Deliver my soul, O Lord, from lying lips, and from a deceitful tongue" (*Domine libera anima mean a labiis iniquis, et a lingua dolosa*). He serves against the enemies of religion, and to convert people to Christianity. This Genius rules religion, theology and morality; he influences chastity and piety in those whose vocation is towards the ecclesiastical state.

The bad Genius rules irreligion, apostates, libertines and renegades.

21st – Nelchael נלכאל. His attribute is "God is One and Unique". He corresponds to the Name Bueg in the language of the Bohemians. His ray begins at the 101st degree up to the 105th degree inclusive, corresponding to the eleventh decade and to the Genius called Sith, under the influence of Mercury. He presides over these days: April 9th, June 20th, August 31st, November 11th, January 22nd. The invocation is made between 6:40 am and 7:00 am. One should pronounce the 14th verse of Psalm 31: "But I trusted in thee, O Lord: I said, Thou art my God. My times are in thy hands[73]" (*Ego autem in te speravi Domine: dixi Deus meus es tu: in manibus tuis sortes meæ*). He serves against calumniators, charms, and works to destroy the power of evil spirits. This Genius rules over astronomy, mathematics, geography and all abstract sciences; he

---

[73] In the King James Version, the last sentence is the first phrase of verse 15 of Psalm 31 – PV.

influences the wise and philosophers. The person born under this influence loves poetry and literature and has a passion for study; he will distinguish himself in mathematics and geometry.

The bad Genius rules ignorance, error and prejudice.

22ⁿᵈ – Ieiaiel ייאל. His attribute is "The Right of God". He corresponds to the Divine Name "Good", in the English language. His ray begins from 106th degree of the sphere up to the 110th inclusive, corresponding to the eleventh decade and to the Genius called Syth, under the influence of Mercury. He rules over the following days: April 10th, June 21st, September 1st, November 12th, January 23rd. The invocation is made from 7:00 am until 7:20 am; one pronounces the 5th verse of Psalm 121: "The Lord is thy protector, the Lord is thy shade upon thy right hand" (*Dominus custodit te; Dominus protection tua, super manum dexteram tuam*). This Genius rules over fortune, renown, diplomacy and commerce; he influences voyages, discoveries and maritime expeditions; he protects against tempests and shipwrecks. The person born under this influence will love commerce, be industrious and will distinguish himself through his liberal and philanthropic ideas.

The bad Genius rules over pirates, corsairs and slaves; he influences maritime expeditions.

23ʳᵈ – Melahel מלהאל[74]. His attribute is "God who Delivers from evil". He corresponds to the Name Dieh in the Hibernian language. His ray begins at the 111th degree of the sphere up to the 115th inclusively, corresponding to the twelfth decade and to the Genius called Chumis, under the influence of the Moon. He rules over the following days: April 11th, June 22nd, September 2nd, November 13th, January 24th. The invocation is made from 7:20 am to 7:40 am, reciting the 8th verse of Psalm 120[75]: "The Lord shall preserve thy going out and thy coming in from this time forth, and even for evermore" (*Dominus custodiat introitum tuum, et exitum tuum: et*

---

[74] The original book had a Vav (ו) incorrectly inserted between the Mem (מ) and Lamed (ל) – PV.
[75] In the Vulgate; Psalm 121: 8 in the KJV, as given here in accordance with the Latin text. – ed.

ex hoc nunc, et usque in sæculum). He serves against arms and to travel in safety. This Genius rules water, all products of the earth and, principally, those plants necessary to the cure of illnesses. The person born under this influence is naturally hardy and capable of undertaking the most perilous expeditions; he distinguishes himself through honorable actions.

The bad Genius influences all that is harmful to vegetation; he causes illnesses and plague.

24th – Hahiuiah ההויה. His attribute is "God Good in Himself". He corresponds to the Divine Name Esar in the Etruscan language. His ray begins from the 116th degree of the sphere to the 120th inclusive, corresponding to the twelfth decade and to the Genius called Thuimis. He rules over the following days: April 12th, June 23rd, September 3rd, November 14th, January 25th. The invocation is made from 7:40 am to 8:00 am; one says the Divine Names with the 18th verse of Psalm 33: "Behold, the eye of the Lord is upon them that fear him, upon them that hope in his mercy;" (*Ecce oculi Domini super metuentes eum: et in eis, qui spirant in misericordia ejus*). He serves to obtain grace and mercy from God. This Genius rules over exiles, fugitive prisoners and condemned prisoners; he works against the discovery of secret crimes, and those men who commit them will escape justice provided they do not fall back into the same criminal ways. He protects against harmful beasts and he protects against robbers and assassins. Those born under this influence will love truth and the exact sciences; they will be sincere in their words and their actions.

The bad Genius rules over harmful beings; he leads men to commit crimes and influences all those who seek to live by illicit means.

25th – Nith-Haiah נתהיה. His attribute is "God who gives Wisdom". He corresponds to the Divine Name of God "Orsy" in the language of the Magi. His ray commences at the 121st degree of the sphere up to the 125th inclusive, corresponding to the thirteenth decade and to the Genius called Charcumis, under the influence of Saturn. This Genius and those, which follow up to the

32nd, belong to the fourth Order of Geniuses, which the Orthodox calls the Choir of Dominations. He rules over the following days: April 13th, June 24th, September 4th, November 15th, January 26th. The invocation is done from 8:00 am till 8:20 am; you say the divine names along with the 1st verse of Psalm 9: "I will praise thee, O Lord, with my whole heart: I will shew forth all thy marvelous works" (*Confitebor tibi Domine in toto corde meo: narrabo omnia mirabilia tua*). He serves to gain wisdom and to discover the truth of hidden secrets. This Genius rules over all the Occult Sciences; he gives revelations in dreams and particularly to those born on the day over which he rules; he influences wise men who love peace and solitude, and those who seek truth and practice the magic of the sages, which is that of God.

The bad Genius rules over Black Magic, which is that of the evil principal, the demon; this consists of making a pact with the same through which he renounces God, he brings evil to mankind, animals and to products of the earth.

26th – Haaiah האאיה. His attribute is "Hidden God". He corresponds to the Divine Names of "Agdi" and "Abdi" in the language of the Sarazins. His ray commences from the 126th degree up to the 130th degree inclusive, corresponding to the thirteenth decade and to the Genius called Aphruimis. He rules over the following days: April 14th, June 25th, September 5th, 1 November 16th, January 27th. The invocation is done from 8:20 am till 8:40 am. The Divine Names are pronounced and the 145th verse of Psalm 118: "I cried with my whole heart; hear me, O Lord: I will keep thy statutes" (*Clamavi in toto corde meo, exaudi me Domine; justificationes tuas requiram*). He serves to win judgments and to render judges favorable. This Genius protects all those who seek the truth; he brings men to the contemplation of divine things; he rules over politicians, diplomats, plenipotentiaries, ambassadors, peace treaties, dealings and all pacts in general; he influences couriers, communications, agents and secret expeditions.

The bad Genius rules over traitors, the ambitious and conspirators.

27th – Ierathel ירתאל. His attribute is "God Who Punishes The Wicked". He corresponds to the Divine Name of "Teos" in the language of the Copts. His ray commences from the 131st degree up to the 135th degree inclusive, corresponding to the fourteenth decade and to the Genius called Hepe, under the influence of Jupiter. He rules over the following days: April 15th, June 26th, September 6th, November 17th, January 28th. The invocation is done from 8:40 am till 9:00 am. The Divine Names are pronounced and the 1st verse of Psalm 139: "Deliver me O Lord, from the evil man: preserve me from the violent man" (*Eripe me Domine ab homine malo, a viro iniquo eripe me*). He serves to confound the wicked and slanderers, and to be delivered from our enemies. This Genius protects those who provoke us and unjustly attack us. He rules over the propagation of light, civilization and liberty. The person born under this influence loves peace, justice, sciences and the arts, and he distinguishes himself in literature.

The bad Genius rules over ignorance, slavery and intolerance.

28th – Seheiah שאהיה. His attribute is "God Who Heals The Ill". He corresponds to the Divine Name of "Adad[76]" in the language of the Assyrians. His ray commences from the 136th degree up to the 140th degree inclusive, corresponding to the fourteenth decade and to the Genius called Sithacer. He rules over the following days: April 16th, June 27th, September 7th, November 18th, January 29th. The invocation is done from 9:00 am till 9:30 am. The Divine Names are pronounced with the 13th verse of Psalm 70: "O God be not far from me: O my God, make haste for my help" (*Deus ne elongeris a me: Deus meus in auxilium meum respice*). He serves against infirmities and thunder. This protects against fires, ruined buildings, collapse, maladies, etc. He rules over health and longevity of life. The person born under this influence will be full of good judgment; he will only act with prudence and circumspection.

The bad Genius rules over catastrophes, accidents and the cause of apoplexies; he influences people who never think before acting.

---

[76] The name *Adad* signifies alone; it comes from the word *sol*, which designates the Sun, to which it corresponds.

6. Influences of the 72 Geniuses

29th – Reiiel רייאל. His attribute is "God Quick to Help". He corresponds to the Divine Name of "Zimi" in the language of the Peruvians. His ray commences from the 141st degree up to the 145th degree inclusive, corresponding to the fifteenth decade and to the Genius called Phupe, under the influence of Mars. He rules over the following days: April 17th, June 28th, September 8th, November 19th, January 30th. The invocation is done from 9:20 am till 9:40 am. The Divine Names are pronounced with the request, and the 4th verse of Psalm 53: "Behold, God is mine helper: the Lord is with them that uphold my soul" (*Ecce enim Deus adjuvat me: et Dominus susceptor est animæ meæ*). He serves against the impious and the enemies of religion, and to be delivered from all enemies both visible and invisible. This Genius rules over all religious sentiment, divine philosophy and meditation. The person born under this influence will be distinguished by his virtues and his zeal to propagate truth; he will make every effort to destroy impiety through his writings and by example.

The bad Genius rules over fanaticism and hypocrisy; he rules over all those who propagate irreligion through writings and dangerous maxims.

30th – Omael ומאאל. His attribute is "Patient God". He corresponds to the Divine Name of "Tura" in the language of the Indians. His ray commences from the 146th degree up to the 150th degree inclusive, corresponding to the fifteenth[77] decade and to the Genius called Phuonisie. He rules over the following days: April 18th, June 29th, September 9th, November 20th, January 31st. The invocation is done from 9:40 am till 10:00 am. The Divine Names are pronounced and the 5th verse of Psalm 71: "For thou art my hope, O Lord God: thou art my trust from my youth" (*Quoniam tu es patientia mea Domine spes mea a juventute mea*). He serves against chagrin, despair and to have patience. This Genius rules over the animal kingdom; he watches over the generation of beings, in order to see special multiply and races perpetuated; he influences chemists, doctors and surgeons. The person born under these influences will distinguish himself in anatomy and medicine.

The bad Genius is the enemy of the propagation of beings; he influences monstrous phenomena.

31ˢᵗ – Lecabel לכבאל. His attribute is "Inspiring God". He corresponds to the Divine Name of "Teli" in the language of the Chinese. His ray commences from the 151ˢᵗ degree up to the 155ᵗʰ degree inclusive, corresponding to the sixteenth decade and to the Genius called Tomi, under the influence of Sol. He rules over the following days: April 19ᵗʰ, June 30ᵗʰ, September 10ᵗʰ, November 21ˢᵗ, February 1ˢᵗ. One invokes the aid of Lecabel to have lights and for useful advantages in one's profession. The invocation is performed between 10:00 am until 10:20 am. The request must be said with the Divine Names and the 16ᵗʰ verse of Psalm 71: "I will go in the strength of the Lord God: I will make mention of thy righteousness, even of thine only" (*Quoniam non cognovi literaturam introibo in potentias Domini: Domine memorabor justitiae tuæ solius*). He rules over vegetation and agriculture. The person born under this influence will love astronomy, mathematics and geometry; he will distinguish himself through his luminous ideas, by resolving the most difficult problems and his talents will make his fortune.

The bad Genius rules over avarice and usury; he influences those who enrich themselves by illicit means.

32ⁿᵈ – Vasiariah ושריה. His attribute is "Just God". He corresponds to the Divine Name "Anot" in the language of the Tartars. His ray commences from the 156ᵗʰ degree up to the 160ᵗʰ degree inclusive, corresponding to the sixteenth decade and to the Genius called Thumis. He rules over the following days: April 20ᵗʰ, July 1ˢᵗ, September 11ᵗʰ, November 22ⁿᵈ, February 2ⁿᵈ. One invokes the aid of this Genius against those who attack us in the courts[78], and to obtain the grace of those who have recourse to the clemency of kings; in this case one must name the name of the person who is attacking you and speak the motive; then pronounce

---

[78] If the person attacked realizes in his soul and conscience that he is wrong, he should consequently invoke this Genius to come to an amiable conclusion with the adverse party, else he will not succeed.

6. Influences of the 72 Geniuses

the Divine Names and the 4th verse of Psalm 33: "For the word of the Lord is right; and all his works are done in truth" (*Quia rectum est verbum Domini, et omnia opera ejus in fide*). The auspicious time runs from 10:20 am till 10:40 am. This Genius rules over justice; he influences nobility, legal executives, magistrates and attorneys. The person born under this influence will have a good memory and speak eloquently with ease, and will be amiable, spiritual and modest.

The bad Genius rules over all the bad qualities of the body and the soul.

33rd – Iehuiah יהויה. His attribute is "God Who Knows All Things". He corresponds to the holy divine name of "Agad" in the language of the Hesperides. His ray commences from the 161st degree up to the 165th degree inclusive, corresponding to the seventeenth decade and to the Genius called Ouestucati under the influence of Venus. He rules over the following days: April 12st, July 2nd, September 12th, November 23rd, February 3rd. This Genius and those, which follow up to the 40th, belong to the Fifth Order of Geniuses, which the Orthodox call the Choir of Powers. The invocation is done from 10:40 am till 11:00 am. One must recite the 11th verse of Psalm 92: "The Lord knoweth the thoughts of man, that they are vanity" (*Dominus scit cogitations hominium quoniam vanæ sunt*). He serves to recognize traitors, to destroy their projects and their machinations. This Genius protects all Christian princes; he keeps their subjects in obeisance. The person born under this influence will love to fulfill all the works of his estate.

The bad Genius rules over insubordinate beings; he provokes the seditious to revolt.

34th – Lehahiah להחיה. His attribute is "Clement God". He corresponds to the Divine Name "Aneb" in the language of the people of the Congo. His ray commences from the 166th degree up to the 170th degree inclusive, corresponding to the seventeenth decade and to the Genius called Thopitus. He rules over the following days: April 22nd, July 3rd, September 13th, November 24th, February 4th. The invocation is done from 11:00 am till 11:20

am, reciting the 3rd verse of Psalm 131: "Let Israel hope in the Lord from henceforth and forever" (*Speret Israël in Domino; ex hoc nunc, et usque in sæculum*). This Genius rules over crowned heads, princes and nobles; he maintains harmony, understanding and peace between them; he influences the obeisance of subjects towards their princes. The person born under this influence will become famous through his talents and his actions; he will have the confidence and favor of his prince, which he will merit because of his devotion, fidelity and the great service which he will render him.

The bad Genius rules over discord; he provokes war, treason and the ruin of nations.

35th – Chavakiah חוקיה. His attribute is "God Who Gives Joy". He corresponds to the Divine Name of "Anup". His ray commences from the 171st degree up to the 175th degree inclusive, corresponding to the eighteenth decade and to the Genius called Aphoso, under the influence of Mercury. He rules over the following days: April 23rd, July 4th, September 14th, November 25th, February 5th. One invokes the aid of this Genius to return to favor with those whom one has offended. The subject must pronounce the request, the Divine Names and mention the person; then you say the 1st verse of Psalm 116: "I love the Lord, because he hath heard my voice and my supplications" (*Dilexi quoniam exaudiet Dominus vocem orationis meæ*). This must be recited each day, until one is reconciled with the person. The favorable time begins from 11:20am till 11:40am. This Genius rules over testaments, successions and all amiable distributions; he supports peace and harmony in families. The person born under this influence will love to live in peace with everybody, even to the cost of his interest; he will make it his duty to repay the fidelity and good offices of those in his service.

The bad Genius causes discord in family arrangements; he provokes unjust and ruinous procedures.

36th – Menadel מנדאל. His attribute is "Adorable God". He corresponds to the Divine Name of "Alla" in the language of the

Moors. His ray commences from the 176th degree up to the 180th degree inclusive, corresponding to the eighteenth decade and to the Genius called Aphut. He rules over the following five days: April 24th, July 5th, September 15th, November 26th, February 6th. This Genius is invoked to retain one's employment, and to preserve the means of existence which one enjoys; one pronounces the request with the Divine Names and the 8th verse of Psalm 26: "Lord, I have loved the habitation of thy house, and the place where thine honor dwelleth" (*Domine dilexi decorum domus tuæ: et locum habitationis gloriæ tuæ*). He serves against calumnies and to deliver prisoners. The auspicious time begins at 11:40 am till 12:00 noon exactly. This Genius gives light to distant people who have received no news for a long time; he brings exiles back to their native land and uncovers mislaid or disturbed belongings.

The bad Genius rules and protects all those who seek to flee abroad to escape justice.

37th – Aniel אניאל. His attribute is "God of Virtues". He corresponds to the Divine Name of God "Abda" in the language of the ancient Philosophers. His ray commences from the 181st degree up to the 185th degree inclusive, corresponding to the nineteenth decade and to the Genius called Souchoë, under the influence of the Moon. He rules over the following days: April 25th, July 6th, September 16th, November 27th, February 7th. The invocation is done from midday till 12:20 pm. The Divine Names are pronounced and the 7th verse of Psalm 79: "Turn us again, O God of hosts, and cause thy face to shine; and we shall be saved" (*Deus virtutum converte nos: et ostende faciem tuam: et salvi erimus*)[79]. He serves to give victory and to raise the siege of a town. This Genius rules over the sciences and the arts; he reveals the secrets of nature and inspires wise philosophers with their meditations. The person born under this influence will acquire celebrity through his talents and his enlightenment, and he will distinguish himself among the wise.

---

[79] The verse was quoted as being the 8th verse of Psalm 79 – PV.

The bad Genius rules over perverse spirits; he influences charlatans and all those who excel in the art of misleading men.

38th – Haamiah העמיה. His attribute is "God, the Hope of All the Children of the Earth". He corresponds to the Great Name of God "Agla" (*God Three In One*). According to the Kabbalists, this Name is drawn from the mysterious verse in Scripture: לעולם אדני אתה גיבר, which in English signifies: 'You are the strong God forever'.[80] It's composed of the first letters of these four words, beginning from the right to left.[81] The ray of this Genius commences from the 186th degree up to the 190th degree inclusive, corresponding to the nineteenth decade and to the Genius called

---

[80] See Kircher. *Œdipus Egyptiacus*, Vol. 2, page 115.

[81] By this means you have the key of the 72 Hebrew verses written around the talismans of the 72 Geniuses which are found in the Kabbalistic sphere. Each of these verses contains the name of God and the attribute of the Genius to which it corresponds.

The Abbé de Villars recounts wonderful things while speaking of the Great Name AGLA, in his work entitled *Le Comte de Gabalis* (see the third conversation). The best edition is that by Amsterdam, by Jacques Lejeune in 1700. It assures us that with this name one may work infinite marvels, even when pronounced by a profane mouth; it claims that those who desire to convince themselves of the truth of this must raise their imagination and their faith, and then turn towards the East, while performing all that is written in the Kabbalistic Rite.

Wise Philosophers say that this Name was revealed to Jacob when he saw the ladder of 72 rounds in a dream, with the 72 angels climbing to and descending from the place called the Door of Heaven; and they claimed that it was by this (Word) that Joseph was delivered from his brothers and interpreted dreams, notably those of the Pharaoh.

The Kabbalists write this name of the mysterious wand which is used during Kabbalistic experiments, and this is how it's done: cut a one year-old virgin branch of hazel [curiously the words 'noisetier' and 'coudrier' are used here, both which mean 'hazel' – PV], meaning that the tree has never fruited, and no branch has been cut or broken, which may easily be found in a shrubbery of new trees. The branch should be cut between eleven and twelve at night, under influences favorable to the experiment one wishes to perform. One must have a new knife which has never bene used, and hold it aloft while cutting the branch and reciting certain words, face turned towards the East; then it must be blessed and on the wider end the name AGLA, in the middle the word ON and on the narrowest end the word TETRAGRAMMATON. These three Names should each be accompanied by a cross and their mysterious characters ; and when proceeding to evocations, strike the air in a cross with the wand towards the four quarters of the world, beginning in the East, then the South, West and North, each time saying the following words: *I conjure three, Genius… to obey me immediately; by the Living God, by the True God, by the Holy God,* and beat the air each time in the form of a cross.

As all know the analogy of the circular figure with unity, which is the perfect symbol of God, it's for that reason one should enclose the mysterious character within it, and in the middle of a triangle, every time one proceeds to any evocations (see the frontispiece).

Serucuth. He rules over the following days: April 26th, July 7th, September 17th, November 28th, February 8th. One invokes him with the Divine Names to acquire all the treasures in heaven and earth; one must recite the 9th verse of Psalm 90: "Because thou hast made the Lord, which is my refuge, even the most High, thy habitation" (*Quoniam tu es Domine spes mea: altissimum posuisti refugium tuum*). The Kabbalists say that this Psalm works against thunder, arms, ferocious beasts and infernal spirits (*see the Kabbalah of the Psalms*). This Genius rules over all religious cults, and above all those which relate to God; it protects all those who seek truth.

The bad Genius rules over error and falsehood and influences all those who have no religious principles.

39th – Rehael רהעאל. His attribute is "God Who Received Sinners". He corresponds to the Divine Name of "Goot" in the language of the Scottish. His ray commences from the 191st degree up to the 195th degree inclusive, corresponding to the twentieth decade and to the Genius called Techout, under the influence of Saturn. He rules over the following days: April 27th, July 8th, September 18th, November 29th, February 9th. The invocation is done from 12:40 pm till 1:00 pm. One must recite the 13th verse of Psalm 29: "Hear, O Lord, and have mercy upon me: Lord, be thou my helper" (*Audivit Dominus, et misertus est mei: Dominus factus est meus adjutor*). He serves as a cure for maladies and to obtain the mercy of God. This Genius rules over health and long life; he influences paternal and filial love, and the obeisance and respect of children for their parents.

The bad Genius is called *Terre-Morte* or *Terre-Damnée*[82] following the expression of Eteilla in his Philosophy of High Sciences, page 83. He is the most cruel and treacherous of all; he influences infanticides and parricides.

40th – Ieiazel ייזאל. His attribute is "God Who Rejoices". He corresponds to the Divine Name of "Goed" in the language of the Belgians. His ray commences from the 196th degree up to the 200th

---

[82] *Dead-Earth* or *Damned-Earth* – PV.

degree inclusive, corresponding to the twentieth decade and to the Genius called Aterchinis. He rules over the following five days: April 28th, July 9th, September 19th, November 30th, February 10th. The invocation is done from 1:00 pm till 1:20 pm. The request is voiced with the Divine Names and the 14th verse of Psalm 88: "Lord, why castest thou off my soul? Why hidest thou thy face from me?" (*Ut quid Domine repellis orationem meam: avertis faciem tuam a me*). This Psalm has marvelous properties; it serves to deliver prisoners, give consolation and to be delivered from one's enemies. This Genius rules over printing and libraries; he influences men of letters and artists. The person born under this influence will love speaking, design, and all sciences in general.

The bad Genius rules over all evil qualities of the body and soul; he influences somber spirits and those who flee society.

41st – Hahahel ההאל. His attribute is "God in Three Persons". He corresponds to the Divine Name of "Gudi" in the language of the Irish. His ray commences from the 201st degree up to the 205th degree inclusive, corresponding to the twenty-first decade and to the Genius called Chontare, under the influence of Jupiter. He rules over the following days: April 29th, July 10th, September 20th, December 1st, February 11th. This Genius, and those who follow, up to the 48th, belongs to the fifth order of Geniuses, which the Orthodox call the Choir of Virtues. One invokes this Genius from 1:20 pm till 1:40 pm, pronouncing the 2nd verse of Psalm 120: "Deliver my soul, O Lord, from lying lips, and from a deceitfujl tongue" (*Domine libera animam meam a labiis iniquis et a lingua dolosa*). He serves against enemies of religion, the impious and slanderers. This Genius rules over Christianity; he protects missionaries and all the Disciples of Christ, who announce the words of the Scripture to Nations; he influences pious souls, prelates, ecclesiastics and all those related to the priesthood. The person born under this influence distinguishes himself by his greatness of soul and his energy; he is completely devoted to the service of God and does not fear martyrdom for Christ.

The bad Genius rules over apostates, renegades and all those who dishonor the priesthood through their scandalous behavior.

42ⁿᵈ – Mikael מִיכאל. The Kabbalists give him the following attributes: "Virtue of God, House of God, Like unto God". He corresponds to the Divine Names of "Buib" or "Biud" in the language of the Canadians. His ray commences from the 206th degree up to the 210th degree inclusive, corresponding to the twenty-first decade and to the Genius called Arpien. He rules over the following days: April 30th, July 11th, September 21st, December 2nd, February 12th. The invocation is done from 1:40 pm till 2:00 pm exactly on says the request with the Divine Names and the 7th verse of Psalm 121: "The Lord shall preserve thy going out and thy coming in from this time forth, and even for evermore" (*Dominus custodit te ab omni malo; custodiat animam tuam Dominus*). He serves to assist for travel in safety. This Genius rules monarchs, princes and nobles; he keeps their subjects subservient, uncovers conspiracies and all those who seek to destroy their persons and governments. The person born under this influence will become involved in political affairs; he will be curious and will want to learn the secrets of private offices and foreign news, and he will distinguish himself in affairs of State through his knowledge of diplomacy.

The bad Genius rules over traitors; he influences malevolence and all those who propagate false information.

43ʳᵈ – Veualiah וליה. His attribute is "Dominating King". He corresponds to the Divine Name of "Solu" in the language of the Californians. His ray commences from the 211th degree up to the 215th degree inclusive, corresponding to the twenty-second decade and to the Genius called Stochene, under the influence of Mars. He rules over the following days: May 1st, July 12th, September 22nd, December 3rd, February 13th. The invocation is done from 2:00 pm till 2:20 pm, pronouncing the 13th verse of Psalm 88: "But unto thee have I cried, O Lord; and in the morning shall my prayer prevent thee" (*Et ego ad te Domine clamavi: et mane oratio mea praeveniet te*). He serves to destroy the enemy and for deliverance from slavery. This Genius rules over peace and influences the prosperity of empires; he affirms tottering thrones and kingly power. The person born under this influence will love the military state and glory; he will be continually engaged in those sciences which are in rapport with the Genius of war; he will become famous through the means of arms, and will attract the confidence of his prince through the services we renders him.

The bad Genius puts discord between princes; he influences the destruction of empires; he supports revolutions and party spirit.

44th – Ielahiah ילהיה. His attribute is "Eternal God". He corresponds to the Divine Name of "Bosa" in the language of the Mexicans. His ray commences from the 216th degree up to the 220th degree inclusive, corresponding to the twenty-second decade and to the Genius called Sentacer. He rules over the following days: May 2nd, July 13th, September 23rd, Decembe 4th, February 14th. One invokes this Genius to obtain success in a useful enterprise; one should state the request with the Divine Names and the 108th verse of Psalm 119: "Accept, I beseech thee, the freewill offerings of my mouth, O Lord, and teach me thy judgements" (*Voluntaria oris mei bene placita fac Domine: et judicia tua doce me*). He is good for getting the protection of magistrates and to win a lawsuit. This Genius protects against arms; he gives victory. The person born under this influence will love to travel in order to learn and will succeed in all his undertakings; he will distinguish himself through his military talents and his bravery, and his name will be famous in the pomp of glory.

The bad Genius rules over war and causes all the calamities which arise from it; he influences all those who violate surrenders and massacre their prisoners without pity.

45th – Sealiah סאליה. His attribute is "Mover of All Things". He corresponds to the Divine Name of "Hobo" in the language of the people of Quito. His ray commences from the 221st degree up to the 225th degree inclusive, corresponding to the twenty-third decade and to the Genius called Sesme, under the influence of the Sun. He rules over the following days: May 3rd, July 14th, September 24th, December 5th, February 15th. The invocation is done from 2:40pm till 3:00pm. One must pronounce the 18th verse of Psalm 94: "When I said, my foot slippeth; thy mercy, O Lord, held me up" (*Si dicebam: motus est pes meus: misericordia tua Domine adjuviabat me*). He serves to confound the evil and the haughty; he lifts up all those who are humiliated and fallen. This Genius rules over vegetation; he bears life and health to all that breathe and influences the principal agents of Nature. The person born under this influence will love to learn; he will have many resources and facilities.

The bad Genius rules over the atmosphere; he incites great heat or cold, great aridity or excessive humidity.

46th – Ariel עריאל. His attribute is "Revealing God". He corresponds to the Divine Name of "Pino" in the language of the people of Paraguay. His ray commences from the 226th degree up to the 230th degree inclusive, corresponding to the twenty-third decade and to the Genius called Tepiseuth. He rules over the following days: May 4th, July 15th, September 25th, December 6th, February 16th. One invokes this Genius to have revelations; one makes the request with the Divine Names and the 9th verse of Psalm 145: "The Lord is good to all: and his tender mercies are over all his works" (*Suavis Dominus universes: et miserationes ejus super omnia opera ejus*). He serves to thank God for the gifts He has sent us. The favorable hour begins at 3:00 pm until 3:20 pm. This Genius discovers hidden treasures; he reveals the greatest secrets of Nature and he shows the objects of one's desires in dreams. The person born under this influence is blessed with a strong and subtle spirit; he will have original ideas and sublime thoughts; he will be able to resolve the most difficult problems; he will be discreet and will act with much circumspection.

The bad Genius causes tribulations of spirit; he brings men to commit the greatest indiscretions and influences feeble people.

47th – Asaliah עשליה. His attribute is "Just God, Who Points To Truth". He corresponds to the Divine Name of "Hana" in the language of the people of Chile. His ray commences from the 231st degree up to the 235th degree inclusive, corresponding to the twenty-fourth decade and to the Genius called Sieme, under the influence of Venus. He rules over the following days: May 5th, July

15th, September 26th, December 7th, February 17th. The invocation is done from 3:20 pm till 3:40 pm, pronouncing the 24th verse of Psalm 104: "O Lord, how manifold are thy works! In wisdom hast thou made them all: the earth is full of thy riches"(*Quam magnificata sunt opera tua Domine! Omnia in sapientia fecisti: impleta est terra possessione tua*). He serves to praise God and to rise towards Him when he sends us light. This Genius rules over justice, men of probity, and over those who raise their spirit to the contemplation of Divine things. The person born under this influence will have an agreeable character; he will be passionate to acquire secret light.

The bad Genius rules over immoral and scandalous acts, and over all those who spread dangerous and chimerical schemes.

48th – Mihael מיהאל. His attribute is "God, Rescuing Father". He corresponds to the Divine Name of "Zaca[83]" in the language of the Japanese. His ray commences from the 236th degree up to the 240th degree inclusive, corresponding to the twenty-fourth decade and to the Genius called Senciner. He rules over the five following days: May 6th, July 17th, September 27th, December 8th, h February 18th. The invocation is done from 3:40 pm till 4:00 pm, pronouncing the 2nd verse of Psalm 98: "The Lord hath made known his salvation: his righteousness hath he openly shewed in the sight of the heathen" (*Notum fecit Dominus salutare suum: in conspectu gentium revelatit justitiam suam*). He serves to preserve peace and union between married couples. This Genius protects those who turn to him. They will have presentiments and secret inspiration about all that will happen to them. He rules over the generation of beings and he influences friendship and conjugal fidelity. The person born under this influence will be passionate for love; he will love walking and all pleasure in general.

---

[83] The Divine Name Zaca corresponds to Zacael and to Psalm 42, "Like as the hart…" etc. (see this subject in the *Kabbalah of Psalms*). He serves to deliver souls from Purgatory, to obtain all spiritual and temporal benefits, and to have revelations in dreams. The request must be just and agreeable to God (according to Lenain).

The bad Genius rules over luxury, sterility and inconstancy; he creates discord between married couples and causes jealousy and inquietude.

49th – Vehuel והואל. His attribute is "Great and High God". He corresponds to the Divine Name of God "Mara" in the language of the inhabitants of the Islands of the Philippines. His ray commences from the 241st degree up to the 245th degree inclusive, corresponding to the twenty-fifth decade and to the Genius called Reno, under the influence of Mercury. He rules over the following days: May 7th, July 18th, September 28th, December 9th, February 19th. This Genius and those, which follow up to the 56th belong to the seventh Order of Geniuses, which the Orthodox call the Choir of Principalities. The invocation is done from 5:00 pm till 5:20 pm. The request is pronounced with the Divine Names and the 3rd verse of Psalm 145: "Great is the Lord, and greatly to be praised; and his greatness is unsearchable" (*Magnus Dominus et laudabilis nimis et magnitudinia ejus non est finis*). One should recite the Psalm in its entirety when one is tested by afflictions and when one has a vexed spirit. He serves to make one enflamed towards God, to bless Him and to glorify Him, when one is touched with admiration. This Genius rules over great people and those who raise themselves and distinguish themselves through their talents and virtues. The person born under this influence will have a sensitive and generous nature; he will be held in esteem and will distinguish himself in literature, jurisprudence and diplomacy.

The bad Genius rules over egotistical men; he rules hate and hypocrisy.

50th – Daniel דניאל. His attribute is "Sign of Mercy" and, according to others, the Genius of Confessions[84]. He corresponds to the Divine Name of "Pola" in the language of the Samaritans. His ray commences from the 246th degree up to the 250th degree inclusive, corresponding to the twenty-fifth decade and to the Genius called Eregbuo. He rules over the following days: May 8th, July 19th, September 29th, December 10th, February 20th. The

---

[84] Kircher, *Œdipus Egyptiacus*, Vol. 2, pp. 266 and 267.

invocation is done from 4:20 pm till 4:40 pm, reciting the 8th verse of Psalm 103: "The Lord is merciful and gracious, slow to anger, and plenteous in mercy" (*Miserator et misericors Dominus: longanimis, et multum misericors*). He serves to obtain God's mercy, and to receive consolation. This Genius rules over justice, counsels, attorneys and magistrates in general. He gives inspiration to those who are encumbered by many things, and do not know how to take decisions. A person born under this influence will be industrious and active in business; he will love literature and will distinguish himself through his eloquence

The bad Genius rules over those who live by their wits, and all those who hate work and who seek to live by illicit means.

51st – Hahasiah ההשיה. His attribute is "Concealed God". He corresponds to the Divine Name of God "Bila" in the language of the Barsians. His ray commences from the 251st degree up to the 255th degree inclusive, corresponding to the twenty-sixth decade and to the Genius called Sesme, under the influence of the Moon. He rules over the following days: May 9th, July 20th, September 30th, December 11th, February 21st. The invocation is done from 4:40 pm till 5:00 pm, pronouncing the 31st verse of Psalm 104: "The glory of the Lord shall endure forever: the Lord shall rejoice in his works" (*Sit gloria Domini in saeculum: laetabitur Dominus in operibus suis*). He serves to raise the soul to the contemplation of Divine things and to uncover the mysteries of wisdom. This Genius rules over chemistry and physics; he reveals the greatest of Nature's secrets, notably the Philosopher's Stone and the Universal Physic. The person born under this influence will love abstract sciences; he will be particularly attracted to the knowledge of the properties and virtues attributed to animals, vegetables and minerals; he will be distinguished in medicine through wonderful cures, and he will make many discoveries useful to society.

The bad Genius rules over charlatans and all those who abuse others' good faith by promising them extraordinary things.

52nd – Imamiah עממיה. His attribute is "God Raised Above All Things". He corresponds to the Name of "Abag" in the language of the Melindais. His ray commences from the 256th degree up to the 260th degree inclusive, corresponding to the twenty-sixth decade and to the Genius called Sagen. He rules over the following five days: May 10th, July 21st, October 1st, December 12th, February 22nd. The invocation is done from 5:00 pm till 5:20 pm, reciting the 17th verse of Psalm 7: "I will praise the Lord according to his righteousness: and will sing praise to the name of the Lord most high" (*Confitebor Domino secundum justitiam ejus: et psallam nomini Domini altissimi*). He is good for destroying the power of enemies and to humiliate them. This Genius rules over all travel in general; he protects prisoners who call upon him; and inspires in them the means to obtain their liberty; he influences all those who seek the truth of good faith, and turn away from their mistakes by making a truly sincere return to God. The person born under this influence will have a strong and vigorous temperament; he will bear adversity with much patience and courage; he will love work and will complete everything he wishes with ease.

The bad Genius rules over pride, blasphemy and evil; he influences coarse and quarrelsome men.

53rd – Nanael נגאאל. His attribute is "God Who Brings Down The Proud". He corresponds to the Divine Name of "Obra"[85] in the language of the Maltese. His ray commences from the 261st degree up to the 265th degree inclusive, corresponding to the twenty-seventh decade and to the Genius called Chomme, under the influence of Saturn. He rules over the following days: May 11th, July 22nd, October 2nd, December 13th, February 23rd. The invocation is done from 5:20 pm till 5:40 pm, by pronouncing the Divine Names and the 75th verse of Psalm 119: "I know, O Lord, that thy judgments are right, and that thou in faithfulness hast afflicted me" (*Cognovi Domine quia æquitas judicia tua: et in veritate tua humiliasti me*). This Psalm is divided into 22 equal parts, corresponding to the 22 Hebrew letters and to the 22 sacred

---

[85] The holy name *Obra* corresponds to Psalm 132, according to the Kabbalah. This Psalm teaches us that all men should love one another as brothers, and that they should be united among themselves and live together. He serves to obtain friendship and the favors of those one desires, and to live in peace with all men.

names of God, which correspond to each of these letters, and which indicate the ladder by which wise men climb towards the contemplation of God. The Kabbalists claim that the Holy Virgin recited it each day (*see the Kabbalah of Psalms*). This Genius rules over the high sciences; he influences religious men, teachers, magistrates and men of law. The person born under this influence will possess a melancholic demeanor; he will pursue a private life, rest and meditation, and he will distinguish himself through his knowledge of the abstract sciences.

The bad Genius rules over ignorance and all bad qualities of body and soul.

54th – Nithanael ניתאל. His attribute is "King of Heaven". He corresponds to the Divine Name of "Bora" in the language of the Zaflanians. His ray commences from the 266th degree up to the 270th degree inclusive, corresponding to the twenty-seventh decade and to the Genius called Chenon. He rules over the following days: May 12th, July 23rd, October 3rd, December 14th, February 24th. The invocation is done from 5:40 pm till 6:00 pm exactly, pronouncing the 19th verse of Psalm 103: "The Lord hath prepared his throne in the heavens: and his kingdom ruleth over all" (*Dominus in coelo paravit sedem suam: et regnum ipsius omnibus dominabitur*). He serves to obtain the mercy of God, and to obtain long life. This Genius rules over emperors, kings, princes and all civilian and ecclesiastical dignitaries. He watches over all legitimate dynasties and over the stability of empires; he gives a long and peaceful reign to princes who have recourse to him and protects all those who wish to remain in their employ. The person born under this influence will become famous through his writings and his eloquence; he will have a strong reputation among the wise, will distinguish himself through his virtues and will merit the confidence of his prince.

The bad Genius rules over the ruin of empires; he causes revolutions and overthrows; he influences all those who unite for the overthrowing of monarchies to seize authority and preferred positions.

6. Influences of the 72 Geniuses

55th – Mebahiah מבהיה. His attribute is "Eternal God". He corresponds to the Divine Name of "Alay" in the language of the people of Ormuz. His ray commences from the 271st degree up to the 275th degree inclusive, corresponding to the twenty-eighth decade and to the Genius called Smat, under the influence of Jupiter. He rules over the following days: May 13th, July 24th, October 4th, December 15th, February 25th. The invocation is done from 6:00 pm till 6:20 pm; the request is pronounced with the Divine Names and the 12th verse of Psalm 102: "But thou, O Lord, shalt endure forever: and thy remembrance unto all generations" (*Tu autem Domine in aeternum permanes: et memoriale tuum in generationem et generationem*).

He is good for obtaining consolation and for those who wish to have children. This Genius rules over morality and religion; he influences those who protect them with all their power and spread them by all possible means. His good works, his piety and his zeal for completing his duties before God and man will distinguish the person born under this influence.

The bad Genius is the enemy of virtue; he influences all those who wish to destroy religion and the princes who protect it in order to prevent the great work of the regeneration of the human race.

56th – Poiel פויאל. His attribute is "God Who Supports the Universe". He corresponds to the Divine Name of "Illi" in the language of the people of Aden. His ray commences from the 276th degree up to the 280th degree inclusive, corresponding to the twenty-eighth decade and to the Genius called Themeso. He rules over the following days: May 14th, July 25th, October 5th, December 16th, February 26th. The invocation is done from 6:20 pm till 6:40 pm; one must pronounce the 15th verse of Psalm 145: "The Lord upholdeth all that fall, and raiseth up all those that be bowed down" (*Allevat Dominus omnes qui corrunt: et origit omnes elisos*). He serves to obtain what one wants. This Genius rules fame, fortune and philosophy. For his modesty, moderation and agreeable humor all will hold the person born under this influence in esteem; he will only make his fortune by talent and his conduct.

The bad Genius rules over ambition and pride; he influences all those who set themselves up as masters and wish to raise themselves above others.

57th – Nemamiah נממיה. His attribute is "Praiseworthy God". He corresponds to the Divine Name of "Popa" in the language of the Sirenians. His ray commences from the 281st degree up to the 285th degree inclusive, corresponding to the twenty-ninth decade and to the Genius called Sro, under the influence of Mars. He rules over the following days: May 15th, July 26th, October 6th, December 17th, February 27th. This Genius and those who follow up to the 63rd belong to the Eighth Order, which the Orthodox call the Choir of Archangels. The invocation is done from 6:40 pm till 7:00 pm, reciting the 11th verse of Psalm 115[86]: "Ye that fear the Lord, trust in the Lord; he is their help and their shield" (*Qui timet Dominum speraverunt in Domino: adjutor eorum et protector eorum est*). He serves to bring prosperity in all things and to deliver prisoners. This Genius rules over great captains, admirals, generals and all those who fight in a just cause. The person born under this influence loves the military state; and he will distinguish himself through his actions, bravery, and greatness of spirit, and he will endure hardship with great courage.

The bad Genius rules over treason, the cause of disagreement among leaders; he influences pusillanimous men and those who attack defenseless people.

58th – Ieialel יילאל. His attribute is "God Who Hears the Generations". He corresponds to the Divine Name of "Para" in the language of the Selamites. His ray commences from the 286th degree up to the 290th degree inclusive, corresponding to the twenty-ninth decade and to the Genius called Epima. He rules over the following days: May 16th, July 27th, October 7th, December 18th, February 28th. The invocation is done from 7:00 pm till 7:20 pm. The Divine Names are pronounced and the 3rd verse of Psalm 6: "My soul is sore vexed: but thou, O Lord, how long?" (*Et anima turbata est valde: sed tu Domine usque quo?*). He serves against

---

[86] Listed as verse 19 of Psalm 113 in the original – PV.

chagrins and cures illnesses, principally problems with the eyes[87]. This Genius rules over Fire; he influences armorers, metalworkers, cutlers and those involved in commerce; he confounds the evil and those who bear false witness. The person born under this influence will be distinguished by his bravery and boldness, and he will be passionate for Venus.

The bad Genius rules over anger; he influences the evil and homicides.

59th – Harahel הרהאל. His attribute is "God Who Knows All Things". He corresponds to the Divine Name of God "Ella" in the language of the Mesopotamians. His ray commences from the 291st degree up to the 295th degree inclusive, corresponding to the thirtieth decade and to the Genius called Isro, under the influence of the Sun. He rules over the following days: May 17th, July 28th, October 8th, December 19th, March 1st. The favorable time begins at 7:20 pm till 7:40 pm; one must pronounce the name of the Genius with his attributes, and the 3rd verse of Psalm 113: "From the rising of the sun unto the going down of the same the Lord's name is to be praised" (*A solis ortu usque ad occasum, laudabile nomen Domini*). He serves against the sterility of women and to make children subservient and respectful towards their parents. This Genius rules over treasures, agents of change, public funds, archives, libraries and all rare and precious closets; he influences printing, the book trade and all those involved in this business. The person born under this influence will love to be instructed in all sciences in general; he will be busy in business, will follow the activities of the Stock Exchange, will speculate successfully and be distinguished by his probity, talents and fortune.

The bad Genius rules over the enemies of illumination; he causes ruin and destruction through fire; he influences embezzlement and fraudulent bankruptcy.

60th – Mitzrael מצראל. His attribute is "God Who Comforts the Oppressed". He corresponds to the Divine Name of "Gena" in the language of the people of Tibet. His ray commences from the 296th

---

[87] On this subject see the Enchiridion of Pope Leo, page 4.

degree up to the 300th degree inclusive, corresponding to the thirtieth decade and to the Genius called Homoth. He rules over the following days: May 18th, July 29th, October 9th, December 20th, March 2nd. The invocation is done from 7:40 pm till 8:00 pm, pronouncing the 18th verse of Psalm 145: "The Lord is righteous in all his ways, and holy in all his works" (*Justus Dominus in omnibus viis suis: et sanctus in omnibus operibus suis*).

He serves to heal spiritual ills and for deliverance from those who persecute one; he rules over illustrious people who are distinguished by their talents and virtues; he influences the fidelity and obeisance of subordinates towards their superiors. The person born under this influence will unite all the fine qualities of body and soul; he will distinguish himself through his virtues, spirit, and agreeable humor and will have a long life.

The bad Genius rules over all insubordinate beings and influences all bad physical and moral qualities.

61st – Umabel ומבאל. His attribute is "God Above All Things". He corresponds to the name of "Sila" following the language of the ancient Bethulians. His ray commences from the 301st degree up to the 305th degree inclusive, corresponding to the thirty-first decade and to the Genius called Ptiau, under the influence of Venus. He rules over the following days: May 19th, July 30th, October 10th, December 21st, March 3rd. The invocation must be done from 8:00 pm till 8:20 pm: one pronounces the Divine Names and the 2nd verse of Psalm 113: "Blessed be the name of the Lord from this time froth and for evermore" (*Sit nomen Domini benedictum, ex hoc nunc et usque in sæculum*). He serves to obtain a person's friendship. This Genius rules over astronomy and physics; he influences all those who distinguish themselves in these fields. The person born under this influence will love travel and all honest pleasures; he will have a sensitive heart and love will cause him grief.

The bad Genius rules over libertines and particularly those who deliver themselves up to passions contrary to the order of nature.

6. Influences of the 72 Geniuses

62ⁿᵈ – Iah-hel יההאל. His attribute is "Supreme Being". He corresponds to the Divine Name of "Suna" following the language of the ancient Carmanians. His ray commences from the 306ᵗʰ degree up to the 310ᵗʰ degree inclusive, corresponding to the thirty-first decade and to the Genius called Oroasoer. He rules over the following days: May 20ᵗʰ, July 31ˢᵗ, October 11ᵗʰ, December 22ⁿᵈ, March 4ᵗʰ. The invocation is done from 8:20 pm till 8:40 pm; one must pronounce the 159ᵗʰ verse of Psalm 119: "Consider how I love thy precepts: quicken me, O Lord, according to thy lovingkindness" (*Vide quoniam mandata tua dilexi Domine, in misericordia tua vivifica me*). He serves to acquire wisdom. This Genius rules philosophers, enlightened ones and all those who wish to retire from the world. The person born under this influence will love tranquility and solitude; he will precisely fulfill the duties of his state and will be distinguished by his modesty and virtues.

The bad Genius rules over those who commit scandals; he rules over luxury, inconstancy and divorce; he provokes disunion between spouses.

63ʳᵈ – Anauel ענואל. His attribute is "Infinitely Good God". He corresponds to the Divine Name of God "Miri" in the language of the Cambodians. His ray commences from the 311ᵗʰ degree up to the 315ᵗʰ degree inclusive, corresponding to the thirty-second decade and to the Genius called Asau, under the influence of Mercury. He rules over the following days: May 21ˢᵗ, August 1ˢᵗ, October 12ᵗʰ, December 23ʳᵈ, March 5ᵗʰ. The invocation is done from 8:40 pm till 9:00 pm, pronouncing the Divine Names and the 11ᵗʰ verse of Psalm 2: "Serve the Lord with fear, and rejoice with trembling" (*Servite Domino in timore: et exultate ei cum tremore*). He serves to convert nations to Christianity and to confound those who are its enemies. This Genius protects against accidents, he preserves health and cures illnesses; he rules over commerce, bankers, businessmen and clerks. The person born under this influence will have a subtle and ingenious spirit; he will distinguish himself through his industry and his actions.

The bad Genius rules over folly and prodigality; he influences all those who ruin themselves through their bad conduct.

64th – **Mehiel** מהיאל. His attribute is "God Who Vivifies All Things". He corresponds to the Divine Name of "Alli" in the language of the Mongols. His ray commences from the 316th degree up to the 320th degree inclusive, corresponding to the thirty-second decade and to the Genius called Astiro. He rules over the following days: May 22nd, August 2nd, October 13th, December 24th, March 6th. The invocation is done from 9:00 pm till 9:20 pm, pronouncing the Divine Names with the 18th verse of Psalm 33: "Behold, the eye of the Lord is upon them that fear him, upon them that hope in his mercy" (*Ecce oculi Domini super metuentes eum: et in eis, qui sperant super misericordiam ejus*). This Psalm is good against adversities; he grants the prayers and wishes of those who hope in the mercy of God. This Genius and those who follow, up to the 72nd, belong to the Ninth Order, which the Orthodox call the Choir of Angels. This Genius protects against rabies and ferocious animals; he rules over the wise, teachers, orators and authors; he influences printing and bookshops and all those who engage in this type of business. The person born under this influence will distinguish himself in literature.

The bad Genius rules over all false wise men; he influences controversies, literary disputes and criticism.

65th – **Damabiah** דמביה. His attribute is "God Fountain of Wisdom". He corresponds to the Divine Name of "Tara" following the language of the Gymnosophs. His ray commences from the 321st degree up to the 325th degree inclusive, corresponding to the thirty-third decade and to the Genius called Ptebiou, under the influence of the Moon. He rules over the following days: May 23rd, August 5th, October 14th, December 25th, March 7th. The invocation is done from 9:20 pm till 9:40 pm pronouncing the 13th verse of Psalm 90[88]: "Return, O Lord, how long? And let it repent thee concerning thy servants" (*Convertere Domine usquequo? Et deprecabilis esto super servos tuos*). He serves against sorcery and to obtain wisdom and success in useful enterprises. This Genius rules overseas, rivers, springs, maritime expeditions and naval

---

[88] Identified as verse 15 in Psalm 89 in the original – PV.

construction; he influences sailors, pilots, fishing and all those for work in this line of commerce. The person born under this influence will distinguish himself in marine affairs through his expeditions and discoveries, and he will amass a considerable fortune.

The bad Genius causes tempests and shipwrecks; he influences unhappy expeditions.

66th – Manakel מנקיה. His attribute is "God Who Supports and Maintains All Things". He corresponds to the nName of "Pora" in the language of the Brahmans. His ray commences from the 326th degree up to the 330th degree inclusive, corresponding to the thirty-third decade and to the Genius called Tepisatras. He rules over the following days: May 24th, August 4th, October 15th, December 26th, March 8th. The invocation is done from 9:40 pm till 10:00 pm, reciting the 21st verse of Psalm 3: "Forsake me not, O Lord: O my God, be not far from me" (*Ne derelinquas me Domine Deus meus; ne discesseris a me*). He serves to appease God's anger and to cure epilepsy. He rules over vegetation and aquatic animals; he influences sleep and dreams. The person born under this influence will unite all the good qualities of body and soul; he will bring about friendship and goodwill among all good people through his pleasantness and through the sweetness of his character.

The bad Genius rules over all bad physical and moral qualities.

67th – Eiael איעאל. His attribute is "God, Delight of the Children of Men". He corresponds to the Divine Name of "Bogo" in the language of the Albanians. His ray commences from the 331st degree up to the 335th degree inclusive, corresponding to the thirty-fourth decade and to the Genius called Abiou, under the influence of Saturn. He rules over the following days: 25th May, 5th August, 16th October, 27th December, 9th March. The invocation is done from 10:00 pm till 10:20 pm; one pronounces the request with the Divine Names and the 4th verse of Psalm 37: "Delight thyself also in the Lord; and he shall give thee the desires of thine heart" (*Delectare in Domino et dabit tibi petitiones cordis tui*). He serves to receive consolation in adversity and to acquire wisdom. This

Genius rules over change, the preservation of monuments and long life; he influences the Occult Sciences; he reveals truth to those who have recourse to him in their works. The spirit of God will illuminate the person born under this influence; he will love solitude and will be distinguished in the high sciences, principally astronomy, physics and philosophy.

The bad Genius rules over error, prejudice and those who propagate erroneous schemes.

68th – Habuhiah הבויה. His attribute is "God Who Gives Freely". He corresponds to the Divine Name of "Depos" in the language of the Peloponnesians. His ray commences from the 336th degree up to the 340th degree inclusive, corresponding to the thirty-fourth decade and to the Genius called Archatapias. He rules over the following days: May 26th, August 6th, October 17th, December 28th, March 10th. The invocation is done from 10:20 pm till 10:40 pm, reciting the 1st verse of Psalm 106: "Praise ye the Lord, O give thanks unto the Lord; for he is good: for his mercy endureth forever" (*Confitemini Domino, quoniam bonus: quoniam in saeculum misericordia ejus*). He serves to preserve health and to cure diseases. This Genius rules agriculture and fertility. The person born under this influence will love the countryside, hunting, gardens and all things connected with agriculture.

The bad Genius rules over sterility; he causes famine and plague; he influences insects which harm produce from the soil.

69th – Rochel ראהאל. His attribute is "God Who Sees All". He corresponds to the Divine Name of "Deos" in the language of the Cretans. His ray commences from the 341st degree up to the 345th degree inclusive, corresponding to the thirty-fifth decade and to the Genius called Chontare, under the influence of Jupiter. He rules over the following days: May 27th, August 7th, October 18th, December 29th, March 11th. The invocation is done from 10:40 pm till 11:00 pm exactly, pronouncing the 5th verse of Psalm 16: "The Lord is the portion of mine inheritance and of my cup: thou maintaineth my lot" (*Dominus pars hæreditatis meæ, et calicis mei: tu es, qui restitues hæreditatem meam mihi*). He serves to find lost or hidden objects, and to know the person who has removed them. This Genius rules renown, fortune and succession. He influences jurisconsults, magistrates, attorneys, solicitors and notaries. His knowledge of morality, custom and the spirit of the laws of all people will distinguish the person born under this influence at the bar.

The bad Genius rules over reports, testaments and bequests which are made to the detriment of legitimate inheritors; he influences all those who cause the ruin of families, by provoking high fees and interminable court cases.

70th – Jabamiah יבמיה.[89] His attribute is "Word Which Produces All Things". He corresponds to the Divine Name of "Aris" in the

---

[89] The Abbé de Villars says that this name expresses the *Eternal Fecundity of God* (see the Comte de Gabalis, 4th interview). We find this work in the *Recueil des voyages imaginaries et romans cabalistiques* ('Collection of Imaginary Journeys and Kabbalistic Novels', Vol. 34. The author tells a singular story on this subject: "When Noah floated upon the vengeful waves which inundated the whole world, the women who were saved in the Kabbalistic Ark, which the second father of the world had built, were reduced to a small number. That great man, weeping to see the terrifying chastisement with which the Lord punished the crimes caused by the love which Adam had had for his Eve, and seeing that Adam had lost his posterity by preferring Eve over the daughters of the Elements; Noah, I tell you, who had become wise because of the fatal example of Adam consented for Vesta, his wife, to be given over to the Salamander Oromastis, Prince of igneous substances, and persuaded his three children to hand over their three wives as well to the Princes of the other three Elements. In a very short time, the world was repopulated with men so heroic, so wise and so admirable, that their posterity, dazzled by their own virtues, believed themselves to be gods. One of Noah's children, Ham, rebelling against the advice of his father, couldn't resist the charms of his wife, just as Adam couldn't resist the charms of his Eve. But just as Adam's sin had blackened all the souls of his descendants, the lack of accommodation which Ham had for the Sylphs marked all his posterity black; from which, according to the Kabbalists, comes the horrible color of the Ethiopians, and of all those hideous people who were commanded to inhabit the torrid zone, as punishment for the profane ardor of their father. Noah left the Ark, and seeing that Vesta, his wife, had grown more beautiful because of the relationship she had with her lover Oromasis, became passionate for her. Ham, fearing that his father would populate the Earth with children just as black as his Ethiopians, bided his time, waited until the good old man was full of wine, and chastised him mercilessly.

"Oromasis, whose jealousy didn't extend to not feeling pity for his rival's disgrace, taught his son Zoroaster, also called Japheth, the Name of Almighty God which expressed His Eternal Fecundity: Japheth pronounced the redoubtable name JABAMIAH six times alternately with his brother Shem, walking backwards towards the Patriarch; and they

language of the Boetians. His ray commences from the 346th degree up to the 350th degree inclusive, corresponding to the thirty-fifth decade and to the Genius called Thopibui. He rules over the following days: May 28th, August 8th, October 19th, December 30th, March 12th. The invocation is done from 11:00 pm till 11:20 pm. The Divine Names are pronounced and the 1st verse of Genesis: "*In the beginning God created the heaven and the earth.*" This Genius rules over the generation of beings and phenomena of Nature; he protects those who desire to regenerate themselves, and to reestablish in themselves that harmony which was broken by the disobedience of Adam, which they will accomplish by raising themselves before God and purifying those parts which constitute the nature of man through the elements: thus they will regain their rights and their original dignity. They will once more become the masters of nature and will enjoy all the prerogatives which God gave them at their creation. The person born under this influence will be distinguished by his genius; he will be considered one of the great luminaries of philosophy.

The bad Genius rules over atheism and all those who spread dangerous writings; he influences critics and literary disputes.

71st – Haiaiel הייאל. His attribute is "God, Master of the Universe". He corresponds to the Name of "Zeut" in the language of the Phrygians. His ray commences from the 351st degree up to the 355th degree inclusive, corresponding to the thirty-sixth decade and to the Genius called Ptibiou, under the influence of Mars. He rules over the following days: May 29th, August 9th, October 20th, December 31st, March 14th. The invocation is done from 11:20 pm till 11:40 pm, pronouncing the 30th verse of Psalm 109: "I will greatly praise the Lord with my mouth; yea, I will praise him

---

restored the old man completely. This story, being misunderstood, led the Greeks to say that the oldest of the Gods had been castrated by one of his children."

We see in the *Lettres cabalistiques*, that salvation to the Kabbalists was in Jabamiah and through Jabamiah. [It goes without saying that in every book from the 18th or early 19th Century we will read ideas which are morally abhorrent to modern times. However, this is what was written, and in the interest of history the words of Abbé de Villars are translated faithfully here. Incidentally, the reference to castration is of course to Uranus' castration by his son Cronos – PV].

among the multitude" (*Confitebor Domino nimis in ore meo: et in medio multorum laudabo eum*). He serves to confound evil and to be delivered from all those who wish to oppress one. This Genius protects all those who have need of him; he gives victory and peace; he influences weapons, arsenals, fortresses and all connected with the military genius. The person born under this influence will have a lot of energy; he will love the military state and will be distinguished by his bravery, talents and actions.

The bad Genius rules over discord; he influences traitors and all those who become famous because of their crimes.

72nd – Mumiah מומיה. His attribute is represented by the "Omega", which symbolizes the end of all things; he rules over Thrace or Rumelia. His ray commences from the 356th degree up to the 360th and last degree of the sphere, corresponding to the last decade and to the Genius called Atembui. He rules over the following days: May 30th, August 10th, October 21st, January 1st, March 14th. The invocation is done from 11:40 pm till midnight precisely; one must pronounce the Divine Names, namely *Alpha* and *Omega*, with the name and attributes of the Genius, and the 7th verse of Psalm 116: "Return unto thy rest, O my soul; for the Lord hath dealt bountifully with thee" (*Convertere anima mea in requiem tuam: quia Dominus beneficit tibi*). One must have a talisman, which is on the frontispiece, with that of the Genius written on the other side, which should be prepared under favorable influences as indicated in the Chapter on Kabbalistic Astrology. This Genius protects in mysterious operations; he brings success in all things and brings all things to their conclusion; he rules over chemistry, physics and medicine; he influences health and longevity. The person born under this influence will be distinguished in medicine; he will become famous through his marvelous cures, will unveil many secrets of nature which will lead to the prosperity of the children of earth, and he will devote his labors and his care to ease the poor and the sick.

The bad Genius rules over despair and suicide; he influences all those who hate their life and the day that they were born.

In the previous Chapters I explained the manner of knowing the Geniuses which influence the Universe, Nature and man. Form this we can see that the Geniuses rule each ten days of the year. Firstly, we see by means of the Second Table, that the first Genius rules from March 20th to 24th inclusive, which makes five days; and from the Third Table, that this first Genius also rules over five other days, by the effect of the five revolutions which take place every 72 days each 72 days, since March 20th to May 30th makes 72 days, and May 31st is the 73rd, corresponding to the first Genius, and so forth.

Everyone knows that the ancient philosophers only recognized four Elements, being: Fire, Air, Water and Earth which, according to their doctrine, corresponded with the four first numbers 1, 2, 3 and 4; to the four seasons being: spring, Summer, Autumn, Winter; and to the four Cardinal Points being: East, South, West and North. It's because of all the consequences of these principles that the invocation of the Geniuses must be made in the season which corresponds to their Element, by turning towards the part of the world they govern. It's important to know this important point if you wish to proceed to perform the evocations successfully. Here is the procedure I use:

The result of the horoscope for November 17th, which is done by the method indicated in the example at the end of Chapter 4, gives three Geniuses, being the 49th, the 27th and the 31st. If we divide these numbers separately by four, the remainder from each division indicates their Element and the part of the world over which they govern.

EXAMPLE

Firstly, I divide 49 by 4; the remainder is 1, which indicates Fire, the first Element, and the Eastern part, corresponding to Spring.

Then I divide 27 by the same number, giving a remainder of 3, which indicates Water, the 3rd Element, and the West, corresponding to the season of Autumn.

Finally, by dividing the number 31 by 4, the remainder is also 3, which indicates the third Element.

By this mean it's easy to know from which Element they are, the part of the world where they govern, and the Season they rule.

7. *The Geniuses of the Third Class and Their Mysteries*

Having made known in Chapter 2 the various celestial hierarchies that make up the nine choirs of Angels, the names of the Intelligences that influence the planets, with the Divine Names corresponding to the 22 Hebrew letters and the Three Worlds, and having spoken about the 72 Geniuses that influence everything that exists in the Universe, I've yet to speak about the Geniuses of the Third Class, called, by the Philosophers, the Elemental Peoples. Among the most famous authors who have dealt with the nature of the gods are Iamblicus and Porphyry; the first saying that the Ancient Egyptians and Assyrians were convinced that the Geniuses were spread throughout the Universe, and that they all contributed to the government of the world through a common providence; they claimed that they existed in Fire, in Air, in Water, and in Earth. All wise Philosophers agree that the Elements are inhabited, namely, Fire by Salamanders, Air by Sylphs, Water by Nymphs or Undines, and Earth by Gnomes or Pygmies; and they say that Salamanders are the most beautiful and most perfect creatures of the Elements, because they're composed of the most subtle parts of Fire, conglobed and organized by the action of the Universal Fire, which is the principle of all the movements of Nature.

The Sylphs are composed of the purest atoms of Air; the Sages claim that their women and their daughters are of extraordinary beauty. The love knowledge and the wise.

The Nymphs or Undines are composed of the subtlest parts of Water; they have few males, and the females are of great numbers. Their beauty surpasses the daughters of men, and all the most beautiful creatures of the human race a thousand-fold.

The Earth is filled up to the center by Gnomes or Pygmies: they are the guardians of treasures, mines and gemstones. Their women are small, and their habits are very rich and quite curious. These peoples follow the principles of Nature in all things; their morals and their laws are admirable; they are enemies of the ungodly, the ignorant and the libertines.

They have great respect for Divinity and their prayers are sublime. Here is the one which the Salamander who answered in the Temple of Delphi wished to reveal to men, according to Porphyry's account:

PRAYER OF THE SALAMANDERS
who live in the realm of Fire

Immortal, eternal, ineffable and uncreated Father of all things, who are borne upon the incessantly rolling chariot of Worlds which are always turning; Ruler of the ethereal immensity where the throne of thy power is elevated; from whose height thy dread-inspiring eyes discover all things, and thy exquisite and sacred ears hear all; Listen to thy children whom thou hast loved from the beginning of the ages; for thy golden, great, and eternal majesty is resplendent above the world and the starry heavens. Thou art raised above them O sparkling fire! There thou dost illumine and support thyself by thine own splendor; and there comes forth from thine essence overflowing streams of light which nourish thine infinite spirit. That infinite spirit nourishes all things and renders this inexhaustible treasure of substance always ready for the generation which fashions it and which receives in itself the forms with which thou hast impregnated it from the beginning. From this spirit those most holy kings who surround thy throne, and who compose thy court, derive their origin. O Father Universal! Only One! O Father of blessed mortals and immortals! Thou hast specially created powers who are marvelously like thine eternal thought and adorable essence. Thou hast established them superior to the angels who announce to the world thy wishes. Finally, thou hast created us in the third sort[90] in our Elemental Empire. There our continual employment is to praise thee and adore thy wishes. There we incessantly burn with the desire of possessing thee, O Father! O Mother! the most tender of all mothers! O admirable archetype of maternity and pure love! O Son, the flower of sons! O

---

[90] This third sort is man.

Form of all forms; soul, spirit, harmony and number of all things. We adore thee.[91]

This is how the Elemental peoples worship the Supreme Being, without having any right to eternal glory; for philosophers say that their souls are mortal. However, they live for several Centuries, not being subject to corruption, and having no bad principle in them, because they are composed of only one Element; but what is time in comparison to eternity? There are many similarities between Adam and these creatures, because being composed of the purest of what there was of the Elements, he contained within himself all the perfections of these four kinds of peoples, and he was their natural king. But Adam gave in the trap of the serpent, who persuaded him easily, telling him that *Eve, having found the principle of his life in his side, he had to seek the duration of his own in Eve's womb.* Thus, Adam tasted the forbidden fruit by giving himself to Eve, and disobeyed God, according to the formal order he had received from him not to touch her; and so, he neglected the covenant of the Elemental peoples for which God had especially created them.[92]

From that moment harmony was broken by his disobedience; he no longer had any relationship with these substances which were so pure and so subtle, and he took on a nature inferior to theirs. The incontinence of these first spouses and the perversities of their descendants shocked the Elemental peoples to the point that they were completely disgusted with the human race. Noah's wife did everything to restore relations with them; but their reconciliation wasn't so complete that they didn't behave with a good amount of reserve; they all became private, only working with certain people whose conduct was wise and regular, and especially those who devote all their time to the search for the truth.

The first sages of the world, speaking to God face to face, complained to him of the misfortune of these peoples, and God,

---

[91] For the English translation the translator has used the most commonly available version which has withstood the test of time for many decades. It is better to use a prayer imbued with the power of many recitals, than to attempt a second translation which would lack such a power – PV.

[92] This doctrine is derived from the *Comte de Gabalis* by Abbé de Villars, 4th Interview.

whose mercy is boundless, revealed to them that it wasn't impossible to find a remedy for this evil; for, the Kabbalists say, just as man, through the covenant he made with God, was made a participator in Divinity, so the Elemental peoples can be made participants of immortality, by the covenant they may contract with the children of wisdom. It follows from this that those who are predestined to will have the glory and happiness of making the nymph or sylph who makes an alliance with them immortal.[93]

Thus, the man who wishes to regenerate himself and regain his First Dignity and his power over the Elements, must purify and exalt the Element of Fire that is within him. He only has to concentrate the Fire of the world in a glass globe by means of concave mirrors, and it is here the artifice that all the ancients have religiously hidden from the profane, and which the Divine Theophrastus discovered. He formed a solar powder in this globe which, having purified itself from the mixture of the other Elements, became in a short time sovereignly proper to exalt the Fire which is within us, and it makes us, in a way, of an igneous nature; from then on the inhabitants of the sphere of Fire become our inferiors, and, delighted to see the restoration of our mutual harmony, they had for us all the friendship and all the respect they had for Adam; and they desire the covenant of the Wise in order to acquire immortality.

With regard to the Sylphs, Nymphs, and Gnomes, it's easier to attract them to oneself, since their existence being much shorter than that of Salamanders, they seek the covenant of the Wise more eagerly. Just close a glass full of conglobed Air, Water or Earth, and leave it exposed to the sun for a month, then separate the Elements following the principles of Hermetic Science. Each of these Elements, thus purified, is called the raw material by Philosophers, which is what, according to them, God used to create the Universe; this material becomes an marvelous magnet for attracting Nymphs, Sylphs and Gnomes, if one takes a certain small dose of it every day for some time; then the Sylphs, the inhabitants of the Air, will become visible to your eyes, and Nymphs and

---

[93] On this subject see the book entitled *des Préadamistes* (Concerning the Pre-Adamites).

Gnomes, guardians of the treasures, will come out of the Earth and offer you their riches. And thus, without writings, without ceremonies, and without mysterious words, one becomes absolute master over all these peoples; they don't require any worship from the Sage, knowing full well that he is nobler than them. This is how Nature teaches its children to repair the Elements by means of the Elements, because man can do everything in the Elements.

All Philosophers agree that in certain circumstances man can obtain from God a superior power to command the Intelligences, and be obeyed by means of evocations; they claim that one must prepare in a certain way, that one must observe the favorable influences, especially since the secrets of Kabbalistic Astrology are the secrets of all religions.

Agrippa reports three ways of evoking Geniuses: the first is natural; it is done by means of mixtures with which they have sympathy; the second is done by the stars when their influences are favorable; the third is Divine: it is done through God's help, Divine Names, and Sacred Ceremonies.

Besides that, there are censings which have a lot of virtue in attracting Geniuses, which modern Philosophers call Invisible Agents, and there are others to drive away the evil ones; you have to know them, know how to mix them, and how to use them appropriately them.

Here is the composition of the incenses corresponding to the Planets, the Elements and the Seven Says of the Week. according to the doctrines of Agrippa.[94]

Incense of the Sun corresponding to Sunday, and the Element of Fire

Take a quarter of an ounce of each of the following drugs: saffron, balm wood, laurel seed, aloe, clove, myrrh and frankincense. Add three grains of musk and three grains of ambergris. All these things must be powdered. They are mixed with the blood of a white rooster or with rose water, into which put

---

[94] Agrippa's *Occult Philosophy*, Book 1, p. 112. They are also found in the *Petit-Albert*, but Jupiter's perfume isn't listed there.

tragacanth; then form small grains in the form of pills, to use when they are dry, throwing them three by three onto hot coals.

Incense of the Moon corresponding to Monday, and the Element of Earth

Take the head of a frog, dry it with the eye of a bull; then take a equal parts of white poppy seed, frankincense, camphor, storax, benzoin or olibanum: mix these drugs[95] with the blood of a young goose or turtle-dove; form a paste, out of which make small grains to use as required; only put three at a time onto hot coals, and you will observe the same thing for the others.

Incense of Mars, corresponding to Tuesday, and the Element of Fire

Take equal parts of the following drugs, namely: sulfur, armaniac, and euphorbia, with the root of the two hellebores, and a piece of black wood from a tree called bdellium; put it all together with the blood and brains of a raven or a black cat; then form into small grains.

Incense of Mercury corresponding to Wednesday, and the Element of Water

Mix together gum mastic, frankincense, aloe wood, good storax and benzoin; add cloves, cinquefoil, powered agate stone; mix all this with the brain of a fox or stag, and magpie blood; then form into small grains.

---

[95] The Magi say that the most wonderful incense, corresponding to the Influences of the Moon, is the blood of a virgin girl the first time she... *Occult Philosophy*, Volume 1, p. 104.

Incense of Jupiter corresponding to Thursday, and the Element of Air

It is composed of ash seeds, aloe wood, storax, benzoin gum and powdered azure stone; to it is added pieces of peacock feathers (which are the sacred bird of Juno, Jupiter's wife): all these drugs must be powdered; they must be mixed with swallow's or stork's blood.

Incense of Venus corresponding to Friday, and the Element of Air

It consists of musk, ambergris, aloe wood, dried roses, and red coral; pulverize all these drugs; add two or three sparrow brains, and mix it all together with turtle-dove or pigeon blood.

Incense of Saturn corresponding to Saturday, and the Element of Water

It is made of black poppy seed, henbane seed, myrrh, and mandrake root; add powered lodestone, if you have any, and mix it all with black cat's blood; make small grains for you to use as needed.

All perfumes must be made in a small earthenware chafing dish, having a triangular shape. The fire should be composed of bay or hazel wood; everything you use, that is: drugs, wood, tinder, match and candle must be new, and not used for any profane use; that is why you must procure them yourself. The fire must also be new, for the incense of the day must be lit by the rays of the sun which should be concentrated using a burning lens; and at nighttime use a flint which is good for this use, which you yourself must pick up in a field; that is how all those who are initiated into some Mystical Rites burn incense in honor of all the Agents of Nature.

Here is what the author of *Threicia*[96] tells us about this, page 361

"But the day is not made without observance. You will begin by making sacrifices or libations to the gods, and you will not go to rest in your bed from the cares of the day until you have done this again; you will offer them incense and each house will have a censer for this purpose, which will continually attest to you the presence of the gods." And in another place, on page 373, he says the following, speaking about the gods who influence the Elements and the Earth: "You shall make no journey without making viatic sacrifices before your departure and upon your return. You depend in upon the gods for everything; you can do nothing by yourself in this unfortunate world; you don't even have your own thoughts. At every occasion in life you will sacrifice to the gods; you will invoke them, whether they are for pain or pleasure; you will not approach a country without invoking the Genius of the place[97] and all the gods who preside over it. When you see a city, you will pray to the guardian gods to be auspicious to you, as well as to those who inhabit it; you will not see a forest without worshipping the fauns and nymphs which inhabit it; you will not see a plain or a mountain, without worshipping the gods who rule there.[98] The Earth is in Heaven; some Philosophers will understand me well; but other Philosophers won't understand me: but it is not to them that I speak. You will not spoil the wells, nor the fountains; you will not sully the Elements; you will not destroy any fruit tree, and you will cut down others except out of necessity, for fear of distorting the Nature which you embrace, since you are in unity. The hearth of your house will be sacred to you; it is your domestic altar; that is where the power of Vesta and of your tutelary gods resides. Be careful not to commit any indecency to your home, for the gods

---

[96] See the book titled *Thréicie, or la seule Voie des sciences divines et humaines*. Paris, pub. Moutardier, printer-bookseller, Quai des Augustins, n.28; Year VII edition.
[97] See *Thréicie*, pp. 377, 378, 379 and 384.
[98] The author, from whom I took this passage to serve as an authority on my system, should have added, according to the consequences he advances, that all the times that our eyes open to the light, and when we look at the great everything, we must worship the Great Being. The same is true of the spirit; all the times we awaken in sleep, our first thought should be for God…

would punish it. *Beware of raising your dress indecently before your hearth, said Hesiod, for the gods reside there.* That is where you will make the sacrifices and libations of your family. What is more holy, more filled with al religion, said Cicero, than the home of every citizen? There are the altars, the hearths, the Penates; there are contained the sacred things of the family, the religions, the ceremonies. If I didn't tell you: I give you the religion that is emanated from the breast of Divinity, I would say to you: I give you the religion of heroes. I throw myself out of bed, said Eneas, and with a cry of joy, I extend my supplicating hands towards heaven. *I pour upon the hearth pure gifts*, intemerata dona, *and joyful to have acquitted myself of this duty, I will announce to my father the vision of the gods...* And elsewhere: "Saying this, he lights the covered fires at the hearth"; *sapitos ignes* does not mean extinct, otherwise, it would have been necessary to relight them: it awakens the Lares of Pergamos, the sanctuary of the chaste Vesta; there is made "a sacrifice of pure flour, and, filling an censer with incense, he makes it burns it in honor of the gods; it is this incense which I said every house must have for this purpose; this is where you will exercise all your rites, waiting for truth to have public temples...

"You will perform no worship, no invocation, no sacrifice, without being purified by washing the body or at least the hands; religion is the expression of what is, and these acts are symbols which express invisible actions, and which operate them. *Without having washed your hands, says Hesiod, you cannot offer wine to Jupiter or to all the other gods in the morning, and they will not listen to your prayers.* If you lack water, you will cleanse yourself in the fire; if you have neither water nor fire, you will purify yourself in the air, asking that the water that takes away everything, will take away your stain. In the water in which you will wash you will place the salt of wisdom, which will sanctify it. You will sanctify the table with salt, and you will not omit salt in any of your sacrifices. For worship, you will present yourself first before the gods, turned in the morning to face the East, at noon and in the evening towards the South, in the evening facing the South, as well as upon going to bed: there is the heart of the world and the hearth. That is how, in Sophocles, Deianira sending her husband Hercules the robe which was to be so fatal to him, said: let him appear before the gods in this robe; you will then hold up the right hand, which is the hand of power, the thumb touching the index finger, to your mouth, because it is your words which must worship the words of the gods and speak to them in their language, *ob ore orare*; then you will prostrate before them; you will then turn around describing a circle: the Romans turned from right to left; the Celts, your ancestors, – O Europeans! – turned from left to right. I would tell you to choose; but you have seen that these are Roman Rites which you must follow; you are only stripped away parts of the Roman Empire. In this manner you will see all the gods and you will be seen; and then you will sit in their repose and in their unity. Great goddess, I do not believe in disclosing your mysteries by saying these things; and whether you offer incense or the parts of the victim you must burn, which are the fats and the intestines, you will wave them in the form of a cross from East to West, from South to North; you will draw a cross[99] by which everything is done, which is the symbol of the power of the gods, of the future and eternal life. The cross within the circle making four right angles, is what the Ancients called *ferctum obmovere*."[100]

It follows from this that the religion of the Magi is the expression and worship of all that is, following the inscription of Isis: *I am all that is, and no one has yet been able to lift the veil that covers me...*

---

[99] It's for this reason that Magi strike the air in crosses with the mysterious rod, turning to the four parts of the world and the four angles of the circle; which must correspond to the four cardinal points, when they make their evocations.
[100] See *Thréicie*, p. 379.

8. *Kabbalistic Astrology with Favorable Influences to Compose the Talismans of the Geniuses*

Philosophers say that Heaven dominates the Earth, and that all the stars influence one another. They've observed that the strongest influences occur when large conjunctions take place, and they say that the two upper planets cross the entire circle of the four triplicities[101] of the heavens in 796 years, which is 199 years for each triplicity; but the greatest changes occur when these conjunctions double the circle of the four triplicities, because the planet Mars, which reverses great things, was in a position diametrically opposed to where it was when the great conjunctions of the planets took place at the cardinal point of the four triplicities, six years before the time when the common era[102] places the birth of Jesus Christ. This is how the author of *Thréicie* reports, page 2 *et seq.*, where he claims that these great conjunctions took place at the cardinal point of the four triplicities under the sign of Aries, where they doubled their circle in the year of the common era 1585; it follows from this that if one wants to take the trouble to compare the eras, from 1585, going back 796 years in periods of 796 years, we will be able to see the causes that have made great changes on the Earth at all these remarkable times; for if we compare it with ancient and modern history, we will see that all these conjunctions correspond first to the Empire of Augustus, the Roman Revolution, the Founding of Rome, the Empire of Alexander and that of Cyrus; then the beginnings of the Mede and Assyrian monarchies, as well as the division of the Assyrian Empire under Sardanapalus, and

---

[101] 'Triplicities' is a way of categorizing the 12 Signs of the Zodiac in Astrology into four groups of 3 (hence the term 'triplicities'). Each season contains 3 Zodiacal signs, known as 'Cardinal', Fixed' and 'Mutable'. For example, in Spring we find Aries (Cardinal – meaning it welcomes in the season); Taurus (Fixed – meaning the season is firmly established); and Gemini (Mutable – meaning the season is preparing to change or 'mutate' into the next one, Summer) – PV.

[102] Note that, while it is odd to see this term used back in the early 1800s rather than B.C. (Before Christ) and A.D. (Anno Domini), this was a result of the French Revolution and the de-emphasizing of religious terms in the calendar – PV.

back from that time to the time when the great cataclysm of the world (the Flood) was located. We find the double circle of the triplicities and that great cataclysm in the same period; and we find the double circle again when we fix the creation of the present world.

Thus, beginning from the year 1585, and descending from period to period, that is, of 796 years, we will arrive at the year 1786[103], when the second triplicity took place, by completing their double circle; then we will project the various changes which have taken place since 1788.

It's not surprising that these monarchies, completing their double circle, have experienced great changes in which various events produced by human passions have taken place, and it's likely that they will continue to experience terrible tremors, since they establish themselves at the cardinal point of their triplicity. The result is that these influences aren't regarded as mere illusion by all who observe them.

On the division of Time

The measure of time, according to the Mages and Kabbalists, is divided by the septenary[104] cycle; all Nations have experienced this cycle, and they have all sanctified the seventh day, whatever the basis of their cycle; some peoples of the islands of the Indian Sea celebrate Tuesday; the Indians of the Malabar coast celebrate Thursday; the Arabs and Mahommedans celebrate Friday; and the Jews Saturday; the Mages sanctify Sunday; the Egyptians, Chaldeans, Persians and Romans also sanctify the day of the Sun. All the Nations didn't create this cycle based upon what they saw; for if they had taken the planet closest to us for their own cycle, the

---

[103] Bear in mind that the author says that 796 years represents around 199 years for each triplicity. Thus, 1786 is around 199 years after 1585 (1784 to be precise). Since the effects are felt over a period of 4 or so years, this encompasses the year 1788. For more examples of numerical operations being applied to history, see the translated text of Papus' *The Science of Numbers* (pub. Rose Circle books 2020), part of the book *The Numerical Theosophy of Saint-Martin & Papus*, and in particular Chapters 9 - 11 – PV.

[104] That is, 7-year – PV.

first day would have been that of the Moon, and the second day of Mercury; and if they had taken as their cycle the furthest planet away, the first day would have been that of Saturn, and the second that of Jupiter, etc..

The Sages of all Nations observed that the number of planets corresponded to the number of actions of the Creation of this world, and that they affected all the divisions of day and night; that is why they assigned four planets to the four divisions of day and night, dividing the twenty-four hours into four equal parts; from which comes the sacred quaternary, by which everything is done, as seen in the following Table:

TABLE OF CYCLES

Which indicates the planets that correspond to the seven quaternaries, the seven days of the week, and the twenty-eight Houses of the Moon

---

The quaternary is composed of four different planets; they each rule six hours every six hours, starting from midnight to midnight, as follows:

Sunday is the first quaternary, whose first hour of the day begins at midnight by the Sun until 6 a.m.; Mars begins from 7 a.m. exactly until noon; Jupiter rules from 1 o'clock precisely hour until 6 o'clock in the evening; Saturn from 7 p.m. precisely until midnight, and so on.

Monday is the 2nd quaternary, whose first hour begins with the Moon[105], the 7th Mercury, the 13th Venus, and the 19th the Sun.

Tuesday is the 3rd quaternary, whose first hour begins with Mars, the 7th Jupiter, the 13th Saturn, and the 19th the Moon.

Wednesday is the 4th quaternary, whose first hour begins with Mercury, the 7th Venus, the 13th the Sun, and the 19th of Mars.

---

[105] This is easier to understand in French, where Monday is *lundi* (Moon = *lune*); Tuesday is *mardi* (Mars); Wednesday is *mercredi* (Mercury); Thursday is *jeudi* (Jupiter), Friday is *vendredi* (Venus), and Saturday is *samedi* (Saturn) – PV.

Thursday is the 5th quaternary, whose first hour begins with Jupiter, the 7th Saturn, the 13th the Moon, and the 19th Mercury.

Friday is the 6th quaternary, whose first hour of the day begins with Venus, the 7th the Sun, the 13th Mars, and the 19th Jupiter.

Saturday is the 7th quaternary, the first hour of the day begins with Saturn, the 7th the Moon, the 13th Mercury, and 19th Venus.

It follows from this that by joining the 7 quaternaries one after the other, in the order shown above, it will be seen that they are the planets which correspond to the 28 Houses of the Moon, and to the four quarters of its revolution, as represented in the following order:

DAYS OF THE MOON

1st quarter	2nd quarter	3rd quarter	4th quarter
1st Sun	8th Sun	15th Sun	22nd Sun
2nd Mars	9th Mars	16th Mars	23rd Mars
3rd Jupiter	10th Jupiter	17th Jupiter	24th Jupiter
4th Saturn	11th Saturn	18th Saturn	25th Saturn
5th Moon	12th Moon	19th Moon	26th Moon
6th Mercury	13th Mercury	20th Mercury	27th Mercury
7th Venus	14th Venus	21st Venus	28th Venus

The 29th day corresponds to the Sun, and the 30th to Mars.

It follows from this that the Moon passes through the seven quaternaries during its revolution, that is, that it encounters the seven planets four times.

These first two tables are the basis and foundation of all Kabbalistic Astronomy; so, whenever the days of the week aren't in correspondence with the days of the Moon, the influences are bad; therefore that Moon is unfortunate; and notice that whenever the Moon renews itself on a Sunday, that month is fortunate, because then the planets are in correspondence with the Moon; and be especially careful to note that whenever the Moon comes together in equal number with the Sun, that is, when it renews itself on the day when the Sun enters one of the twelve Signs of the Zodiac, and that that day is a Sunday, then it will encounter a

8. Kabbalistic Astrology with Favorable Influences

conjunction of favorable influences, to operate in the mysteries of the planet that corresponds to the sign which rules the month. The sage must observe it and prepare accordingly, according to the principles of the Kabbalistic Rite, in order to profit from it and use it in the utmost secrecy...

It was from that doctrine that the Magi, and all those who had been initiated into the Mysteries of the Lamb, Mithras, those of Eleusis and Isis, etc., etc., observed the influences which ruled over the birth and death of humans. They claimed that the soul was a material substance, infinitely subtle, emanating from the eternal fire that shines in the Sun and in the stars, and that it was part of that substance they called Ether. It was for that reason that they observed under which face of the Moon and in which month souls freed themselves from the bonds of the body, in order to return to the luminous abode from which they had originally descended; and they believed that the souls of those who died during the first day of the Moon until the 15th, when it had a favorable aspect with the planets, as we've said above; and especially when the light had vanquished the darkness, that is, from March 20th to September 19th, for then the days are longer than the nights, that soul immediately went back unobstructed to the Principle which had created it.

But for those who died in the last fortnight of the Moon, that is, from September 21st to March 19th, and when the influences of the Moon were unfavorable, the Magi then claimed that the soul experienced all the alterations of light, because the principle of darkness triumphed over Nature, and the nights were longer than the days.

The ancient Indian and Chaldean Astrologers divided the revolution of the Moon into 28 equal parts, which they called the 28 Houses, each of which consisted of 12 degrees 51 minutes and 26 seconds. Each House had its names, attributes and mysteries; as in the following Table:

TABLE OF THE 28 HOUSES OF THE MOON

Containing the Divine Names that Correspond to the 22 Hebrew Letters, According to Kircher's System, with the Names of the Geniuses Corresponding to the 12 Signs of the Zodiac

———

The First House of the Moon begins on the 1ˢᵗ degree of Aries[106] to the 12ᵗʰ; it corresponds to the fist Hebrew letter *aleph* א[107] from which comes the Name *Aiah* איה, which means *Infinite God*. The Geniuses who rule this House are called, according to the Kabbalists, Enediel[108], and according to the Persians, Ormuzd.[109]

The 2ⁿᵈ House begins on the 12ᵗʰ degree 51 minutes and 22 seconds of Aries to the 25ᵗʰ degree of the same sign; it corresponds to the letter *beth* ב, from which comes the Name *Biah* ביה, which means *Path of Wisdom*. The Geniuses who rule over the 2ⁿᵈ day are called Enediel and Bhaman.

3ʳᵈ House begins on the 25ᵗʰ degree 42 minutes and 51 seconds of Aries, up to the 8ᵗʰ degree of Taurus; it corresponds to the letter *gimel* ג from which comes the name *Giah* גיה, which means *God of Retribution*. The Geniuses of the 3ʳᵈ day are called Amixiel, and Ardibeisth.

The 4ᵗʰ House begins on the 8ᵗʰ degree 34 minutes 17 seconds of Taurus, up to the 21ˢᵗ degree of Taurus[110]; it corresponds to the letter daleth ד, from which comes the name *Diah* דיה, which means *Gate of Light*. The Geniuses of the 4ᵗʰ day are called Azariel and Sarivar.

---

[106] Strictly speaking this is misleading, because if the sphere of 360° is divided into 12 Zodiacal signs, the first sign, Aries, actually begins at 0°. Also, some of the calculations in this Table are not entirely accurate, and the precise number of degrees, minutes and seconds are given in some cases and not in others. This Table has been retained as is, with changes only made in the case of clear errors. However, a more accurate Table of the Ranges and Zodiacal Signs for the 28 lunar days is provided in Appendix B – PV.
[107] Kircher, *Œdipus Egyptiacus*, Vol. 2, p. 305 *et seq*.
[108] Agrippa's *Occult Philosophy*.
[109] See the Table of Months, *l'Origine des Cultes*, Vol. 7, p. 142.
[110] The original incorrectly stated 'up to the 4ᵗʰ degree of Gemini' – PV.

The 5th House begins on the 21st degree 25 minutes and 34 seconds of Taurus, up to 4th Degree of Gemini; it corresponds to the letter *heh* ה, from which comes the name *Eiah* היה; which means *God of Gods*. Gabriel and Isphendarmaz rule over the 5th day of the Moon.

The 6th House begins on the 4th degree 17 minutes and 9 seconds of Gemini, up to 17th degree of the same Sign; it corresponds to the letter *vav* ו, from which comes the name *Viah* ויה (*Founding God*). Dirachiel and Churdad rule over the 6th day of the Moon.

The 7th House begins on the 17th degree 8 minutes and 34 seconds of Gemini up to the end of that Sign; it corresponds to the letter *zayin* ז, from which comes the name Ziah זיה; and its attribute is *Shining and Luminous God*. The 7th day is under the influence of Seheliel, Scheliel and Murdad.

The 8th House begins on the first quarter of the moon, that is, from the first degree of Cancer to the 12th degree of the same sign; it corresponds to the letter *heth* ח, from which comes the name *Hiah* חיה; its attribute is *Merciful God*. The Geniuses of the 8th day are Amaediel, Amnediel and Deybadur.

The 9th House begins on the 12th degree 51 minutes and 22 seconds of Cancer up to the 25th degree of the same Sign; it corresponds to the letter *teth* ט, from which comes the name *Tiah* טיה; its attribute is *God of Beauty*. The Geniuses of the 9th day of the Moon are called Barbiel, Adur and Azur.

The 10th House begins on the 25th degree 42 minutes and 52 seconds of Cancer up to the 8th degree of Leo; it corresponds to the letter *yod* י, from which comes the name *Yiah* יהי; its attribute is *Principle of all Things*. The Geniuses ruling the 10th day of the Moon are called Ardefiel and Aban.

The 11th House begins on the 8th degree 34 minutes and 17 seconds of Leo up to the 21st degree of the same Sign; it corresponds to the letter *kaph* כ, from which comes the name *Kiah* כיה; its attribute is *Unchanging God*. The Geniuses of the 11th day are called Neciel and Chûr.

The 12th House begins on the 21st degree 25 minutes and 43 seconds of Leo up to the 4th degree of Virgo; it corresponds to the letter *lamed* ל, from which comes the name *Liah* ליה; its attribute is *God of the Paths of Wisdom*. The Geniuses corresponding to the 12th day of the Moon are called Abdiziel, Abdizuel and Mâh.

The 13th House begins on the 4th degree 17 minutes and 9 seconds of Virgo up to the 17th degree of the same Sign; it corresponds to the letter *mem* מ, from where comes the name *Miah* מיה; its attribute is *Hidden God*. The Geniuses who govern 13th day of the Moon are called Zaxemiel, Jazeriel and Tir.[111]

The 14th House begins on the 17th degree 8 minutes and 34 seconds of Virgo, until the end of that Sign; it corresponds to the letter *nun* נ, from which comes the name *Niah* ניה; its attribute is *God of the Gates of Light*. The Geniuses corresponding to the 14th day of the Moon are called Egrediel, Ergediel, Gjush and Ghûsh.

The 15th House begins on the full moon, that is, from the 1st degree of Libra, up to the 12th degree of the same Sign; it corresponds to the letter named *samekh* ס, from which the name *Siah* סיה; its attribute is *God who Supports*. The Geniuses ruling the 15th day of the Moon are called Ataliel and Deybamihr.

The 16th House begins on the 12th degree 51 minutes and 22 seconds of Libra, up to the 25th degree of the same Sign; it corresponds to the letter *ayin* ע, from where comes the name *Aiah* עיה; its attribute is *God Who Saves*. The Geniuses of the 15th House are called Azertel, Azernel and Mihr.

The 17th House beging on the 25th degree 42 minutes and 51 seconds of Libra up to 8th degree of Scorpio; it corresponds to the letter *peh* פ, from which comes the name *Piah* פיה; its attribute is *God of Praise*. The Geniuses corresponding to the 17th day of the Moon are called Adriël and Sarûsh.

The 18th House begins on the 8th degree 34 minutes and 17 seconds of Scorpio up to the 12th degree of the same Sign; it corresponds to the letter *tzaddi* צ, from which comes the name *Tziah* ציה; its attribute is *God of Justice*. The Geniuses ruling the 18th day of the Moon are called Egibel, Egibiël and Resh.

The 19th House begins on the 21st degree 25 minutes and 43 seconds of Scorpio up to the 4th degree of Sagittarius; it

---

[111] Tir, according to the Persians, is the name of the planet we call Mercury; it corresponds to the 13th day of the Moon. See Zoroaster or the Zend-Avesta, Vol. 2; also see Dupuis, Vol. 2, p. 93.

corresponds to the letter *qoph* ק, from which comes the name Qiah קיה; its attribute is *Just God*. The Geniuses of this House are called Amatuel, Amutiel and Phevardin.

The 20th House begins on the 4th degree 17 minutes and 9 seconds of Sagittarius, up to the 17th degree of the same Sign; it corresponds to the letter *resh* ר, from which comes the name *Riah* ריה; its attribute is *God the Leader*. The geniuses of the 20th day are called Kiriël and Behram.

The 21st House begins on the 17th degree 8 minutes and 34 seconds of Sagittarius until the end of the same Sign; it corresponds to the letter *shin* or ש, from which comes the name *Shiah* שיה its attribute is *God the Savior*. The Geniuses of this House are called Bethuël, Beth-Naël and Ram.

The 22nd House begins on the last quarter of the Moon, that is, from the degree of Capricorn to the 12th degree of the same Sign; it corresponds to the letter *tau* ת, from which comes the name *Tiah* תיה; its attribute is interpreted as *The End of All Things*. The Geniuses ruling the 22nd day of the Moon are called Geliel and Bâd.

The 23rd House begins on the 12th degree 51 minutes and 22 seconds of Capricorn up to the 25th degree of the same Sign; it corresponds to the final kaph letter ך from which comes the name *Casiah* ךסיה[112]; its attribute is *God of Grace*. The Geniuses ruling the 23rd day of the Moon are called Kequiël, Requiël and Deybadin.

The 24th House begins on the 26th degree 42 minutes and 51 seconds of Capricorn up to 8th degree of Aquarius; it corresponds to the final letter *mem* ם[113], from which comes the name *Miah*; its attribute is *God Who Supports*. Geniuses dominating the 24th. Moon Day are named Abrinel, Ainael and Din.

---

[112] The fact that the 23rd through the 27th Houses being each Hebrew word with a final letter caused some debate. However, I am grateful to Aaron Leitch for doing some research on the topic, which revealed the fact that using what we term 'final' letters to end words is a relatively recent grammatical rule, and that previously both forms were used interchangeably – PV.

[113] In the original this is listed as *samekh* (ס), which is an understandable error given its similarity with the final *mem*. However, this led to a copying of the rest of the attributes of that incorrect letter. Similarly, the name has been altered from *Siah* to *Miah*. Since this was an error in the original 1823 book, we must assume that, since the name is the same as the regular *mem*, the meaning (*God Who Supports*) remains the same – PV.

The 25th House begins on the 8th degree 34 minutes and 17 seconds of Aquarius, up to 21st degree of the same Sign; it corresponds to the final letter nun ן, from which comes the name *Niah* ניה; its attribute is *God of Light*. The geniuses of the house are named Aziel and Ard.

The 26th House begins on the 21st degree 25 minutes and 43 seconds of Aquarius, up to the 4th degree of Pisces; it corresponds to the final letter peh ף, where comes the name *Phiah* פיה; its attribute is *God of Eloquence*. The Geniuses ruling the 26th day are called Tagriël and Ashtad.

The 27th House begins on the 4th degree 17 minutes and 9 seconds of Pisces up to 17th degree of the same Sign; it corresponds to the final letter tzaddi ץ, from which comes the name *Tzaddiah* צדיה; its attribute *Just God*. The Geniuses corresponding to the 27th day of the Moon are called Alheniel and Azuman.

The 28th and the Moon's last House begins on the 17th degree 8 minutes and 34 seconds of Pisces until the end of the same Sign; it corresponds to the letter O, which refers to the circle and the end of the revolution of the Moon, from which comes the name *Oiah* ויה; its attribute is *God Who Contains All That Is*. The Geniuses of the 28th House are called Amnixiel and Zamyâd.

The 29th and the 30th days correspond to Marisphand and Adiram.

DISTRIBUTION OF THE PLANETS

During the twelve hours of day and night

The ancient Mages recognized that the number twelve divided up the heavens, especially since six signs of day and six of night rose at all times, regardless of whether the days were long or short; it was because of this that they divided the day and night into twelve equal parts. ("*Are there not twelve hours in the day?*" Jesus Christ in St. John, Ch. 11, v. 9.) They also assigned a planet to each division of the day and night; and since the days aren't equal, it follows that planetary hours aren't either; and if one wishes to know how many minutes compose a particular planet's hour, on any day or in any location, one must perform the following calculation, namely: suppose the length of the day when one wishes to know the influence of the planets is fifteen hours, multiply the number of hours by five, which gives 75 minutes, that is, the 12th part of the day; consequently the 12 planetary hours of that day are each composed of 75 minutes. There remain 9 hours for the night. Multiply that number by 5, to give 45; that is, the 12 hours of the night each consist of 45 minutes. Follow the same process for all times and for any location.

Others perform their calculation as follows: they learn the times of sunrise and sunset; then they add up the number of minutes which make up the day, and that number divided by 12 gives a planetary hour.

We know that Sunday corresponds to the Sun; The Moon to Monday, March to Tuesday, Mercury to Wednesday, Jupiter to Thursday, Venus to Friday and Saturn to Saturday.[114]

Sunday, the hours of the day

The Sun rules the first of the day of Sunday at midnight, the 2nd Venus, the 3rd Mercury, the 4th the Moon, the 5th Saturn, the 6th Jupiter, the 7th Mars, the 8th the Sun, the 9th Venus, the 10th Mercury, the 11th the Moon, the 12th Saturn.

Sunday, the hours of the night

The 1st hour rules Jupiter, the 2nd Mars, the 3rd the Sun, the 4th Venus, the 5th Mercury, the 6th the Moon, the 7th Saturn, the 8th Jupiter, the 9th Mars, the 10th the Sun, the 11th Venus, the 12th Mercury.

Monday, the hours of the day

The 1st hour rules the Moon, the 2nd Saturn, the 3rd Jupiter, the 4th Mars, the 5th the Sun, the 6th Venus, the 7th Mercury, the 8th the

---

[114] Refer to Footnote 107 – PV.

Moon, the 9th Saturn, the 10th Jupiter, the 11th Mars, the 12th the Sun.

Monday, the hours of the night

The 1st hour rules Venus, the 2nd Mercury, the 3rd the Moon, the 4th Saturn, the 5th Jupiter, the 6th Mars, the 7th the Sun, the 8th Venus, the 9th Mercury, the 10th the Moon, the 11th Saturn, the 12th Jupiter.

Tuesday, the hours of the day

The 1st hour rules Mars, the 2nd the Sun, the 3rd Venus, the 4th Mercury, the 5th the Moon, the 6th Saturn, the 7th Jupiter, the 8th Mars, the 9th the Sun, the 10th Venus, the 11th Mercury, the 12th the Moon.

Tuesday, the hours of the night

The 1st hour rules Saturn, the 2nd Jupiter, the 3rd Mars, the 4th the Sun, the 5th Venus, the 6th Mercury, the 7th the Moon, the 8th Saturn, the 9th Jupiter, the 10th Mars, the 11th the Sun, the 12th Venus.

Wednesday, the hours of the day

The 1st hour rules Mercury, the 2nd the Moon, the 3rd Saturn, the 4th Jupiter, the 5th Mars, the 6th the Sun, the 7th Venus, the 8th Mercury, the 9th the Moon, the 10th Saturn, the 11th Jupiter, the 12th Mars.

Wednesday, the hours of the night

The 1st hour rules the Sun, the 2nd Venus, the 3rd Mercury, the 4th the Moon, the 5th Saturn, the 6th Jupiter, the 7th Mars, the 8th the Sun, the 9th Venus, the 10th Mercury, the 11th the Moon, the 12th Saturn.

8. Kabbalistic Astrology with Favorable Influences

Thursday, the hours of the day

The 1st hour rules Jupiter, the 2nd Mars, the 3rd the Sun, the 4th Venus, the 5th Mercury, the 6th the Moon, the 7th Saturn, the 8th Jupiter, the 9th Mars, the 10th the Sun, the 11th Venus, the 12th Mercury.

Thursday, the hours of the night

The 1st hour rules the Moon, the 2nd Saturn, the 3rd Jupiter, the 4th Mars, the 5th the Sun, the 6th Venus, the 7th Mercury, the 8th the Moon, the 9th Saturn, the 10th Jupiter, the 11th Mars, the 12th the Sun.

Friday, the hours of the day

The 1st hour rules Venus, the 2nd Mercury, the 3rd the Moon, the 4th Saturn, the 5th Jupiter, the 6th Mars, the 7th the Sun, the 8th Venus, the 9th Mercury, the 10th the Moon, the 11th Saturn, the 12th Jupiter.

Friday, the hours of the night

The 1st hour rules Mars, the 2nd the Sun, the 3rd Venus, the 4th Mercury, the 5th the Moon, the 6th Saturn, the 7th Jupiter, the 8th Mars, the 9th the Sun, the 10th Venus, the 11th Mercury, the 12th the Moon.

Saturday, the hours of the day

The 1st hour rules Saturn, the 2nd Jupiter, the 3rd Mars, the 4th the Sun, the 5th Venus, the 6th Mercury, the 7th the Moon, the 8th Saturn, the 9th Jupiter, the 10th Mars, the 11th the Sun, the 12th Venus.

Saturday, the hours of the night

The 1st hour rules Mercury, the 2nd the Moon, the 3rd Saturn, the 4th Jupiter, the 5th Mars, the 6th the Sun, the 7th Venus, the 8th

Mercury, the 9th the Moon, the 10th Saturn, the 11th Jupiter, the 12th Mars.

It should be noted that Jupiter and Venus are favorable and joyful planets. Saturn and Mars are very bad. The Sun and Moon are intermediate. Mercury is good with the good planets, and bad with the bad.

The Mages also submitted the 12 Signs of the Zodiac to the 12 hours of the day and night; the first hour begins at precisely midnight with Aries, and the second ends with Pisces in the following order;

Hours of the day

Aries rules from midnight to 1 o'clock.
Taurus, from one o'clock to 2 am.
Gemini, from 2 am to 3 am.
Cancer, from 3 am to 4 am.
Leo, from 4 am to 5 am.
Virgo, from 5 am to 6 am.
Libra, from 6 am to 7 am.
Scorpio, from 7 am to 8am.
Sagittarius, from 8 am to 9 am.
Capricorn, from 9 am to 10 am.
Aquarius, from 10 am 11 am.
Pisces, from 11 am to 12 noon.

Hours of the night

Aries rules from noon to 1 o'clock.
Taurus, etc. (*see the hours of the day*).

Modern Philosophers say that the first Sign must always begin with the Sign which rules the month, and the season in which one is, observing the following:

8. Kabbalistic Astrology with Favorable Influences

From March 20th to April 18th, the Sun is in the Sign of Aries. The 1st hour of day and night must begin with Aries, and the 12th hour ends with Pisces.

From April 19th to May 18th, the 1st hour begins with the Sign of Taurus, and the 12th ends with Aries.

From May 19th to June 17th, the 1st hour begins with Gemini, and the 12th ends with Taurus.

From June 18th to July 17th, the 1st hour begins with Cancer, and the 12th ends with Gemini.

From July 18th to August 16th, the 1st hour begins with Leo, and the 12th ends with Cancer.

From August 17th to September 15th, the 1st hour begins with Virgo, and the 12th ends with Leo.

From September 16th to October 15th, the 1st hour begins with Libra, and the 12th ends with Virgo.

From October 16th to November 14th, the 1st hour begins with Scorpio, and the 12th ends with Libra.

From November 15th until December 14th, 1st hour begins with Sagittarius, and the 12th ends with Scorpio.

From December 15th to January 13th, the 1st hour begins with Capricorn, and the 12th ends with Sagittarius.

From January 14th until February 12th, the 1st hour begins with Aquarius, and the 12th ends with Capricorn.

From February 13th to March 14th, the 1st hour begins with Pisces, and the 12th ends with Aquarius.

EXPLANATION OF THE FOUR TRIANGLES

Fire Triangle

This corresponds to the East and the Spring season; it affects blood, humidity and heat. The Sun is the first leader that rules the day, and Jupiter the second; at night it is the other way around: Jupiter rules the first, the Sun the second, and Saturn shares both empires. Aries is the principle of Fire, Leo is its increase, and Sagittarius the end.

Air Triangle

This corresponds to the South and the Summer season; it is hot and dry and influences bile and anger. Saturn is the first leader ruling the day, and Mercury the second; at night it is the other way around: Mercury rules the first, and Saturn the second: Jupiter shares both empires. Air derives its principle from Gemini[115], Libra is its increase, and Aquarius the end.

Water Triangle

This corresponds to the West and the Autumn season. This season influences melancholy; it is cold and dry. Venus is the first planet that rules in the day, and Mars the second; at night it is the opposite: Mars rules the first, and Venus the second: the Moon shares both empires. Cancer is the first principle of Water, Scorpio is its increase, and Pisces the end.

Earth Triangle

This corresponds to the North and the Winter season; it influences phlegmatics. This season is cold and humid. Venus is the first planet that rules the day, and the Moon the second: at night it is the other way around: the Moon rules the first, and Venus the second: Mars shares both empires. Taurus derives its principle from Earth, Virgo expresses its fertility, and Capricorn the end.

---

[115] Agrippa, *Occult Philosophy*, Book 1.

EXALTATIONS OF PLANETS
and the period when they arrive

According to Dupuis[116], the exaltation of a planet is the place in the heavens where its influence is supposed to be strongest; he claims that the ancients instituted fasts to celebrate their Feasts and Mysteries. According to him, the Feast of Saturn takes place at 21st degree of Libra, which is the place of its exaltation, corresponding to October 6th; the Feast of Jupiter takes place on the 15th degree of Cancer, corresponding to July 2nd; the Feast of Mars comes on the 18th degree of Capricorn, which corresponds to January 1st; the Feast of the Sun comes on March 20th, which is the equinoctial point or the place of its exaltation; the Feast of Venus comes on the 27th degree of Pisces, corresponding to March 11th; the Feast of Mercury comes on the 15th degree of Virgo, corresponding to August 31st; and the Feast of the Moon comes on the 3rd degree of Taurus, corresponding to April 21st.

Concerning the influence of the planets, depending on their positions in the 12 Signs of the Zodiac

Saturn has its throne in Aquarius; then it rules over melancholy. Earth, Air and dark green are associated with it.

Jupiter has its throne in Sagittarius; it rules over Fire mixed with Air; it affects the blood; then the color red is associated with it.

Mars has its throne in Aries; it rules over Fire and anger: the fiery color is associated with it.

The Sun has its throne in Leo; it rules over Fire and Air; the colors yellow and gold are associated with it.

Venus has its throne in Taurus; it rules over Earth and Water; it influences blood and phlegm: the colors green and citron are associated with it.

Mercury has its throne in Gemini; it rules over Water and Air; it influences bile: the color ash grey is associated with it.

---

[116] *Origine des cultes*, Vol. 1, pp. 325 and 253.

The Moon has its throne in Cancer; it rules over Water and phlegm; white is associated with it.

Power and strength of the planets

Saturn is strong and powerful in Capricorn; it governs the Earth and melancholy: then it likes the color black.

Jupiter is strong and powerful in Pisces; it governs Water and Air; it affects the pituitary and blood: the colors blue and green are associated with it.

Mars is strong and powerful in Scorpio; it governs Fire and Earth; it influences phlegm and anger: the color of iron is associated with it.

Venus is strong and powerful in Libra; it governs Air and blood; the colors green and blue are associated with it.

Mercury is strong and powerful in Virgo; it governs Earth and Air; it influences black bile and melancholy: the color of lead is associated with it.

The harmony of the planets

Saturn in Pisces likes Jupiter a little, and Jupiter in Aquarius likes Saturn a little; Mars in Virgo is Mercury's friend; the Sun in Sagittarius is good with Jupiter; Venus in Leo is good with the Sun; Mercury in Aries is good with Mars; the Moon in Cancer is good with the Earth.

Falls of the planets, that is, where they influence a character contrary to their benevolence with respect to the Earth

Saturn is sad in Cancer, and unfortunate in Aries; Jupiter in Gemini, and Capricorn; Mars in Taurus, Libra and Cancer; Sun in Aquarius and Libra; Venus in Aries, Scorpio and Virgo; Mercury in Sagittarius and Pisces; the Moon in Capricorn and Libra.

It should also be noted that not all planets work well together; for example, Mars and Venus are enemies of Saturn: Jupiter, the Sun, Mercury and the Moon are all favorable to it. All planets except Mars, are friends of Jupiter; and all except Venus, are enemies of Mars. Jupiter and Venus love the Sun; Mars, Mercury and the Moon are contrary to it: all planets except Saturn love Venus.

Birds dedicated to the planets

Saturn influences the hoopoe, raven, and owl; Jupiter influences the eagle, peacock and pelican; March influences the vulture, falcon and hawk; the Sun influences the phoenix, the swan and the rooster; Venus influences the dove, turtle-dove and sparrow; Mercury influences the stork, parrot and magpie; the Moon influences the goose, duck and the diver.

Fish dedicated to the planets

Saturn influences the eel; Jupiter influences the dolphin; March influences the barbel and pike; the Sun influences the sea calf; Venus influences the tithymallus; Mercury influences the mugil and trochus[117]; the Moon influences the crayfish.

Animals dedicated to the planets

Saturn influences the donkey, mole, camel, wolf and snake; Jupiter influences the elephant, hart and lamb; March influences the wolf, leopard and hyena; The Sun influences the baboon, lion, ram and horse; Venus influences the goat, calf, bull and rabbit; Mercury influences the dog, hare, fox and monkey; the Moon influences the chameleon, the panther, the hind and the cat.

Trees and plants dedicated to the planets

Saturn influences the asphodel, pine, cypress, black fig, black poppies, black hellebore, great parsley or wild celery, sempervivum, cumin, rue, benzoin, and generally all fragrant roots, such as mandrake root and ageratum.

---

[117] Agrippa's *Occult Philosophy*.

Jupiter influences the bugloss, agrimony, mace, buckwheat, henbane, ear of wheat, mastic, mint, elecampane; darnel, poplar, oak, ash, hazel, pear, apple, vine and plum tree, and all fragrant fruits, such as nutmeg and cloves.

Mars influences garlic, euphorbia, onions, shallots, leeks, radishes, French turnips, mustard, nettle, thistle, peucedanum, plantain, nettle seeds, scammony, small bay, dogwood, and all trees which have thorns, and usually all fragrant trees, such as cypress and balm.

The Sun influences the sunflower, knotweed, peony, celandine, ginger, gentian, dittany, ivy, mint, lavender, marjoram, rosemary, bay leaf, lemon tree, saffron, balm, aloe wood, cloves, pepper, palm and cedar; and in general all kinds of odoriferous gums, such as amber, frankincense, mastic, benzoin, storax, laudanum and musk.

Venus influences verbena, violet, maidenhair, orange, valerian, thyme, coriander, sandalwood, myrtle and boxwood; and all fragrant flowers, such as roses, etc.

Mercury influences the fumatory, pimpernel, marjoram, various species of parsley, cinquefoil, cinnamon, cassia, mace, barks, laurel seed; and all fragrant seeds.

The Moon influences the selenotropion, which is always turned towards the Moon[118] like the sunflower towards the Sun; the palm tree which grows a branch at every moonrise; chinosta grass that grows and decreases like the Moon; hyssop, peony and the olive tree, nicknamed the unblemished lamb or the chaste tree; and all fragrant leaves, such as the leaves of the horse-chestnut, myrtle and laurel.

Precious stones and metals dedicated to the planets

Saturn influences lead, onyx, cornelian, sapphire, jasper and chalcedony; Jupiter influences tin, hyacinth, beryl, emerald, and jasper; Mars influences iron, lodestones, diamond, amethyst, bloodstone, and all kinds of jasper; the Sun influences the carbuncle, chrysolite, iris, heliotrope, jasper, emerald, hyacinth, topaz, chrysoprase and ruby; Venus influences copper, emerald,

---

[118] Agrippa, *Occult Philosophy*, Book 1.

coral and chrysolite; Mercury influences the quicksilver, porphyry, topaz and agate.

Colors dedicated to the planets

The Mages recognized three principal colors when decomposing light, namely: blue, red and yellow; the intermediary colors were only nuances formed from the mixture of two colors combined: red and yellow gave the color orange, blue and red created purple, yellow and blue formed green. They said that white was not a color, that it was simply the emblem of light, just as black represented darkness and chaos; that color is attributed to Saturn; the brightness and the color of azure at Jupiter; red and the color of the fire to Mars; the color of gold and yellow to the Sun. Venus bears the imprint of the morning star; to it is attributed the colors pink and green: the varied or nuanced colors are attributed to Mercury, and white to the Moon.

Influences attributed to the planets

Saturn is the god of time; the ancient Mages represented him devouring his children, that is, the days that flee behind us; he influences old age and decrepitude; he gives the gift of wisdom[119]; he rules the stability of things, longevity of life, and celibacy; he influences imagination, scholars, the high sciences, contemplation of divine things, prelates and ecclesiastics.

Under the influence of the evil principle he causes premature death, change and upheaval; he influences melancholy, ignorance, neglect and laziness.

Jupiter, the god of lightning, is the king of the heavens; he preside at the age when man enjoys his wisdom, and all the empire of his reason; he gives the gift of intelligence; he is naturally hot and humid, but so temperate that he contributes singularly to the spread and preservation of the human species; he rules over Divine power and all matters concerning the priesthood; he influences piety, modesty, fidelity, all that characterizes the generous and virtuous

---

[119] The gifts of the seven planets correspond to the seven gifts of the Holy Spirit.

soul. In relation to the evil principle, he rules pride, disgrace, dishonor, jealousy, vengeance, and all immoral actions.

Mars, the god of war, presides over the virile age when man has all his vigor; he gives the gift of strength; he rules over iron, arsenals, and all that relates to military genius; he influences peace, friendship, gentleness, frankness and greatness of soul. In relation to the evil principle, he causes war, discord, and influences angry and bloodthirsty men.

The Sun, the god of light, is the first Agent of Nature; he presides over sight, beauty of the body, youth and the middle of life; just as he occupies the center of our planetary system, he gives the gift of knowledge, and influences crowned heads, and all that is connected to royal magnificence and majesty; he rules over scholars, fortune, liberality and charity. In relation to the evil principle, he governs pride, selfishness, avarice and arrogance.

Venus is the goddess of love, pleasure, and fertility; she spreads a dew favorable to the vegetation of plants, and to the generation of animals; she gives the gift of piety; she represents adolescence, beauty, amenity, finery, loves, marriages, and anything that flatters the senses. In relation to the evil principle, she influences infertility, jealousy, incest, adultery, and all that belongs to voluptuousness.

Mercury is the messenger of the gods and interpreter of the Divine Light; he represents infancy and gives the gift of counsel; he influences eloquence, poetry, music, astronomy, mathematics and teachers.

The Moon represents the goddess Diana, Apollo's sister; she rules over the night, and influences first youth; she gives it the gift of fear, and she rules over travel and trade, principally that of the sea; she influences freedom, sobriety, culture, aquatic work, and everything related to the navy and fishing. In relation to the evil principle, she controls storms, shipwrecks, prisoners, exiles, denunciation, flattery and voracity.

It follows from everything shown in this Chapter that whenever you make a working under the influence of some planet, you have to use the things that are connected with it; otherwise you will not get any results. Suppose you want to create a talisman under the influence of the Sun; it must be engraved on fine gold, or on a stone that is under its influence, or drawn on the skin of an animal dedicated to it, such as lamb. The lamb must be virgin; it must be sacrificed and prepared by you, following the principles of the Kabbalistic Rite; all things having being prepared in advance, and favorable influences having arrived, you will draw the talisman with a pen and the blood of a bird which is dedicated to the Sun, such as a swan or rooster; then you will cense it with the appropriate drugs and plants: the fire must be made from wood of a tree which is also dedicated to it, such as laurel; and you will follow the same system for all the rest.

9. Favorable Influences
for Composing the Talismans

Explanation of the Mysterious Seal of the Sun

According to Egyptian and Arab traditions, the ancient Astrologers composed the mysterious Seal of the Sun around the first degree of Aries. It's at the moment when it joins with the constellations of the Whale or Sea Monster, and when it joins at the same time with Medusa; which occurs every year on March 20[120]; on this day the Sun enters the Lamb[121] and reaches the point of its exaltation.

The talisman contains 6 columns that represent the number 6, enclosed in a square corresponding to the number 4; these two numbers form the number 10, emblem of unity and of the circle (see Chapter 1). Each column contains 6 squares, the total of which is 36, corresponding to the 36 faces of the heavens, and the 36 Geniuses ruling the sphere, according to the System of the Egyptians.

The number 36 is half of 72, which is the number of 72 Geniuses who govern the 72 quinaries of the heavens, according to the system of the Kabbalists.

Each of these squares contains a mysterious number.[122] If you add all these numbers, either horizontally, vertically or diagonally, you will always have 111, which is the mysterious seal of the Sun; and if you add up the 6 columns, that is, 6 times 111, you will find a total of 666, which is the Number of the Beast[123], according to Revelations. Here is wisdom. It's said that with this seal one can

---

[120] *Origine des Cultes* by Dupuis, Vol. 1, pp. 150 and 252, and Vol. 6, p. 207.
[121] Then we enter the Paschal Season, and we celebrate the Feast of the Lamb, the day of Easter. The Egyptians, the Magi and the Kabbalists celebrate it on March 20th; on this day the Sun enters the 1st degree of Aries: that is how God revealed it to Moses. (*"This month shall be unto you the beginning of the months: it shall be the first month of the year to you."*) Exodus, Ch. 12. v. 2.
[122] This talisman occupies the center of the Kabbalistic sphere.
[123] Revelation of St. John, Ch. 13, vv. 16, 17 and 18.

protect oneself from all adversity, and that everyone should have it.

This talisman is credited with wonderful virtues; the person who wears it upon him will be very successful in all his endeavors; he will be esteemed by all, and will obtain favor from the great; no human power can harm him, and all the invisible powers will fear him.

Here is the passage from *Abenpharagi* on this seal, with the manner in which the Arab Astrologers prepared this talisman; according to Kircher's report, *Œdipus Egyptiacus*, Vol. 2, p. 75; and according to Dupuis, *Origine des cultes*, Vol. 6, p. 355.

"Take 6 drachmas of pure gold (*this is the metal of the Sun*), and make a round plate, on which you will engrave a table characteristic of the seal, on the day and at the time when the Sun is in its exaltation, which is around the 16th degree of Aries or the ram; this being done, you will steam it in the vapor of saffron; you will wash it with rose water in which you will have dissolved musk and camphor; then you will wrap it in a piece of silk stuff of the color of saffron, and carry it upon you. It will make you successful in all your undertakings; everybody will fear you; you will obtain whatever you want from princes and kings, either by asking yourself, or through the person you decide to send to them; you will find what you've lost, and God will spread His blessing upon you and on everything which belongs to you: this figure of the Sun is its seal; its character, which must be engraved on the reverse, contains a great secret (*est magnum secretum*); it is called creator, light, perfect, powerful, glorious, life, virtue, brilliant, radiant: the angels of the Sun are Anaël and Raphaël."[124]

---

[124] Dupuis gives the figure of this talisman in his set of prints for *l'Origine des cultes*, Plate 21. [This is reproduced in Appendix C since it was not included in the original book by Lenain – PV].

DESCRIPTION

FAVORABLE INFLUENCES FOR COMPOSING TALISMANS AND OPERATEING THE MYSTERIOUS RITES

Concerning the influence of the Sun, corresponding to Sunday

In general, the most favorable influence is where there is a combination of extraordinary circumstances. First, the Moon must meet in an equal number with the Sun, which happens every five years, according to the reasons given by the author of *Thréisie, or la seule Voie de sciences divines et humaines*, page 303 et seq.[125]

The Moon must renew itself on a Sunday, when the Sun enters the 1st degree of Aries; then the favorable hour begins at the moment when the conjunction takes place, that is, at the time when the Moon renews itself; there may be an eclipse of the Sun at that moment, and as long as it lasts the moment will be favorable to create the talisman.

The second influence comes when the Moon renews itself on a Sunday, with the Sun entering the 1st degree of Leo; and the person born during these favorable hours will be a being privileged by Nature; he will have an extraordinary genius in terms of science and the arts.

Concerning the influence of the Moon, corresponding to Monday

The first favorable influence of the Moon comes when it renews itself on a Sunday, the Sun making its entrance to the 1st degree of Taurus; then it is necessary to wait for its 3rd day, which will

---

[125] According to the Egyptians, Osiris entered the Moon. Then the great *Panathenaea* were celebrated in Athens; the Romans celebrated the great *Dionysiac*s; the city, the army and the people were purified, and each was regenerated with the new conjunction of the luminaries. The ancients only celebrated the New Moon when they had seen it. Among the Romans, the second pontiff was responsible for discovering it; as soon as he had seen it he alerted the king of sacrifices, and he proclaimed the news for the following day, and when he couldn't see it he ruled himself by the *Ephemerids*.

correspond to the 3rd degree of the same Sign, which is the place of its exaltation.

The second influence comes when it renews itself on a Sunday, the Sun entering the 1st degree of Cancer; then it is necessary to wait until it is in its 9th House, that is to say at its 9th day, which will be a Monday; consequently the 1st, 8th, and 15th hours of that day are favorable to compose the talismans of the Geniuses which are under the influence of the Moon.

Concerning the influence of Mars, corresponding to Tuesday

The first favorable influence of Mars comes when the Moon renews itself on a Sunday, with the Sun entering the 1st degree of Capricorn; then one must wait until it's at its 18th day, which will be a Tuesday, because its 18th House corresponds to Scorpio, which is the home of Mars; then the Sun and Moon will be in number equal to the 18th degree of Capricorn, which is the place of its exaltation.

The second influence comes when the Moon renews itself on a Sunday, with the Sun entering the 1st degree of Aries; then the 3rd and the 18th days of the Moon will each correspond to a Tuesday, and all circumstances will be favorable to create talismans which are under the influence of Mars.

Concerning the influence of Mercury, corresponding to Wednesday

Mercury's first influence comes when the Moon renews itself on a Sunday, with the Sun entering the 1st degree of Gemini; then the 1st Wednesday of the Moon will be favorable to the operations of Mercury.

The second influence occurs when the Moon renews itself on a Sunday, the Sun entering the 1st degree of Virgo; then one must wait until it's at its 15th day; then it will correspond to the 15th degree of Virgo; on that day Mercury reaches the point of its exaltation.

Concerning the influence of Jupiter, corresponding to Thursday

Jupiter's first influence occurs when the Moon renews itself on a Sunday, with the Sun entering the 1st degree of Cancer; then one must wait for the day and the hour when it enters its fullness; then it corresponds with the Sun in the 15th degree of Cancer, which is the god of Jupiter's exaltation.

The second influence occurs when the Moon renews itself on a Sunday, with the Sun entering the 1st degree of Sagittarius; then it's necessary to wait until it is in its 19th House which corresponds to Sagittarius and Jupiter (see page 117).

Concerning the influence of Venus, corresponding to Friday

Venus' first influence occurs when the Moon renews itself on a Sunday, with the Sun entering the degree of Pisces; then it is necessary to wait for it to enter its 17th House, which corresponds to this Sign, that is, when it is at its 27th day; then it will correspond with the Sun to the 27th degree of Pisces, which is the place of exaltation of Venus.

The second influence takes place when the Moon renews itself on a Sunday, with the Sun entering the 1st degree of Taurus; then, the 1st Friday of the Moon will be favorable to operations.

Concerning the influence of Saturn, corresponding to Saturday

Saturn's first influence comes when the Moon renews itself on a Sunday, with the Sun entering the degree of Libra; then it is necessary to wait for the day and time the Moon reaches its last quarter; then it will correspond with the Sun to the 21st degree of Libra, which is the place of Saturn's exaltation of Saturn.

The second influence takes place when the Moon renews itself on a Sunday, with the Sun entering the 1st degree of Capricorn, then we must observe the day and time when the Moon arrives in its last quarter, entering its 21st House, which corresponds to Capricorn.

It's the result of all I've just said that sages must observe the influences of the stars; and when there is a favorable circumstance, it's necessary to prepare in advance to take advantage of it, in order to operate successfully in the mysteries of the planet that will dominate. The person who wishes to take advantage of heavenly influences must never talk nor write down what he has conceived and decided in his mind concerning that subject; only God and the Genius of the soul knows our thoughts. The evil Genius can only know them when we pronounce them; for if your evil Genius manages to penetrate your designs, he will cause all possible problems to make you fail.

10. The Etymology of the Name JEHOVAH with an Explanation of the 12 Chavioth הויות of that Mysterious Name

Having started my first chapter with *alph*a, I finish the last one with *omega*; this is how everything must start and end... otherwise, everything is pointless and without result... My intention, in this book, was to instruct my Brothers and Sisters..., to open the path which leads to Light and Truth: all for the Glory of the Eternal Geometrician and Grand Architect of the Universe...

"[126] יהוה Jehovah derives from the root הוה *havah*, which means it is, it was, it existed; or also היה *haiah*, which is the same thing as the previous one, with the proviso that the former is more common among to the Chaldeans, and the latter among the Hebrews. It refers to *He who is, the Eternal*[127]; it is the true proper name of God, by which He is distinguished from idols which are merely feigned objects and do not exist. This name indicates the eternity of God: the first syllable, י or *je*[128], marks the future time; the second, ה *ho*, the present time; and the third, וה *vah*, time past. This title is given to Jesus Christ, *who is, who was, who shall be*. There is no name in any language of other Nations that corresponds perfectly to it, which expresses the essence according to all the differences of time; for, as Aben-Ezra said concerning Psalm 50, verse 1, it indicates God's eternity and immutability. Of all the Names of God, this is – we repeat – the most appropriate to Him, and the only one which expressly and absolutely describes the essence of the Divine Majesty. Jehovah is composed of the only letters that the Hebrews call *quiescent*, which rest, which have no movement, to show that one finds rest only in God and that one can rest on Him.

"It's probable that the Gentiles learned something about this name through hearsay, and because of that they called their God

---

[126] This etymology was given to me by a distinguished scholar.
[127] *L'Éternel* is usually rendered as 'Lord' in English, but here it is given its actual name – PV.
[128] As well as being the first syllable of 'Jehovah', *je* in French also means 'I' – PV.

10. The Etymology of the Name Jehovah

Jupiter, whom they call *Jovem* in the accusative, answering to the name Jehovah; thus the Latins borrowed their common and ordinary name of *Jupiter* or *Jovis* (This is how *Priscian* maintains that the Hebrews once used that name). For finally what is the difference between the *Jovis* of the Latins and the *Jehovah* of the Hebrews, or rather the *Jehovih*, as it is written in certain places in the Bible?"

It was by this name that Jesus Christ performed miracles, chased away demons, and healed the sick[129]; for that great mysterious name is the word of the M∴[130], which has never been lost. This word is universal, and it produces all things; ultimately, it is the Word[131], by which God created the heavens, the earth, and all that is contained within the space of His infinite circle, and it is formed from the beginning of the Word, that is to say from the first letters of the first four dictions of the first verse of Genesis, Chapter II, according to the Hebrew text.

The heavens	*were completed*	*on the sixth*	*day.*
השמים	ויכלו	השׁשׁי	יום
Haschamaim	*Vaiekullou*	*Haschischi*	*Iom*

It follows from this that it should never be uttered unnecessarily; Holy Scripture teaches us by using these words: *"Thou shalt not take the name of the Lord in vain"*, etc. Exodus, chapter 20, verse 7.

The anagram of this name forms twelve others, called by the Kabbalists the twelve *chavioth* הוות; they each correspond to the 12 Signs of the Zodiac, the 12 hours of the day and of the night, the

---

[129] Father Kircher gives the invocation of the Intelligences which preside over the four parts of the world, in his book: *Œdipus Egyptiacus*, Vol. 2, p. 393, in which he discusses the miracles that Jesus Christ did in that name.
Balthasar Bekker, Doctor of Theology, discusses the same thing in his book *le Monde enchanté*, Vol. 1, p. 181, 1694 edition.
[130] Mason. It's curious to note that Lenain spends much time in the last few pages emphasizing his Masonic background – PV.
[131] Man is the only one among the animals who has the power of speech, which is the Word (see p. 108), by which he can worship and praise God in all possible languages, and in a manner worthy of his Creator. From this, we can see it is the most physical proof that we are created in His Image.

four seasons, and the four Elements. Here they are each in their order, as they were engraved upon the 12 stones of the High Priest's breastplate. (On this subject see the 28th Chapter of Exodus, verse 17 *et seq.*)

3	2	1
יוהה	יההו	יהוה
6	5	4
ההיו	הויה	הוהי
9	8	7
וההי	ויהה	והיה
12	11	10
ההוי	היוה	היהו

These twelve names correspond to twelve mysterious verses of the Bible.

The Kabbalists draw from this mysterious name still more different Divine Names; because being written in Hebrew, with letters punctuated and multiplied by 12, by 42 and by 72, one can form the Name of 12 letters, the Name of 42 letters, and the Name of 72 letters; and all the letters that make up these three Great Names each correspond to a particular Name.

I shall go into the greatest details in this regard in my Second edition, if I am granted the advantage and the favor of seeing my first made welcome.

On the frontispiece of this book we see the first side of the talisman of Jehovah, the explanation of which is contained in the first Chapter, which corresponds to the *alpha*. Since I am at the *omega*, I shall give the explanation of the second side of that talisman. All the Kabbalists agree that Judas, nicknamed Maccabeus, being ready to fight against *Antiochus Eupator*[132], received from an angel this famous sign מכבי, by virtue of which they defied 14 thousand of their enemies and a great number of elephants in their first fight; and 35 thousand in their second.

These four mysterious characters מכבי are formed from the first letters of the four dictions of this verse from Exodus כמין בעלים יהוה

---

[132] Agrippa, *Occult Philosophy*, Book 3.

מי. In Latin it means *que similis tibi in fortibus, Domine*; and in English, *who is like unto Thee among the strong, O Lord?* These four letters, reduced in number, give the number 72[133], which is the number of the Jehovah's Triangle[134], and the 72 Geniuses who are clothed with the 72 attributes of God.

These mysterious characters, as well as the name Jehovah, should be contained within a cross, as follows:

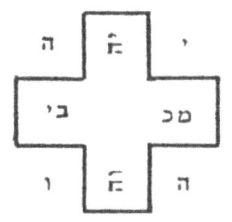

Then enclose it in a circle, around which you will write the mysterious verse above, with the following words: *in hoc signo vinces*. This talisman must be composed under the influence of the Sun (see page 133). It is used to work invocations; it has the same properties as that of the Sun.

The End

---

[133] This is by Theosophical Addition. Remembering that Hebrew letters have a numerical value, the distillation of the word 'Maccabee (מכבי) comes to מ (40) + כ (20) + ב (2) + י (10) = 72 – PV.

[134] Remembering that י = 10, ה = 5 and ו = 6, and that the Triangle contains the cumulative names of God י, יה, יהו and יהוה (see page 20), the sum of these lines is 10 + 15 + 21 + 26 = 72 – PV.

Appendix A: Creation of Names of Geniuses from 3-Letter Names

The root 3 letters are obtained from Verses 19, 20 and 21 of Exodus, Ch. 14 as described in Chapter 3. The suffixes add the name of God, being -AL (-EL, -AEL) or -IH (-IAH, -JAH) to create the name of the Genius.

No.	3-Letter Names	3-Letter Names (English)	Suffix	Genius	Genius (English)
1	והו	VHV	-IH	והויה	Vehuiah
2	ילי	ILI	-AL	יליאל	Jeliel
3	סיט	SIT	-AL	סיטאל	Sitael
4	עלם	ALM	-IH	עלמיה	Elemiah
5	מהש	MHS	-IH	מהשיה	Mahasiah
6	ללה	LLH	-AL	ללהאל	Lelahel
7	אכא	AKA	-IH	אכאיה	Achaiah
8	כהת	KHT	-AL	כהתאל	Cahethel
9	הזי	HZI	-AL	הזיאל	Haziel
10	אלד	ALD	-IH	אלדיה	Aladiah
11	לאו	LAV	-IH	לאויה	Lauviah
12	ההע	HHO	-IH	ההעיה	Hahaiah
13	יזל	IZL	-AL	יזלאל	Iezalel
14	מבה	MBH	-AL	מבהאל	Mebahel
15	הרי	HRI	-AL	הריאל	Hariel
16	הקמ	HQM	-IH	הקמיה	Hakamiah
17	לאו	LAV	-IH	לאויה	Lauviah
18	כלי	KLI	-AL	כליאל	Caliel
19	לוו	LVV	-IH	לוויה	Leuviah
20	פהל	PHL	-IH	פהליה	Pahaliah
21	נלכ	NLK	-AL	נלכאל	Nelchael
22	ייי	III	-AL	יייאל	Ieiaiel
23	מלה	MLH	-AL	מלהאל	Melahel
24	חהו	CHV	-IH	חהויה	Hahuiah
25	נתה	NTH	-IH	נתהיה	Nith-Haiah
26	האא	HAA	-IH	האאיה	Haaiah
27	ירת	IRT	-AL	ירתאל	Ierathel
28	שאה	SAH	-IH	שאהיה	Seheiah
29	ריי	RII	-AL	רייאל	Reiiel
30	ומא	AVM	-AL	ומאאל	Omael
31	לכב	LKB	-AL	לכבאל	Lecabel
32	ושר	VSR	-IH	ושריה	Vasiariah

33	יהו	ICV	-IH	יהויה	Iehuiah
34	להח	LHC	-IH	להחיה	Lehahiah
35	כוק	KVQ	-IH	כוקיה	Chavakiah
36	מנד	MND	-AL	מנדאל	Menadel
37	אני	ANI	-AL	אניאל	Aniel
38	העם	COM	-IH	העמיה	Haamiah
39	רהע	RHO	-AL	רהעאל	Rehael
40	ייז	IIV	-AL	ייזאל	Ieizel
41	ההה	HHH	-AL	ההחאל	Hahahel
42	מיכ	MIK	-AL	מיכאל	Mikael
43	וול	VVL	-IH	וולית	Veuliah
44	ילה	LLH	-IH	ילהיה	Ielahiah
45	סאל	SAL	-IH	סאליה	Sealiah
46	ערי	ORI	-AL	עריאל	Ariel
47	עשל	OSL	-IH	עשליה	Asaliah
48	מיה	MIH	-AL	מיהאל	Mihael
49	והו	VHV	-AL	והואל	Vehuel
50	דני	DNI	-AL	דניאל	Daniel
51	ההש	HCS	-IH	ההשיה	Hahasiah
52	עממ	OMM	-IH	עממיה	Imamiah
53	ננא	NNA	-AL	ננאאל	Nanael
54	נית	NIT	-AL	ניתאל	Nithanael
55	מבה	MVH	-IH	מבהיה	Mebahiah
56	פוי	PBI	-AL	פויאל	Poiel
57	נממ	NMM	-IH	נממיה	Nemamiah
58	ייל	IIL	-AL	יילאל	Ieialel
59	הרה	HRC	-AL	הרהאל	Harahel
60	מצר	MTzR	-AL	מצראל	Mitzrael
61	ומב	VMB	-AL	ומבאל	Umabel
62	יהה	IHH	-AL	יההאל	Iah-hel
63	ענו	ONV	-AL	ענואל	Anauel
64	מחי	MCI	-AL	מחיאל	Mehiel
65	דמב	DMB	-IH	דמביה	Damabiah
66	מנק	MNQ	-IH	מנקיה	Manakel
67	איע	AIO	-AL	איעאל	Eiael
68	הבו	CBV	-IH	הבויה	Habuhiah
69	ראה	RAH	-AL	ראהאל	Rochel
70	יבמ	IBM	-IH	יבמיה	Jabamiah
71	היי	HII	-AL	הייאל	Haiaiel
72	מומ	MVH	-IH	מומיה	Mumiah

Appendix B: 28 Houses of the Moon

This Table accompanies the section on the same name in Chapter 8. Here the values have been calculated exactly, since there are a few errors and inaccuracies in the original list.

Lunar Day	Degrees (Decimal)	Degrees, Min, Secs	Range	
1	12.85714286	12d 51m 26s	0d 0m 0s Aries	- 12d 51m 26s Aries
2	25.71428571	25d 51m 43s	12d 51m 26s Aries	- 25d 42m 51s Aries
3	38.57142857	38d 34m 17s	25d 42m 51s Aries	- 8d 34m 17s Taurus
4	51.42857143	51d 25m 43s	8d 34m 17s Taurus	- 21d 25m 43s Taurus
5	64.28571429	64d 17m 9s	21d 25m 43s Taurus	- 4d 17m 9s Gemini
6	77.14285714	77d 8m 34s	4d 14m 9s Gemini	- 17d 8m 34s Gemini
7	90	90d 0m 0s	17d 8m 34s Gemini	- 30d 0m 0s Gemini
8	102.8571429	102d 51m 26s	30d 0m 0s Gemini	- 12d 51m 26s Cancer
9	115.7142857	115d 42m 51s	12d 51m 26s Cancer	- 25d 42m 51s Cancer
10	128.5714286	128d 34m 17s	25d 42m 51s Cancer	- 8d 34m 17s Leo
11	141.4285714	141d 25m 43s	8d 34m 17s Leo	- 21d 25m 43s Leo
12	154.2857143	154d 17m 9s	21d 25m 43s Leo	- 4d 17m 9s Virgo
13	167.1428571	167d 8m 34s	4d 17m 9s Virgo	- 17d 8m 34s Virgo
14	180	180d 0m 0s	17d 8m 34s Virgo	- 30d 0m 0s Virgo
15	192.8571429	192d 51m 26s	30d 0m 0s Virgo	- 12d 51m 26s Libra
16	205.7142857	205d 42m 51s	12d 51m 26s Libra	- 25d 42m 51s Libra
17	218.5714286	218d 34m 17s	25d 42m 51s Libra	- 8d 34m 17s Scorpio
18	231.4285714	231d 25m 43s	8d 34m 17s Scorpio	- 21d 25m 43s Scorpio
19	244.2857143	244d 17m 9s	21d 25m 43s Scorpio	- 4d 17m 9s Sagittarius
20	257.1428571	257d 8m 34s	4d 17m 9s Sagittarius	- 17d 8m 34s Sagittarius
21	270	270d 0m 0s	17d 8m 34s Sagittarius	- 30d 0m 0s Sagittarius
22	282.8571429	282d 51m 26s	30d 0m 0s Sagittarius	- 12d 51m 26s Capricorn
23	295.7142857	295d 42m 51s	12d 51m 26s Capricorn	- 25d 42m 51s Capricorn
24	308.5714286	308d 34m 17s	25d 42m 51s Capricorn	- 8d 34m 17s Aquarius
25	321.4285714	321d 25m 43s	8d 34m 17s Aquarius	- 21d 25m 43s Aquarius
26	334.2857143	334d 17m 9s	21d 25m 43s Aquarius	- 4d 17m 9s Pisces
27	347.1428571	347d 8m 34s	4d 17m 9s Pisces	- 17d 8m 34s Pisces
28	360	360d 0m 0s	17d 8m 34s Pisces	- 30d 0m 0s Pisces

Appendix C: The Mysterious Seal of the Sun

Since Lenain didn't include the image of the Seal of the Sun to which he extensively refers in Chapter 9, it is reproduced here in three forms: from Image 21 of Dupuis *l'Origine des cultes*; Kircher's *Œdipus Aegyptiacus*; and a contemporary realization by the translator.

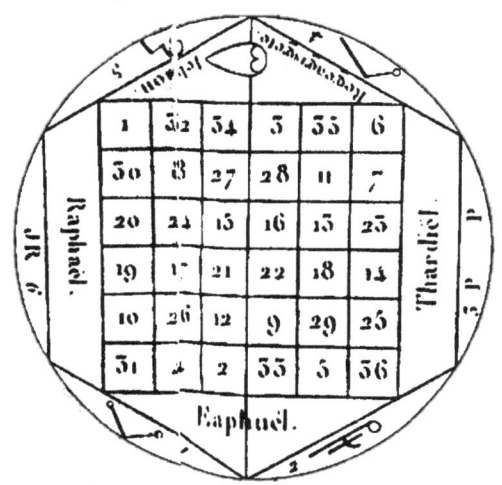

Version from Dupuis *l'Origine des cultes* (1780, rev. 1790), which he attributes to Kircher.

Version from Kircher *Œdipus Egyptiacus* (1652)

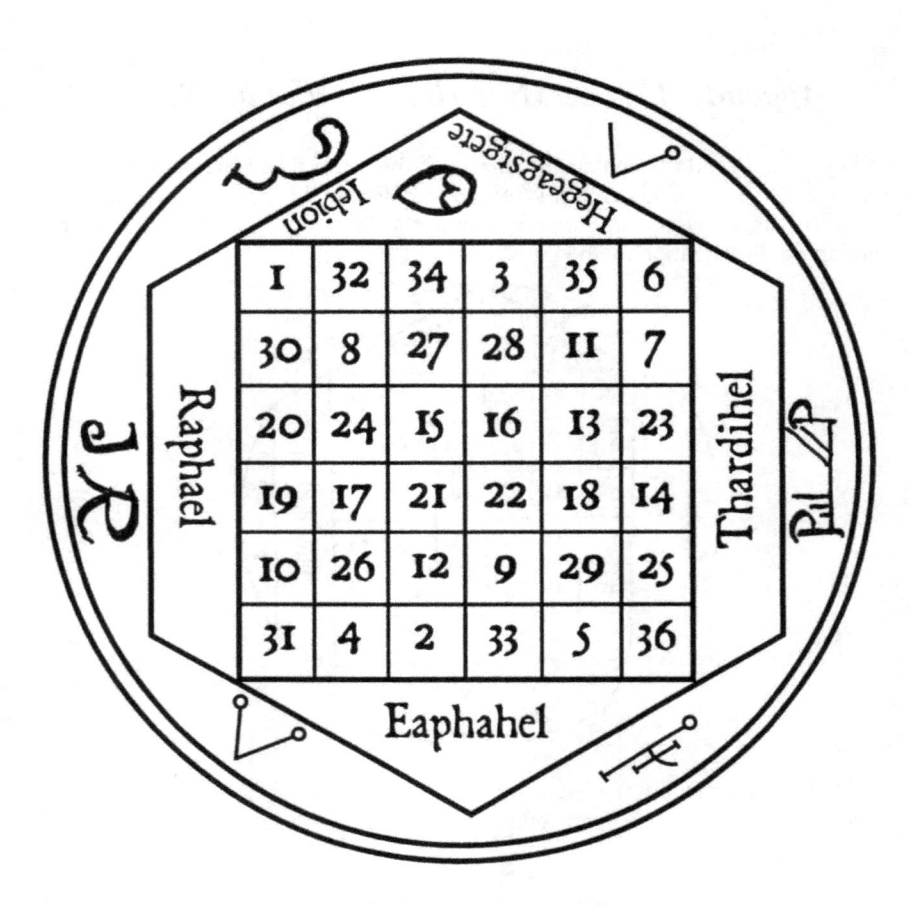

Recreation of Talisman in Kircher's *Œdipus Egyptiacus* by the translator

Appendix D: Sigils of the 72 Geniuses

From the *Table des 72 Anges*, MS Arsenal 2495 at the Bibliothèque de l'Arsenal, Paris, dating from the early 18th Century, and apparently based on the work by Rudd. The table give the number, Hebrew and Anglicized names of the Geniuses, together with their seals.

It's interesting to note that two seals – 50. Daniel and 51. Hahasiah – are reversed in the Arsenal MS 2495, but the order above is found in just about every other book on the topic, including Butler's book The Magus; and on the Golden Dawn side, such books as Zalewski's Kabbalah of the Golden Dawn, Castle Book 2000, pp. 212 -213 and the Ciceros' Tarot Talismans, p. 269, Llewellyn 2006. Even Ambelain took care to reverse them in his hand-drawn reproductions of the sigils in *La Kabbale Pratique*, Éditions Bussière 1992 reprint, p. 289.

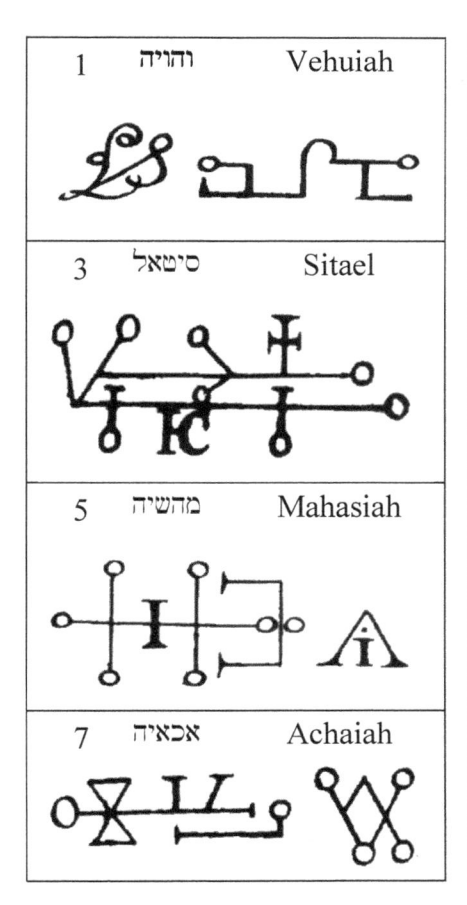

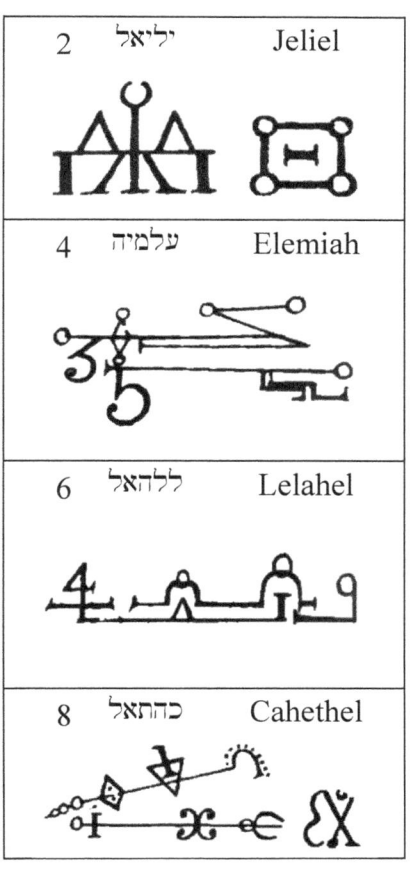

1	והויה	Vehuiah	2	יליאל	Jeliel
3	סיטאל	Sitael	4	עלמיה	Elemiah
5	מהשיה	Mahasiah	6	ללהאל	Lelahel
7	אכאיה	Achaiah	8	כהתאל	Cahethel

150 The Science of the Kabbalah – Lenain

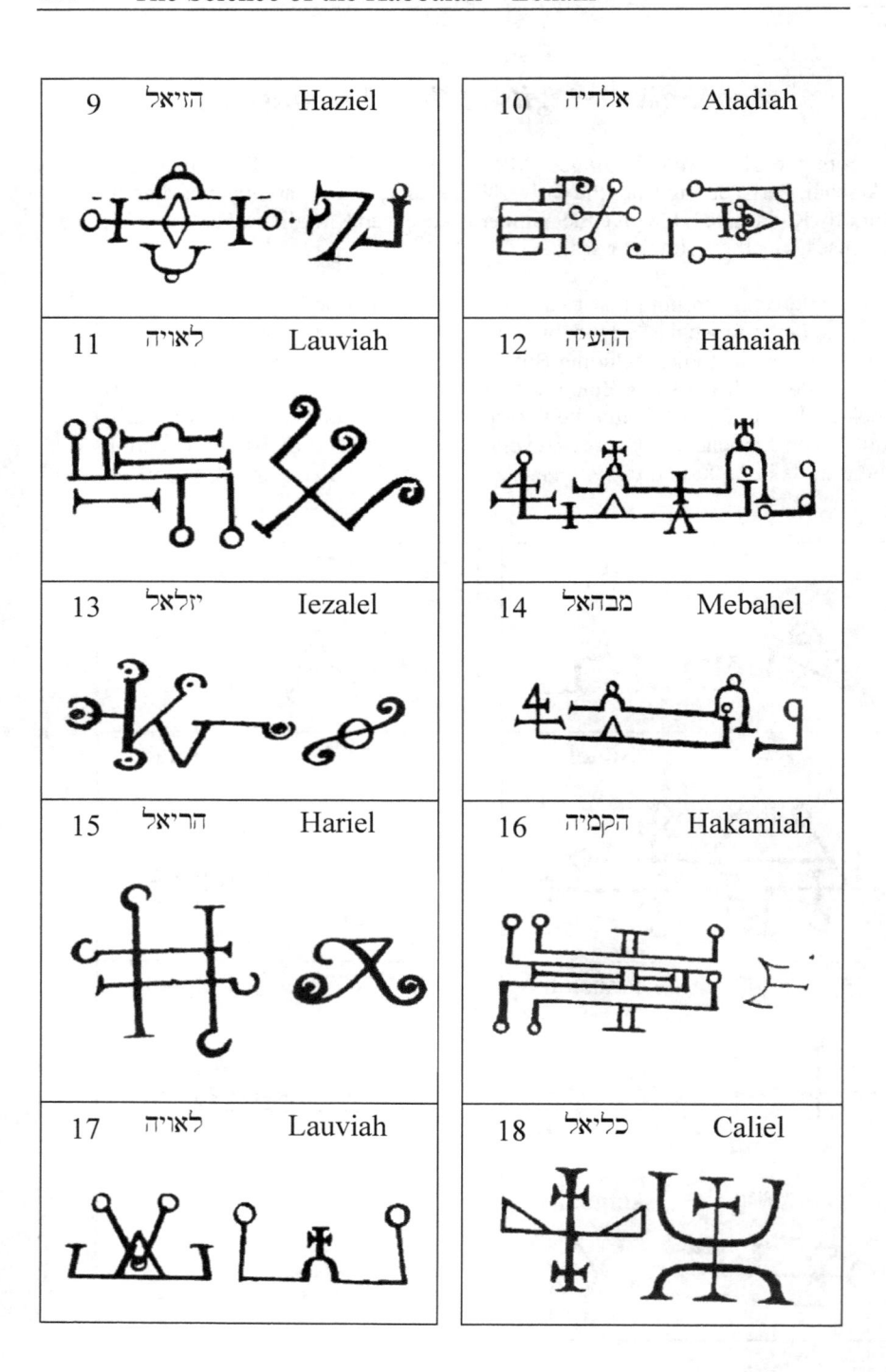

9 הזיאל Haziel	10 אלדיה Aladiah
11 לאויה Lauviah	12 הההעיה Hahaiah
13 יולאל Iezalel	14 מבהאל Mebahel
15 הריאל Hariel	16 הקמיה Hakamiah
17 לאויה Lauviah	18 כליאל Caliel

Appendix D: Sigils of the 72 Geniuses

19	לוויה	Leuviah	20	פהליה	Pahaliah
21	נלכאל	Nelchael	22	ייאל	Ieiaiel
23	מלהאל	Melahel	24	ההויה	Hahuiah
25	נתהיה	Nith-Haiah	26	האאיה	Haaiah
27	ירתאל	Ierathel	28	שאהיה	Seheiah

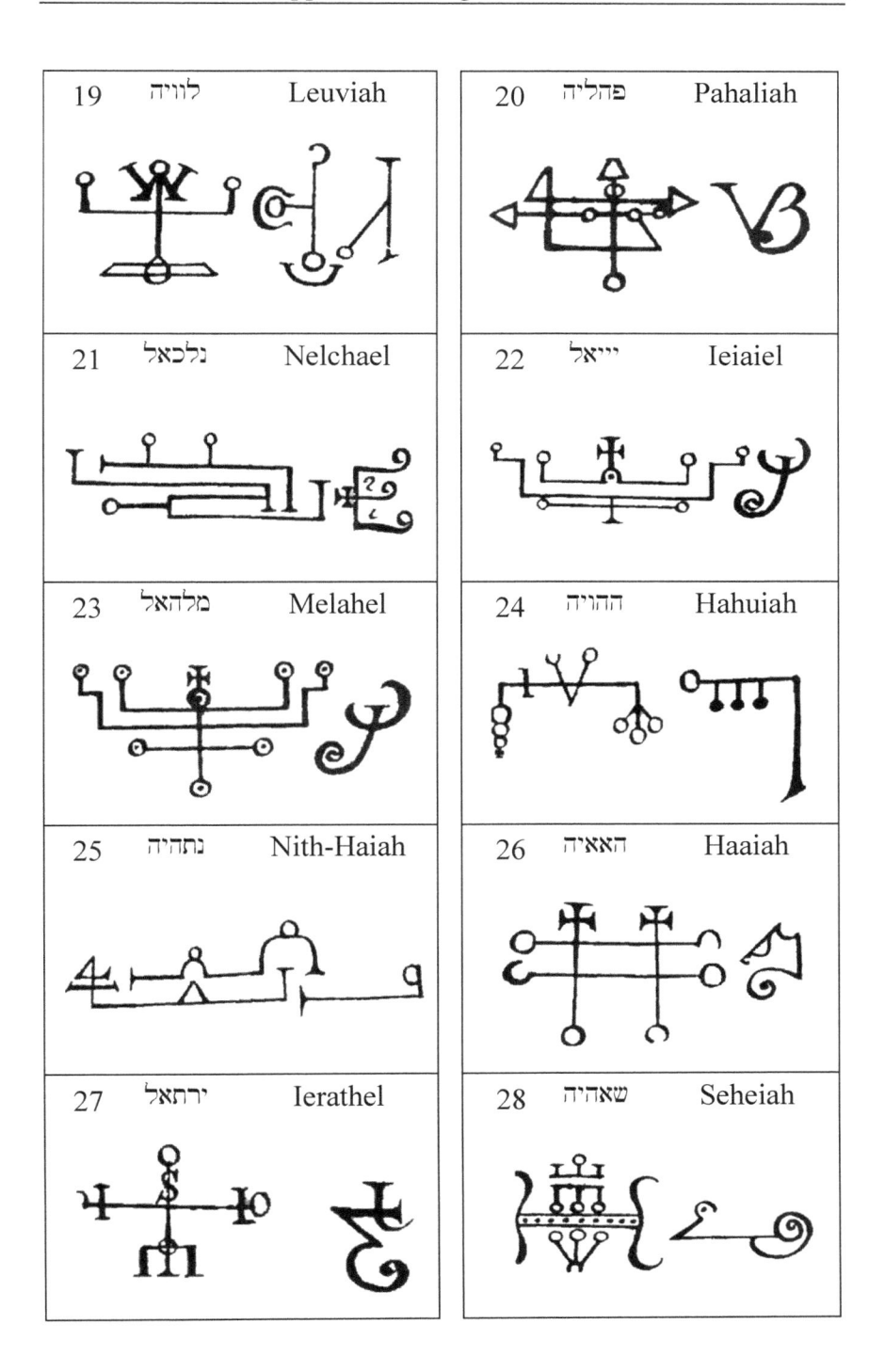

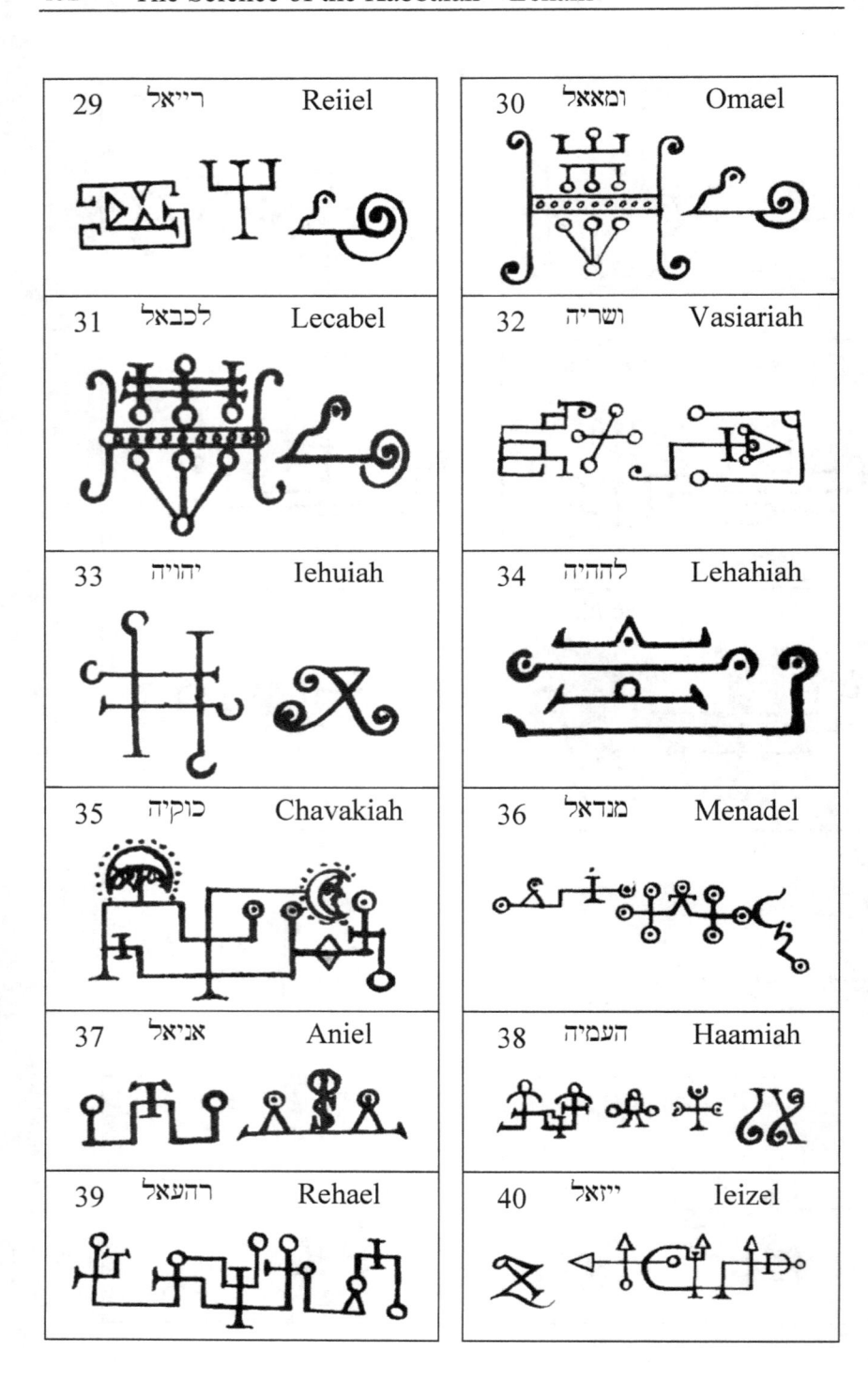

29	רייאל	Reiiel	30	ומאאל	Omael
31	לכבאל	Lecabel	32	ושריה	Vasiariah
33	יהויה	Iehuiah	34	להחיה	Lehahiah
35	כוקיה	Chavakiah	36	מנדאל	Menadel
37	אניאל	Aniel	38	העמיה	Haamiah
39	רהעאל	Rehael	40	ייזאל	Ieizel

Appendix D: Sigils of the 72 Geniuses

41	הההאל	Hahahel
42	מיכאל	Mikael
43	וליה	Veuliah
44	ילהיה	Ielahiah
45	סאליה	Sealiah
46	עריאל	Ariel
47	עשליה	Asaliah
48	מיהאל	Mihael
49	והואל	Vehuel
50	דניאל	Daniel
51	ההשיה	Hahasiah
52	עממיה	Imamiah
53	נאאל	Nanael
54	ניתאל	Nithanael

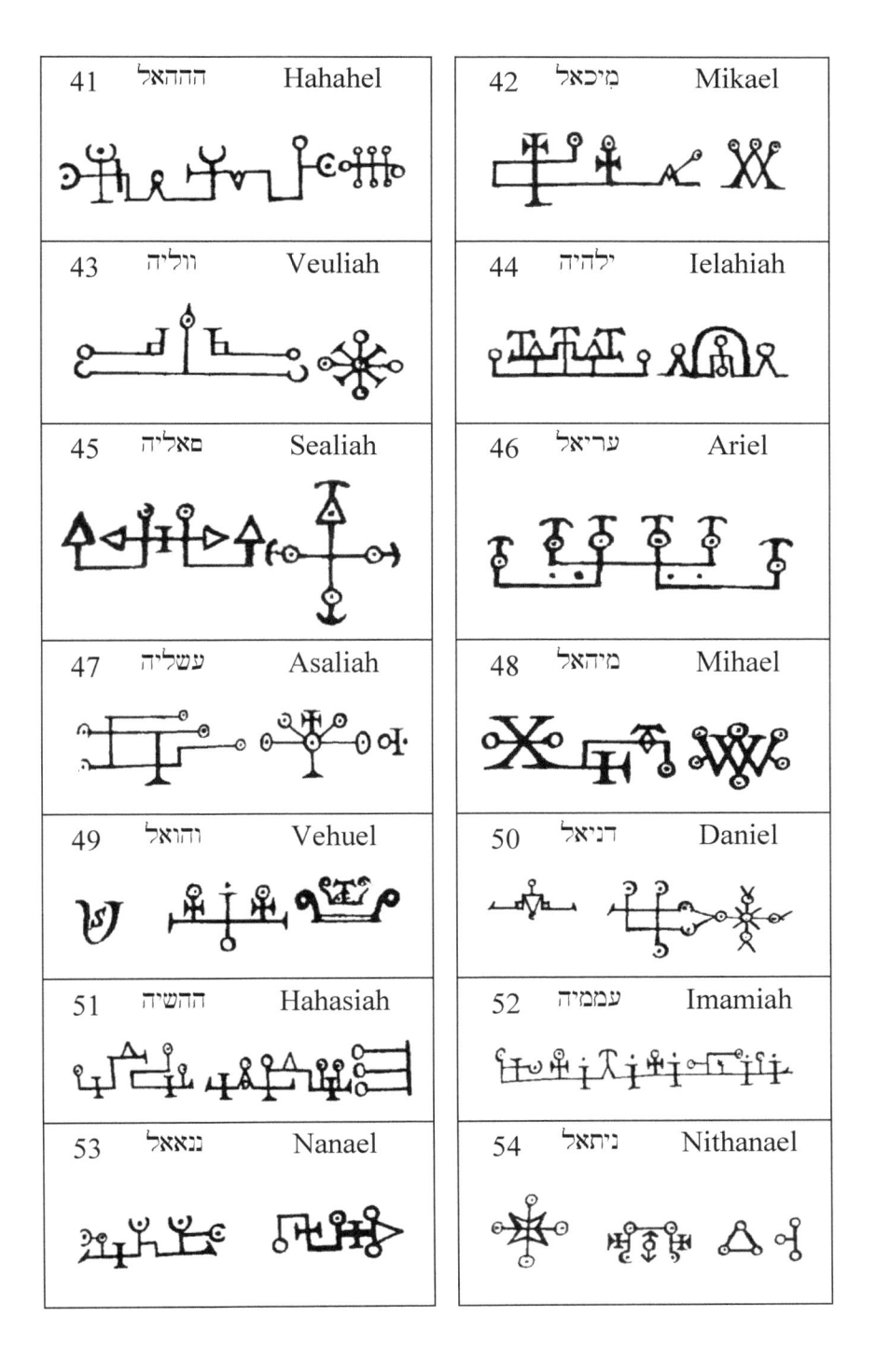

154 The Science of the Kabbalah – Lenain

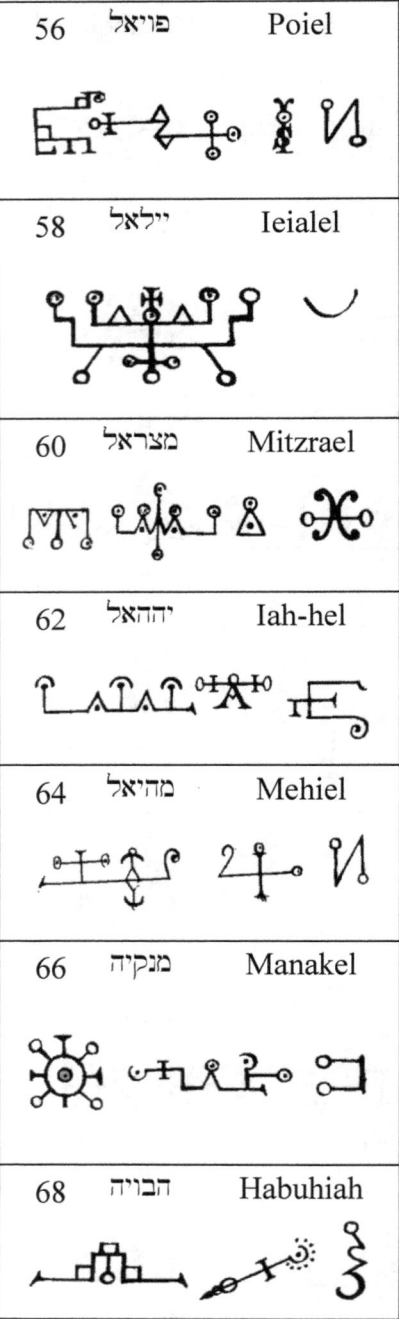

55	מבהיה	Mebahiah	56	פויאל	Poiel
57	נממיה	Nemamiah	58	יילאל	Ieialel
59	הרחאל	Harahel	60	מצראל	Mitzrael
61	ומבאל	Umabel	62	יהחאל	Iah-hel
63	ענואל	Anauel	64	מחיאל	Mehiel
65	דמביה	Damabiah	66	מנקיה	Manakel
67	איעאל	Eiael	68	הבויה	Habuhiah

Appendix D: Sigils of the 72 Geniuses

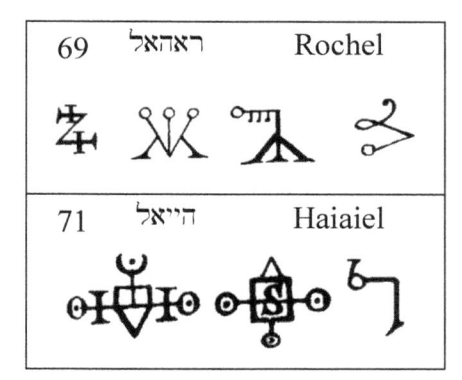

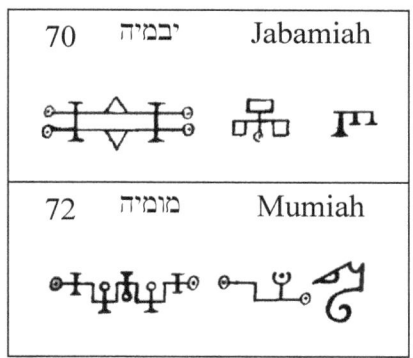

69 ראהאל Rochel	70 יבמיה Jabamiah
71 הייאל Haiaiel	72 מומיה Mumiah

It should be noted that there is a debate over whether these sigils should be used. R. Ambelain famously added them to the first edition of his book *La Kabbale Pratique*, published in 1951, stating that Lenain's book was not usable in the actual construction of seals without them, only to add a warning in 1989 that the sigils were wrongly attributed, and that the sigils were in fact the contrary ones, who use could lead to malefic and very dangerous outcomes, giving examples such as cancer, suicidal obsession, possession, and infestations as consequences. Some have pointed out that, if Ambelain was so concerned about their use, why did they still appear in subsequent editions of the book? The sad truth is that authors have little control over their books once they have signed a contract, and even if Ambelain had asked his publishers to omit the sigils, it is quite likely that they would not have done so, for the simple reason that the sigils look 'cool'. A number of Martinist and other Adepts – particularly in France – hold to this belief and carefully avoid their use. Similarly, many Martinists point out that these sigils have no place in the benign mysticism of Martinism.

Nevertheless, it should be pointed out that these same sigils have been used without adverse effects being reported by the Golden Dawn for over 140 years, and by some Martinist circles since 1951, to name but two groups. The translator would also mention that, a few years earlier he contacted a number of senior Adepts in a number of Orders, including head of Martinists, Golden Dawn, Alchemical and Masonic Rosicrucian groups to verify their experience of working Shemhamephorash rituals using the sigils, and not one person reported adverse effects. For historical reasons, therefore and for completeness the sigils are reproduced here.

However, for those who would prefer not to use these sigils in their work. The translator has also included two other systems of sigils or seals. The first in the Rosicrucian method of drawing the Angelic names upon the Rosicrucian Rose, and using the sigils derived by that method. The second utilizes the series of seals devised by Eliphas Lévi, which may therefore be more speak more clearly to those following the mystical or Martinist paths: in that instance we have most of the seals, and the few which were only described in writing have been created by the translator for this book.

Appendix E: Rosicrucian Sigils of the 72 Geniuses

Another approach to using the Angels is with the seals created from the Rosicrucian Rose, a technique particularly favored by the Hermetic Order of the Golden Dawn. Interestingly, McGregor Mathers visited the Arsenal Library in Paris and transcribed the same sigils of MS 2495 as did Ambelain over 60 years later.

In a system similar to that which Ambelain describes in *La Kabbale Pratique*, the sigils in Appendix D above were placed in a double circle drawn on parchment with the letters of the name around the circle in Hebrew. Interestingly the letters are placed clockwise rather than anti-clockwise (this tradition has been preserved here). Here, however, instead of placing the Arsenal sigils in the center, we have substituted them with Rosicrucian sigils derived from the Rose. This well-known technique utilizes a rose of 22 petals equating to the 22 letters of the Hebrew alphabet, placed in whorls of 3, 7 and 12 petals, on which are placed the 3 'Mother' Letters, the 7 'Double Letters and the 12 'Single' letters. The names are traced out upon this format, a small circle indicating the location of the first letter and the cross bar the location of the last one. A more detailed description can be found in the Ciceros' book *Tarot Talismans*, Llewellyn 2006, pp. 215 – 216.

In the meantime, the translator has created the 72 seals below for easy reference. Note seals 11 and 17 are identical: this is because the names are identical, the same series of letters being used in each. Despite attempts by some writers to distinguish between them, none of the three base letters are 'doubles', that is, all the letters only have one sound, so there cannot be two pronunciations for them.

1 והויה Vehuiah	2 יליאל Jeliel

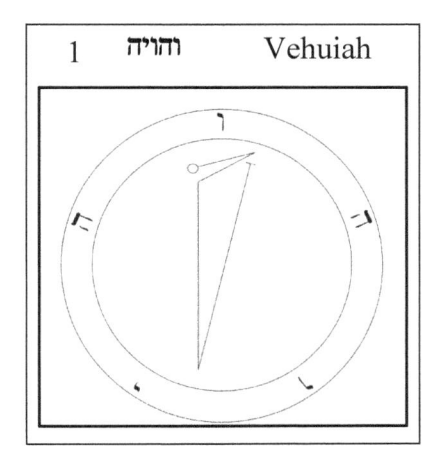

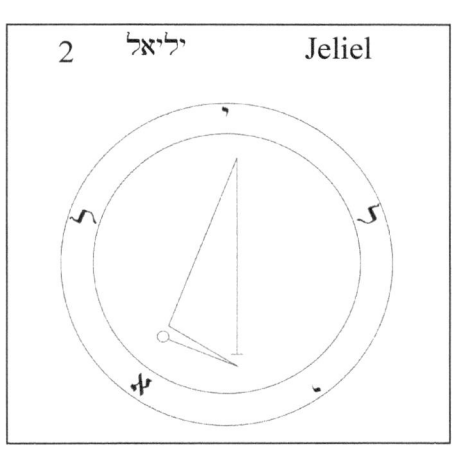

158 The Science of the Kabbalah – Lenain

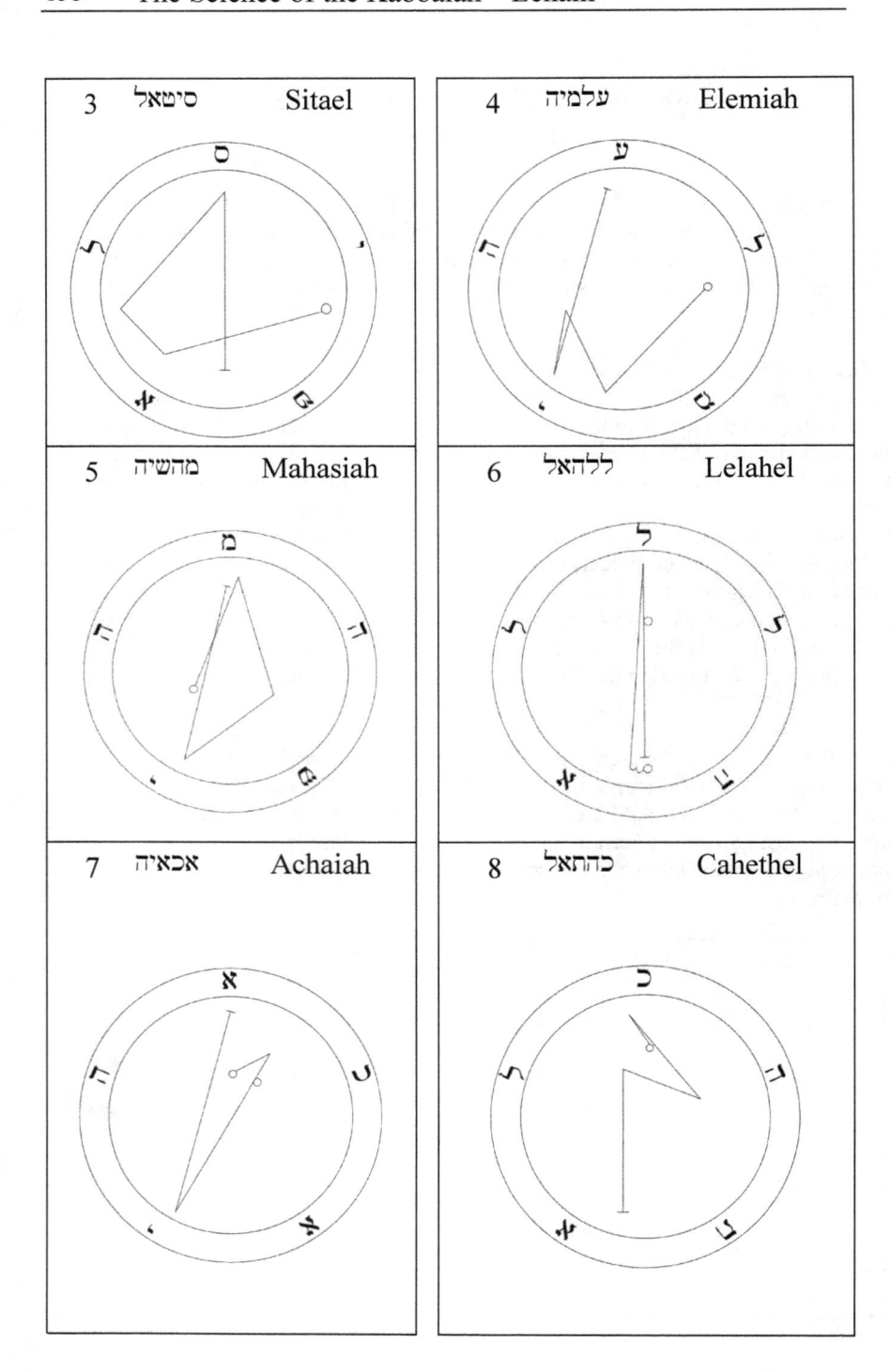

3 סיטאל Sitael	4 עלמיה Elemiah
5 מהשיה Mahasiah	6 ללהאל Lelahel
7 אכאיה Achaiah	8 כהתאל Cahethel

Appendix E: Rosicrucian Sigils

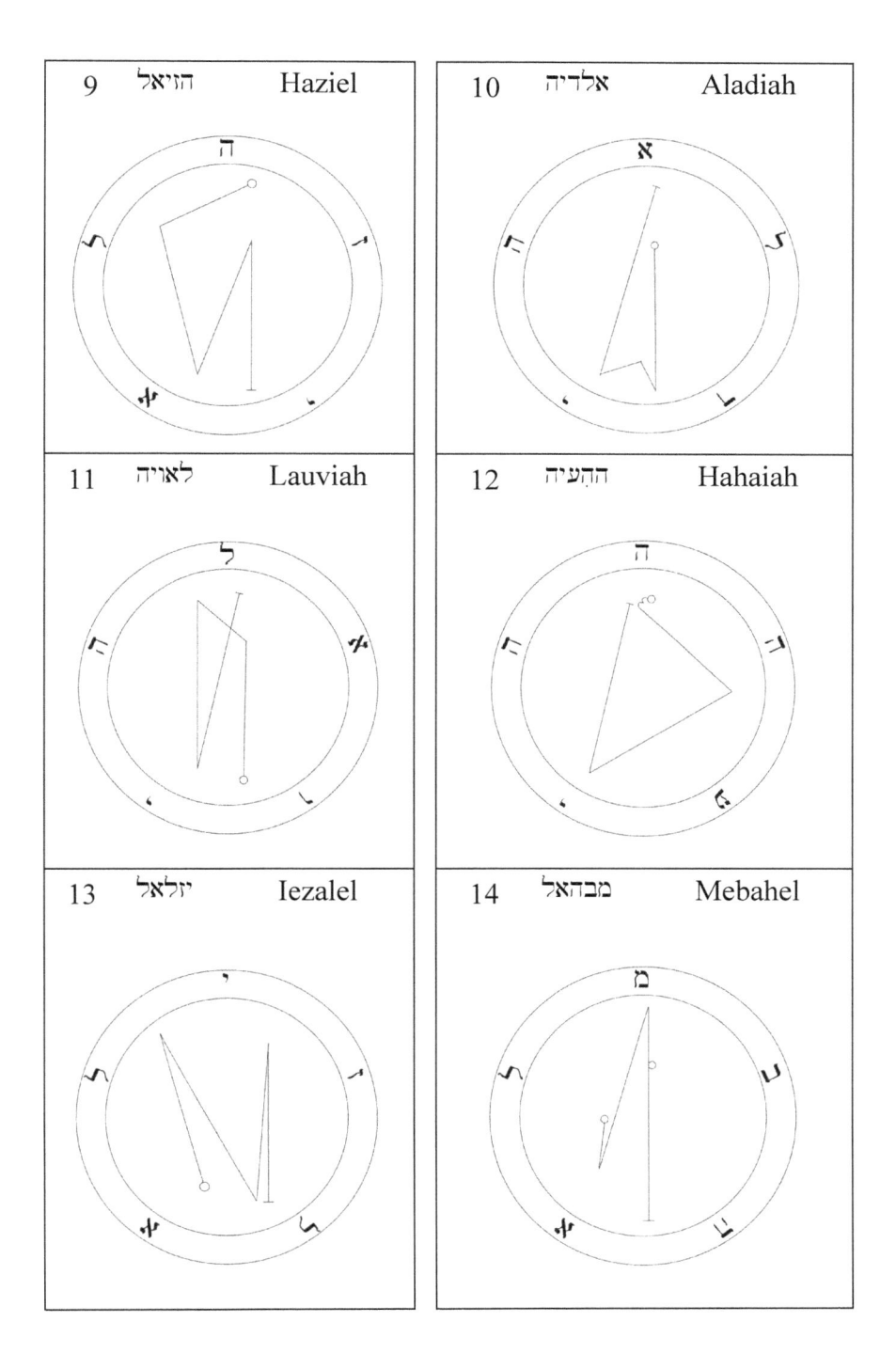

9	הזיאל	Haziel	10	אלדיה	Aladiah
11	לאויה	Lauviah	12	ההעיה	Hahaiah
13	יזלאל	Iezalel	14	מבהאל	Mebahel

160 The Science of the Kabbalah – Lenain

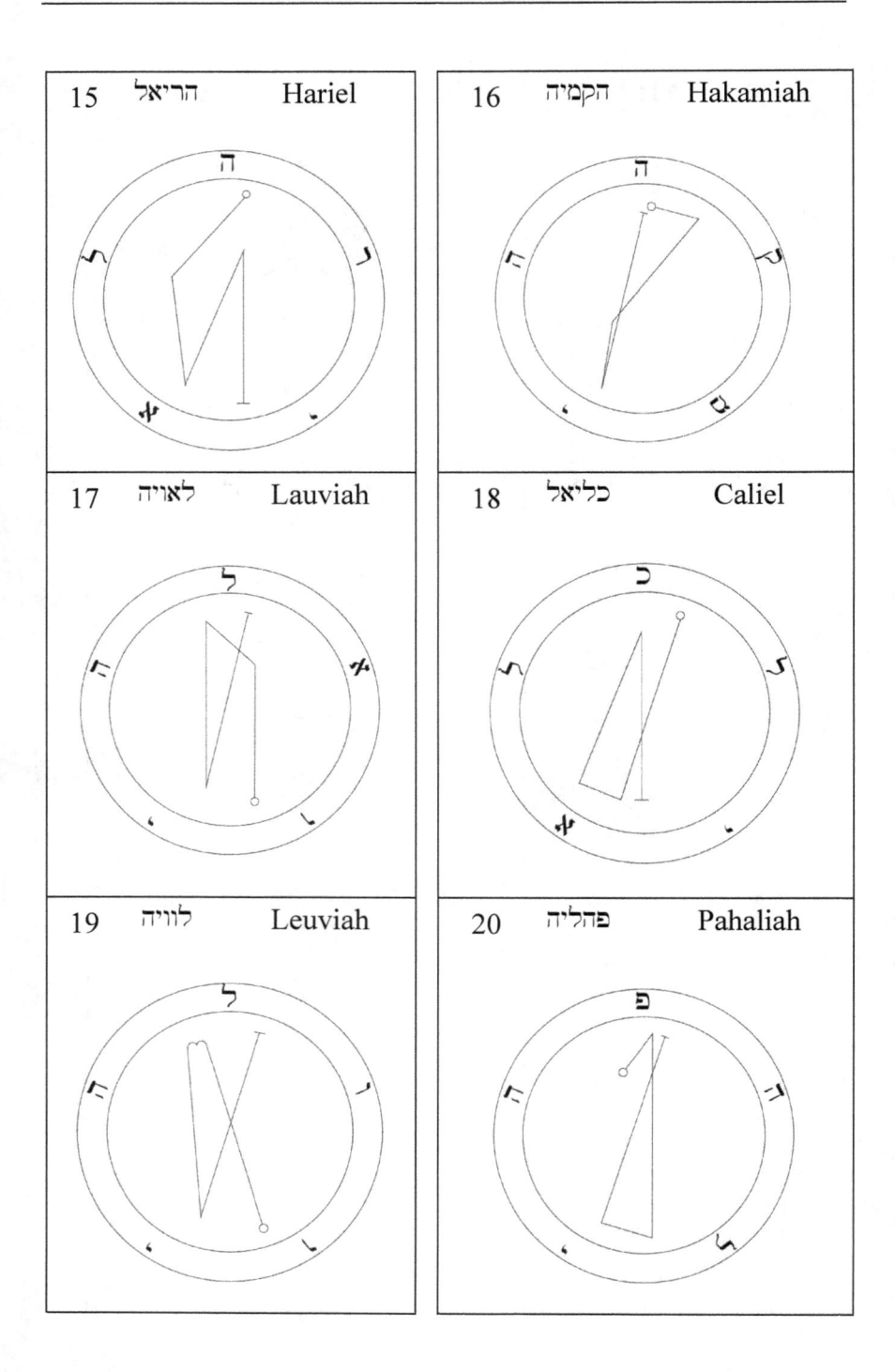

15 הריאל Hariel	16 הקמיה Hakamiah
17 לאויה Lauviah	18 כליאל Caliel
19 לוויה Leuviah	20 פהליה Pahaliah

Appendix E: Rosicrucian Sigils

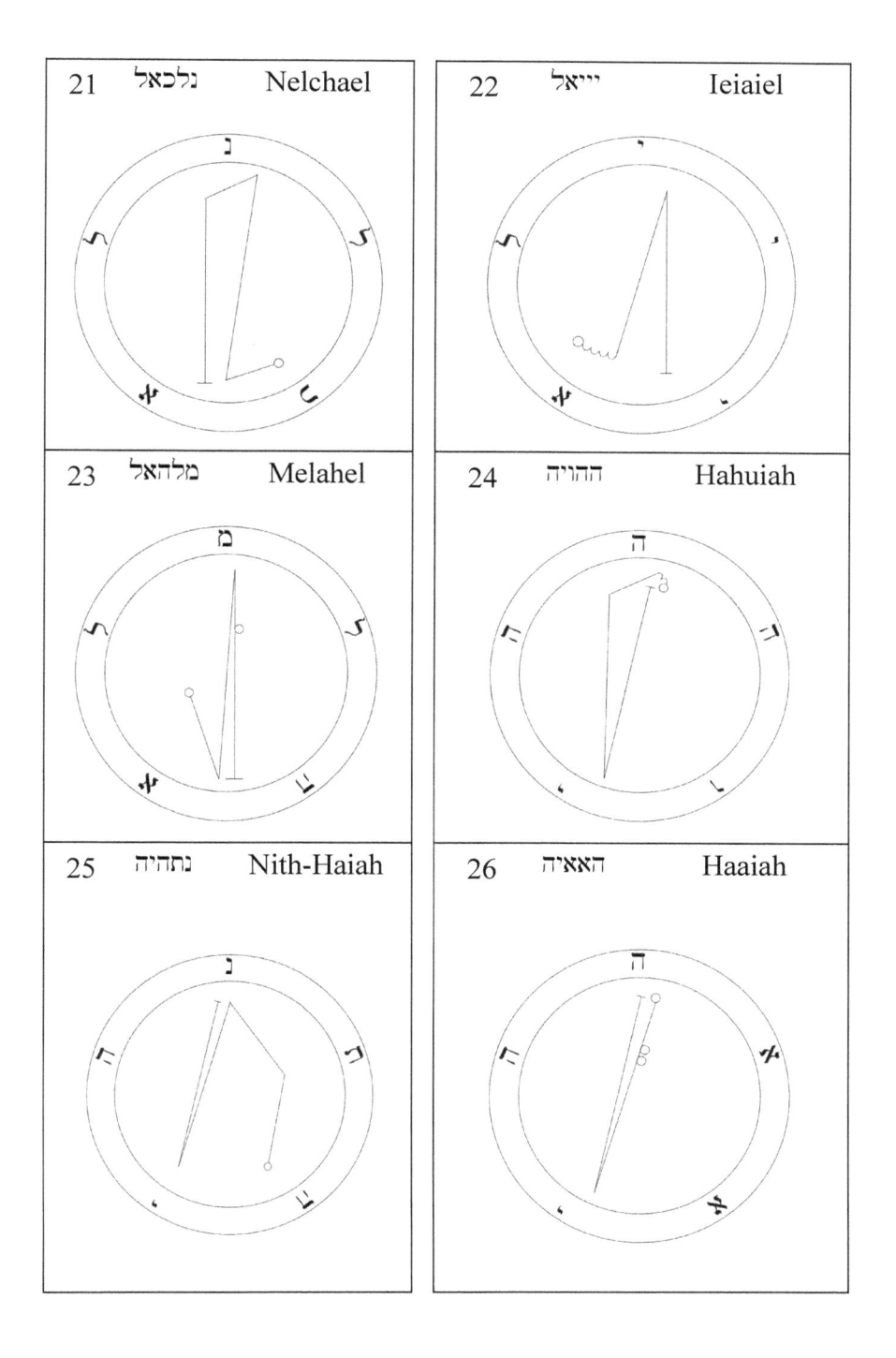

21	נלכאל	Nelchael	22	ייאל	Ieiaiel
23	מלהאל	Melahel	24	ההויה	Hahuiah
25	נתהיה	Nith-Haiah	26	האאיה	Haaiah

162   The Science of the Kabbalah – Lenain

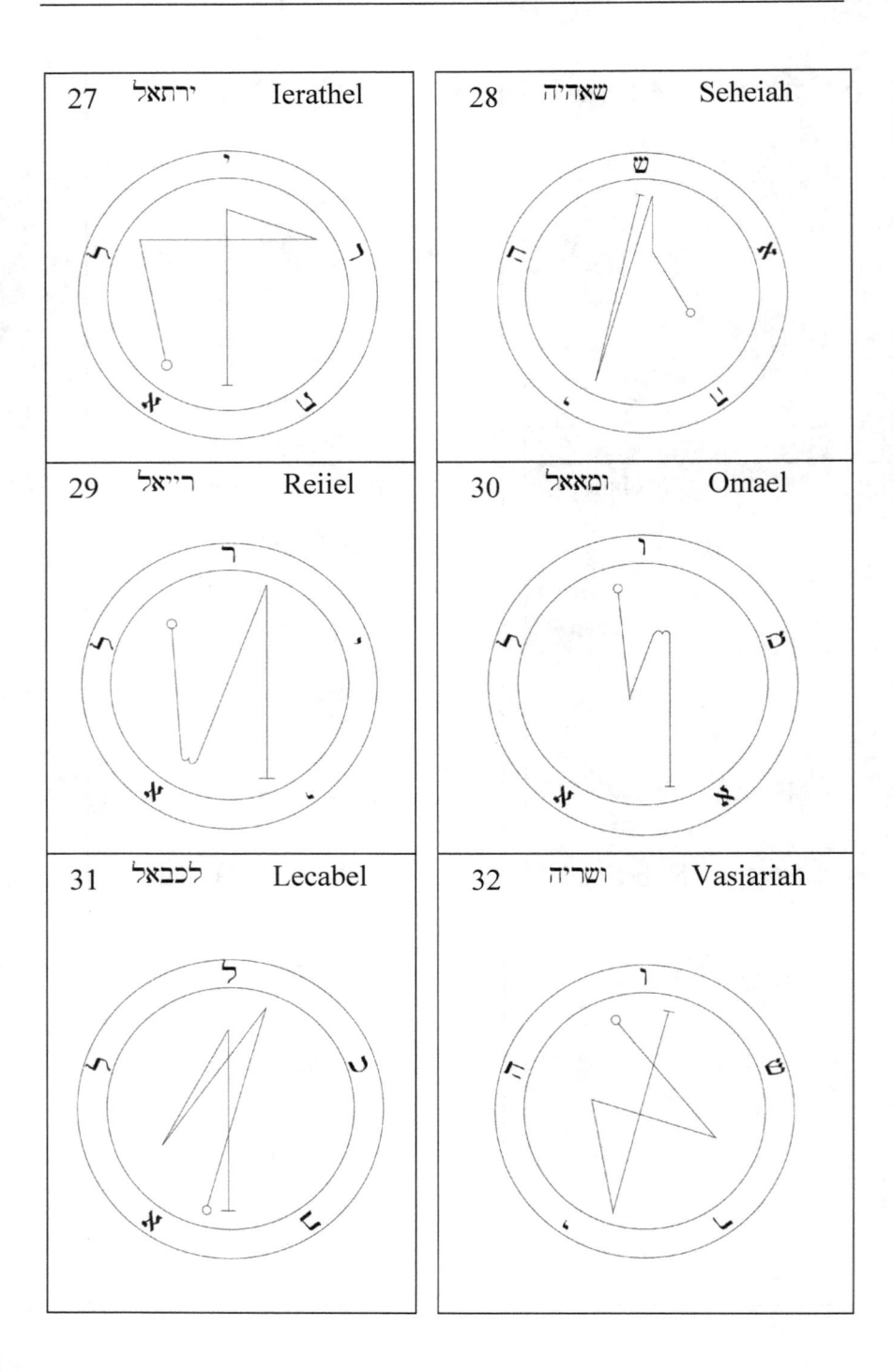

27 ירתאל Ierathel	28 שאהיה Seheiah
29 רייאל Reiiel	30 ומאאל Omael
31 לכבאל Lecabel	32 ושריה Vasiariah

Appendix E: Rosicrucian Sigils

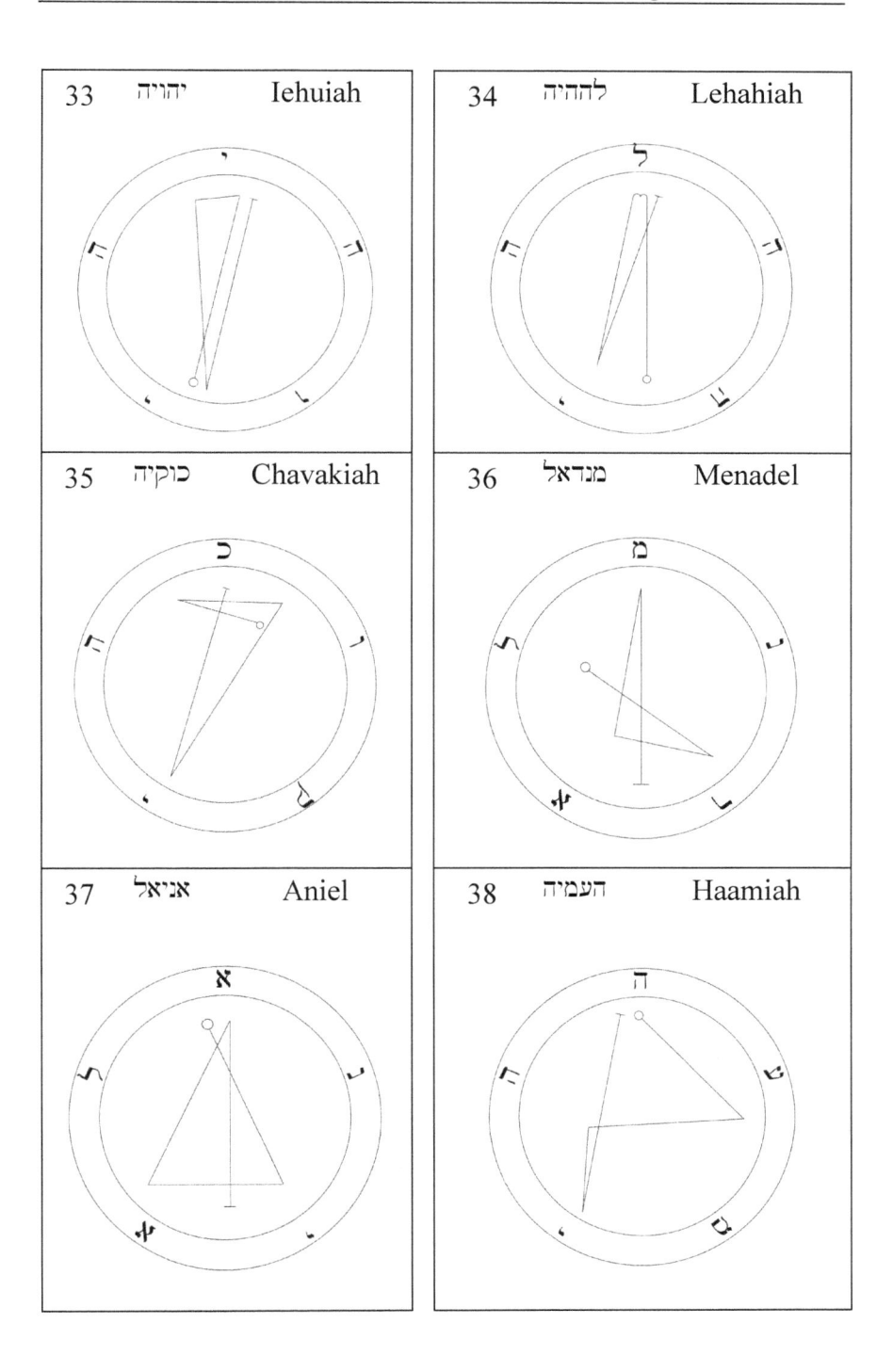

33 יהויה Iehuiah	34 להחיה Lehahiah
35 כוקיה Chavakiah	36 מנדאל Menadel
37 אניאל Aniel	38 העמיה Haamiah

164 The Science of the Kabbalah – Lenain

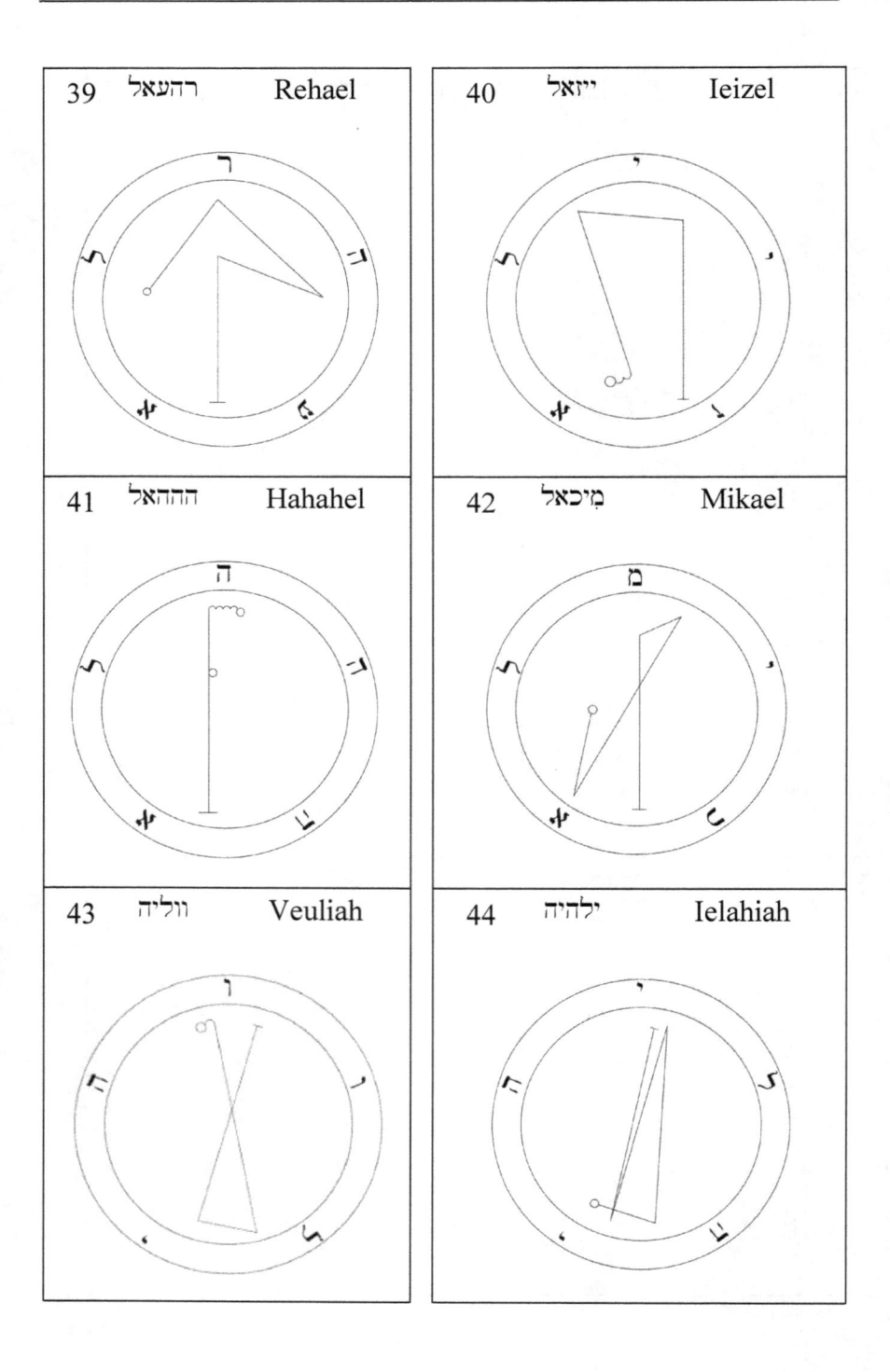

39	רהעאל	Rehael	40	ייזאל	Ieizel
41	ההחאל	Hahahel	42	מִיכאל	Mikael
43	וליה	Veuliah	44	ילהיה	Ielahiah

Appendix E: Rosicrucian Sigils

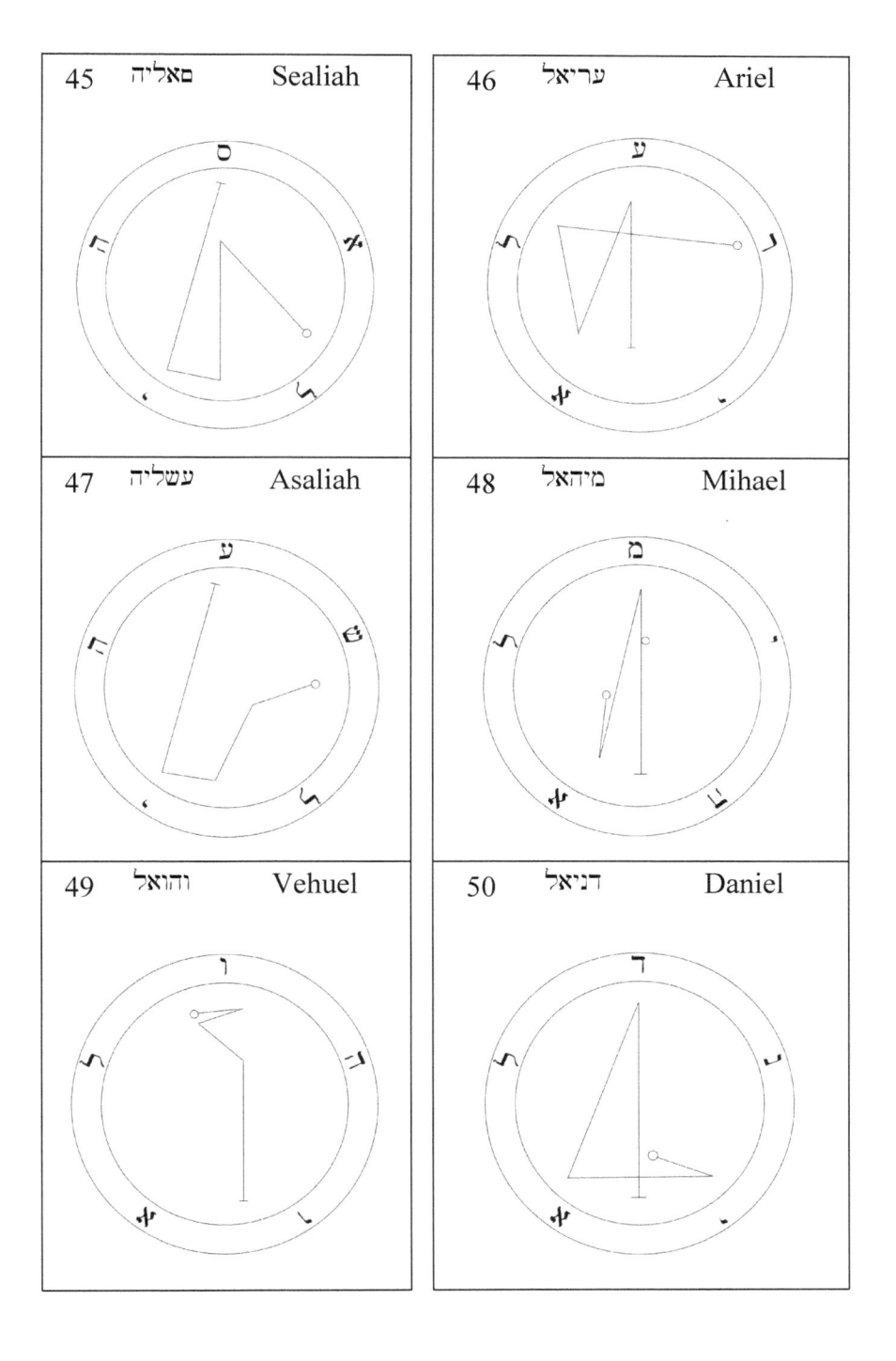

45	סאליה	Sealiah	46	עריאל	Ariel
47	עשליה	Asaliah	48	מיהאל	Mihael
49	והואל	Vehuel	50	דניאל	Daniel

166 The Science of the Kabbalah – Lenain

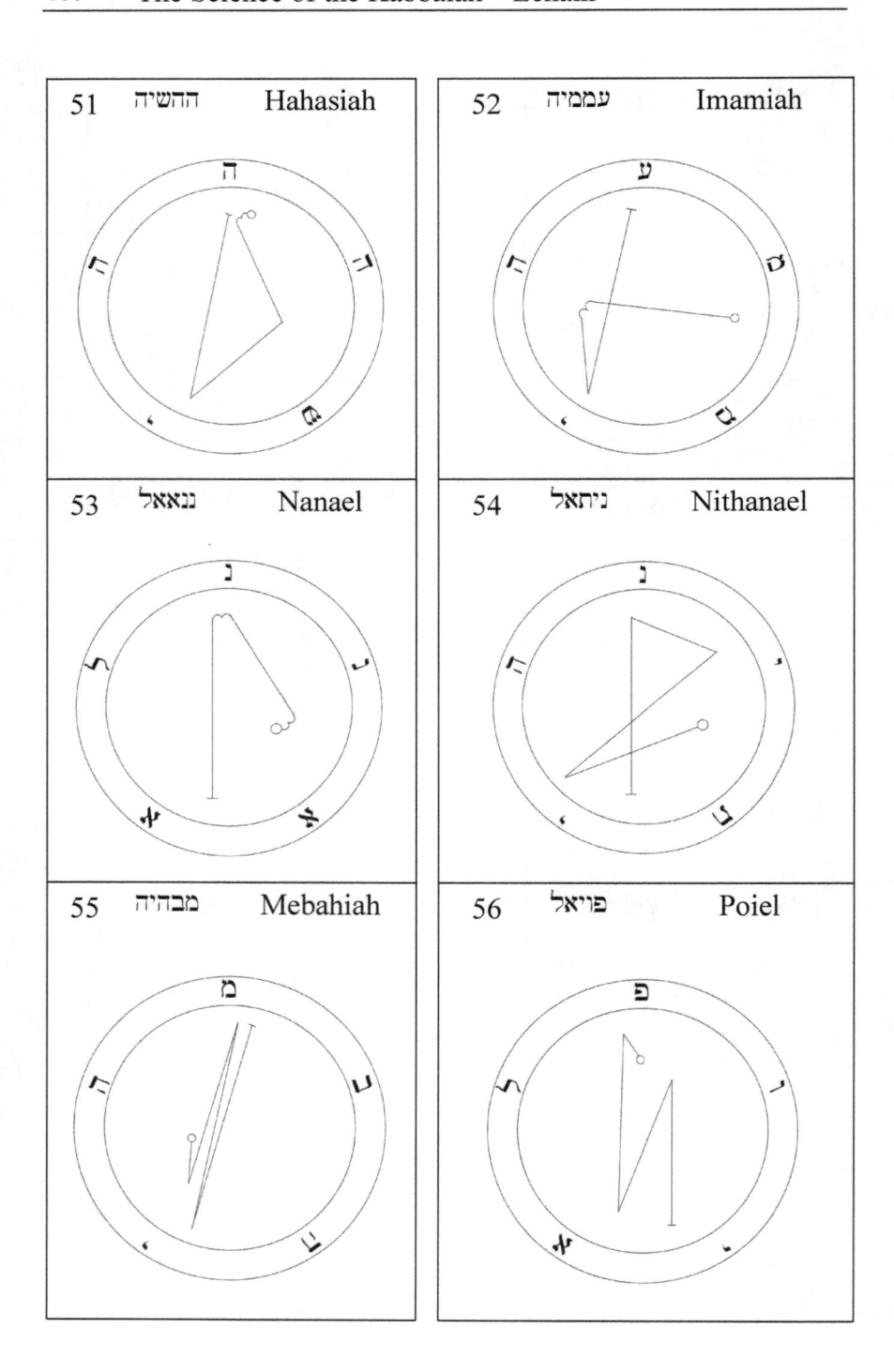

51 ההשיה Hahasiah	52 עממיה Imamiah
53 ננאאל Nanael	54 ניתאל Nithanael
55 מבהיה Mebahiah	56 פויאל Poiel

Appendix E: Rosicrucian Sigils

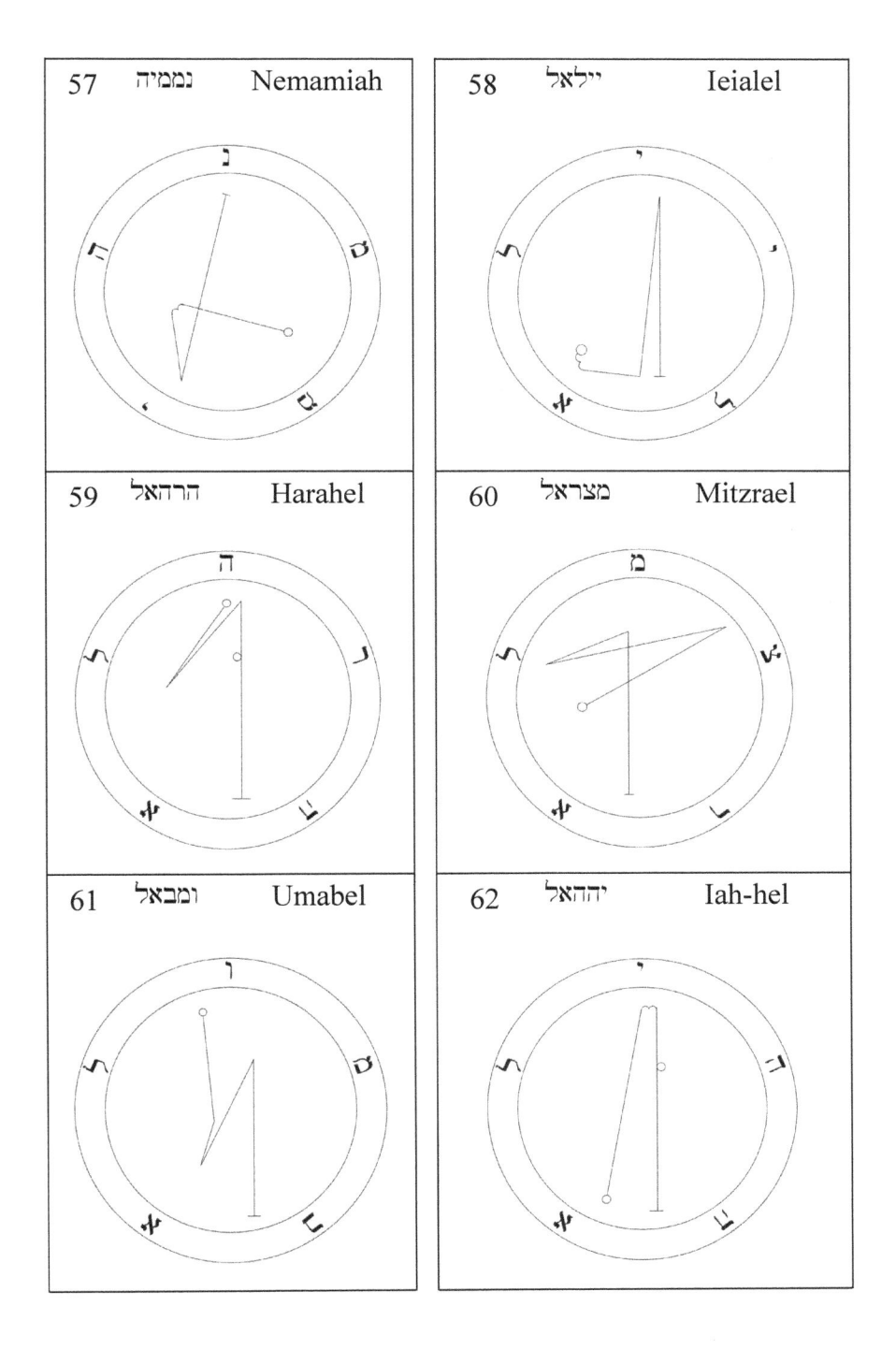

57 נממיה Nemamiah	58 יילאל Ieialel
59 הרהאל Harahel	60 מצראל Mitzrael
61 ומבאל Umabel	62 יההאל Iah-hel

168 The Science of the Kabbalah – Lenain

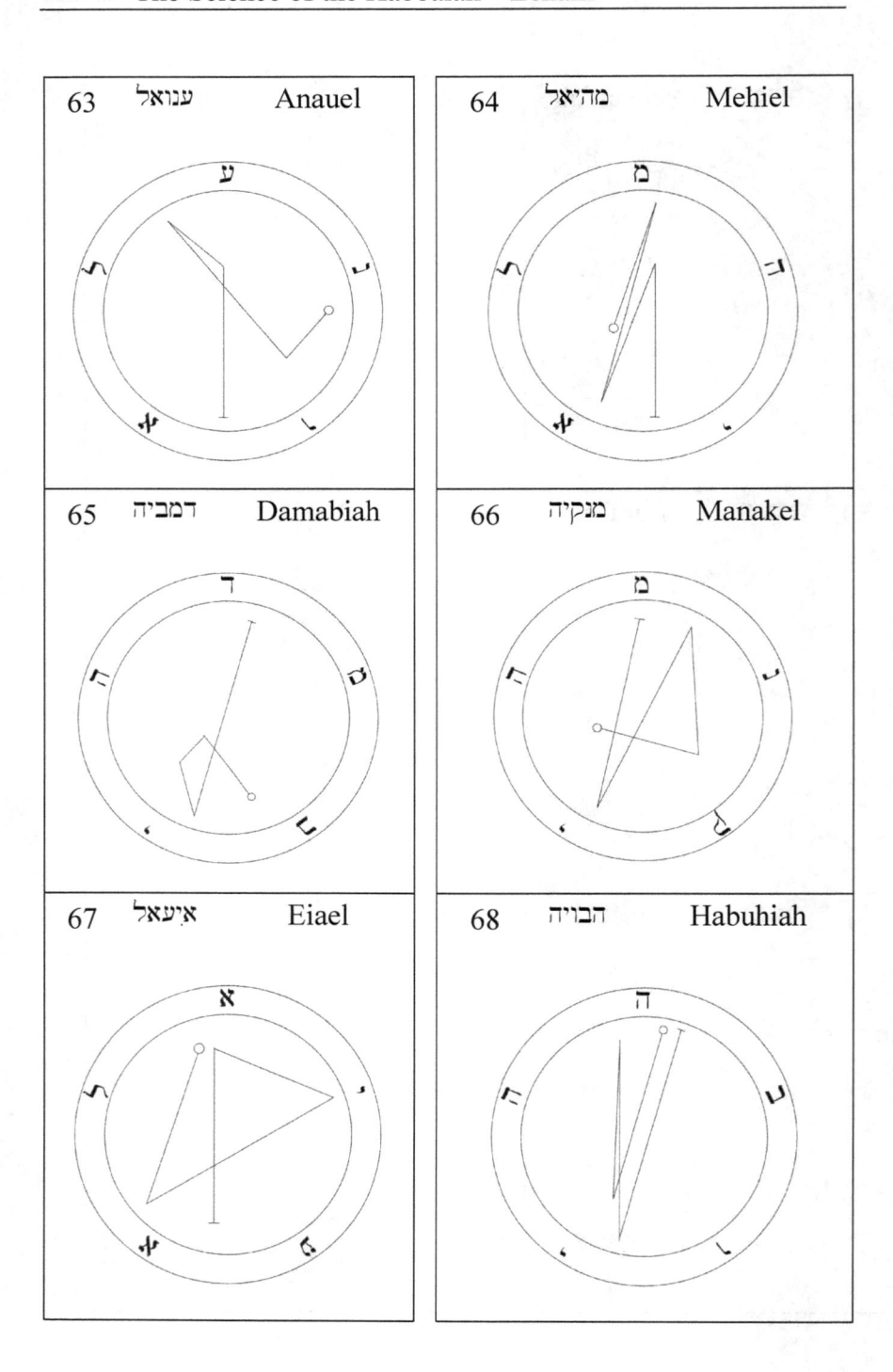

63 עֲנוּאֵל Anauel	64 מְהִיאֵל Mehiel
65 דַמְבִיָה Damabiah	66 מְנָקִיָה Manakel
67 אִיעָאֵל Eiael	68 הַבוּיָה Habuhiah

Appendix E: Rosicrucian Sigils 169

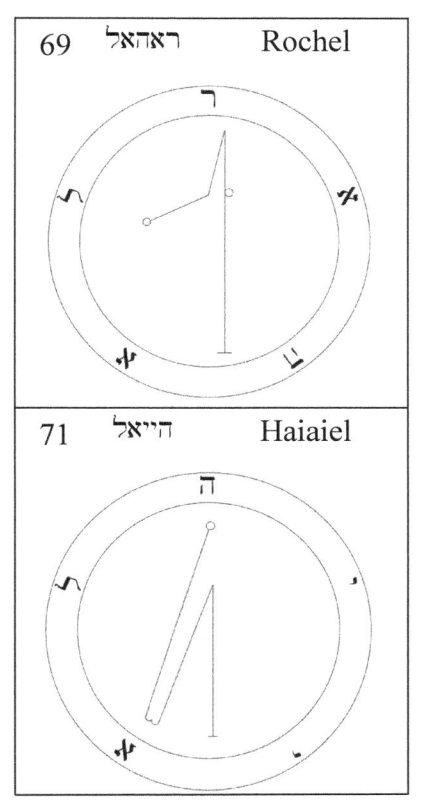

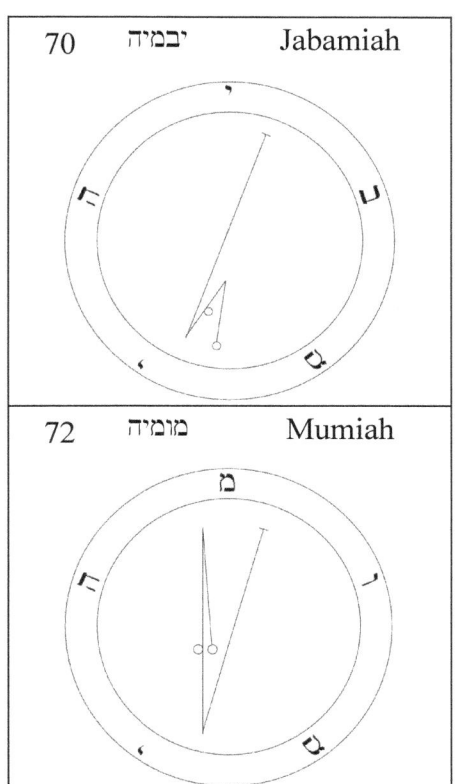

| 69 ראהאל Rochel | 70 יבמיה Jabamiah |
| 71 הייאל Haiaiel | 72 מומיה Mumiah |

Appendix F: Lévi's Seals of the 72 Geniuses

These seals are realized from the *Clefs Majeures et Clavicules de Salomon* by Eliphas Lévi (dated 1860), according to a publication of private papers by the Frères Chacornac in 1895, which was intended for the private use of his disciple Baron Spedalieri. Although the seals were intended to accompany Kabbalistic study, they are equally applicable to rituals based on the Shemhamephorash.

Unfortunately, Lévi's designs are far from complete. While the earlier ones are drawn in some detail, later ones are little more than sketches, and towards the end of the list we find little more than brief one-line descriptions. The translator has therefore attempted to render them in a more usable form, taking cues from earlier seals to recreate later ones.

There has been at least one attempt to recreate the seals prior to this effort. The *Kabalistic and Occult Tarot* of Eliphas Levi (pp. 282 – 290)[135] contains an interpretation of the Seals. However, given the absence of the Latin phrases which Lévi says should be written around the outside (instead the seals follow the Golden Dawn system of placing the Hebrew triads of the Geniuses around the circle), and other differences, the translator decided to create a new set himself.

In order to introduce some consistency, the Latin phrases associated with each Genius have been placed around the circle. Lévi did this for seals 1 through 4 (thought he unexpectedly used Hebrew instead of Latin for seal 4). However, the blank space between the two circles on the subsequent seals lead the translator to presume that this approach was to be followed throughout, and only time or effort prevented Lévi from continuing to write them all out. Secondly it is noticeable that the top seals have a form of Cross at the top of the circle, while the lower ones contain a Star of David. Unfortunately, the seals do not appear in numerical order on the pages of the booklet: the first page containing seals 1 and 4, the second 2 and 5, the third 3 and 6, and so forth. This means seals 1, 2 and 3 have Crosses, and 4, 5 and 6 have Stars of David. This alternation between 3 Crosses and 3 Stars of David has been maintained here. The reason for this becomes evident from the accompanying script: Lévi envisaged these not so much as 72 seals but rather 36 two-sided talismans. These talismans would have image 1 on one side and image 4 on the other. The second image 2 and 5; the third image 3 and 6, and so forth. Thus, each image would have the Star of David on one side and the Cross on the other. However, given the fact that he had a different purpose for these seals and images, they are listed here from 1 to 72 as an alternative to using the Arsenal or the Golden Dawn/Rosicrucian Sigils for creating talismans and invoking the Geniuses.

Finally, while software has been used for most of the design elements, the translator has attempted to introduce hand-drawn elements into each seal where

---

[135] *The Kabalistic and Occult Tarot of Eliphas Levi – A Study Guide*, pub. 2013 by Daath Gnostic Publishing (available at lulu.com) – PV.

sensible. This is to fulfill two requirements: firstly, that perfectly rendered seals can sometimes appear mechanistic and human flaws should be introduced to avoid this; and secondly, to fulfill the old injunction that all magical talismans should contain a human element in their design.

While this feature isn't central to using the seals for the Geniuses, the attentive reader will no doubt detect elements of the Tarot in the seals, which isn't surprising given Lévi's pioneering work on relating the Paths and Sephiroth of the Tree of Life to the Tarot deck. As a clear example, one can see the suit of Cups developed from 22. Ieiaiel onwards. The other suits may be found in a similar manner. In a few instances apparent errors have been corrected. For example, following the sequence of batons, 18. Caliel should contain 9 batons or wands, but only has 8. Another cross baton has been added to following the previous designs to bring the number to 9. However, this isn' the focus of this book, and the translator recommends the seals be used in the order proposed by Lenain.

Similarly, it is evident that these are shorthand notes to his student, implying a summary of things discussed face to face. This can also be seen in such examples as 34. Lehaiah, where the image says '7 Cups'. This is evidently shorthand for drawing out seven individual cups, rather than writing '7 Cups' on the seal!

Some instructions are difficult to read, such as 22. Ieiaiel, where the second word at the bottom looks like 'IARII.IS'. Despite a significant level of research, no obvious solution could be found for what this word should be. Some Hebrew letters are misspelled or reversed. Seal 36. Menadel should have 9 cups but only 6 are present, requiring 3 to be added. Other corrections too numerous to mention have been made to ensure consistency in the progression and correct use of Hebrew letters.

One final point should be made. Firstly, the last several cards are not drawn out, and the descriptions become increasingly vague, requiring the translator to make educated guesses. To give a few examples, seal 64. Mehiel calls for the 'occult sign of the Masonry of Rose-Croix to be engraved'. Since Lévi is quite insistent about following the Kabbalistic approach of using letters and numbers rather than images. In his instructions of the use of the keys he says: "the Hebrews has a horror of using figures in sacred images, and it's for that reason that the figures of the Zohar are almost always drawn solely with letters." Therefore, in this instance the familiar image of the pelican or eagle had to be avoided, and the symbolism of the Most Wise Master's jewel used instead. In a similar manner, 65. Damabiah refers to the Riddle of the Sphynx, which Œdipus solved as being man. Rather than present three images of man in youth, maturity and old age, the Hebrew word 'Adam' has been used instead, following Lévi's comment about the Zohar. The reason why 70. Jabamiah is surrounded by a glory is in order to distinguish it from 71. Haiaiel, which we are told in Lévi's instructions "should be written alone in the center of a talisman of pure gold alone with the particular signs of the Operator's desire." Finally, we are told concerning 72. Mumiah, that "this very occult talisman is proper to control the

Appendix F: Lévi's Seals of the 72 Geniuses   173

power against the terror of dying." This is interpreted to refer to the Seal of Solomon, a symbol often used by Lévi to denote the most profound truth – as in his image of the Great Seal of Solomon, for example. Given that his notes are titled 'Major Keys and Clavicles of Solomon', what could be more fitting for the ultimate seal? 66. Manakel is veiled, suggesting the Grail – a hidden cup ('He who possesses this talisman must hide it carefully from the profane')?

No doubt many will take issue with one or many of the recreations. Since, to my knowledge, nobody has previously attempted to recreate them before, I can only offer this as a first attempt.

Piers A. Vaughan

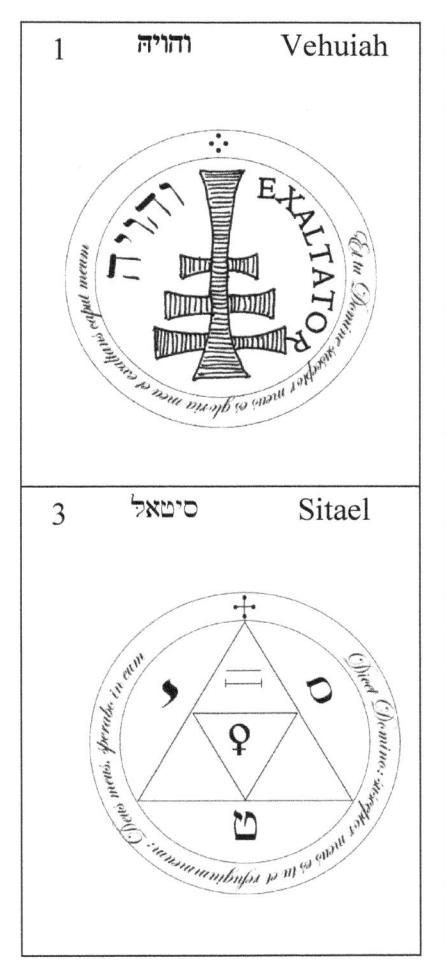

1	והויה	Vehuiah	2	יליאל	Jeliel
3	סיטאל	Sitael	4	עלמיה	Elemiah

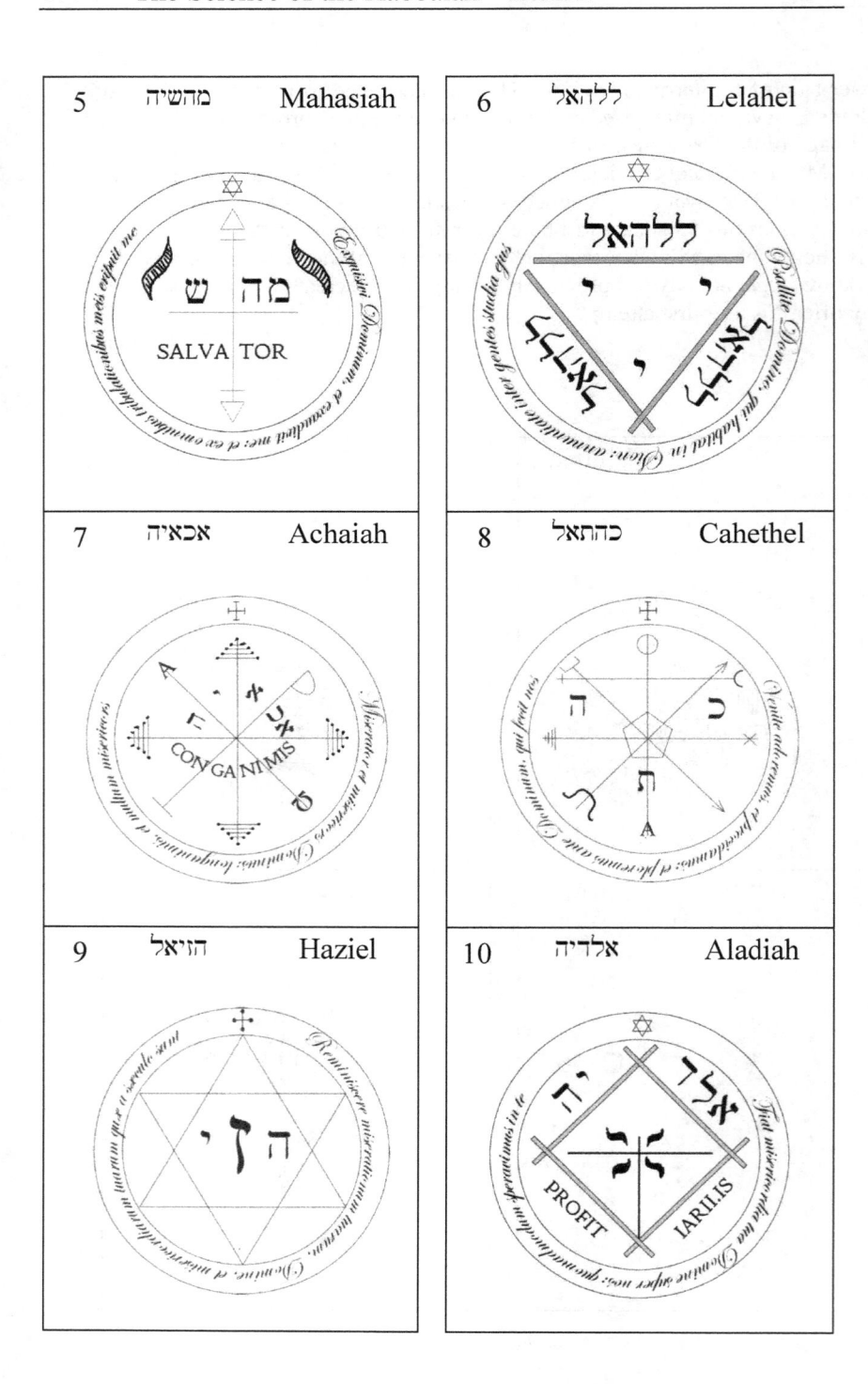

5	מהשיה	Mahasiah	6	ללהאל	Lelahel
7	אכאיה	Achaiah	8	כהתאל	Cahethel
9	הזיאל	Haziel	10	אלדיה	Aladiah

Appendix F: Lévi's Seals of the 72 Geniuses

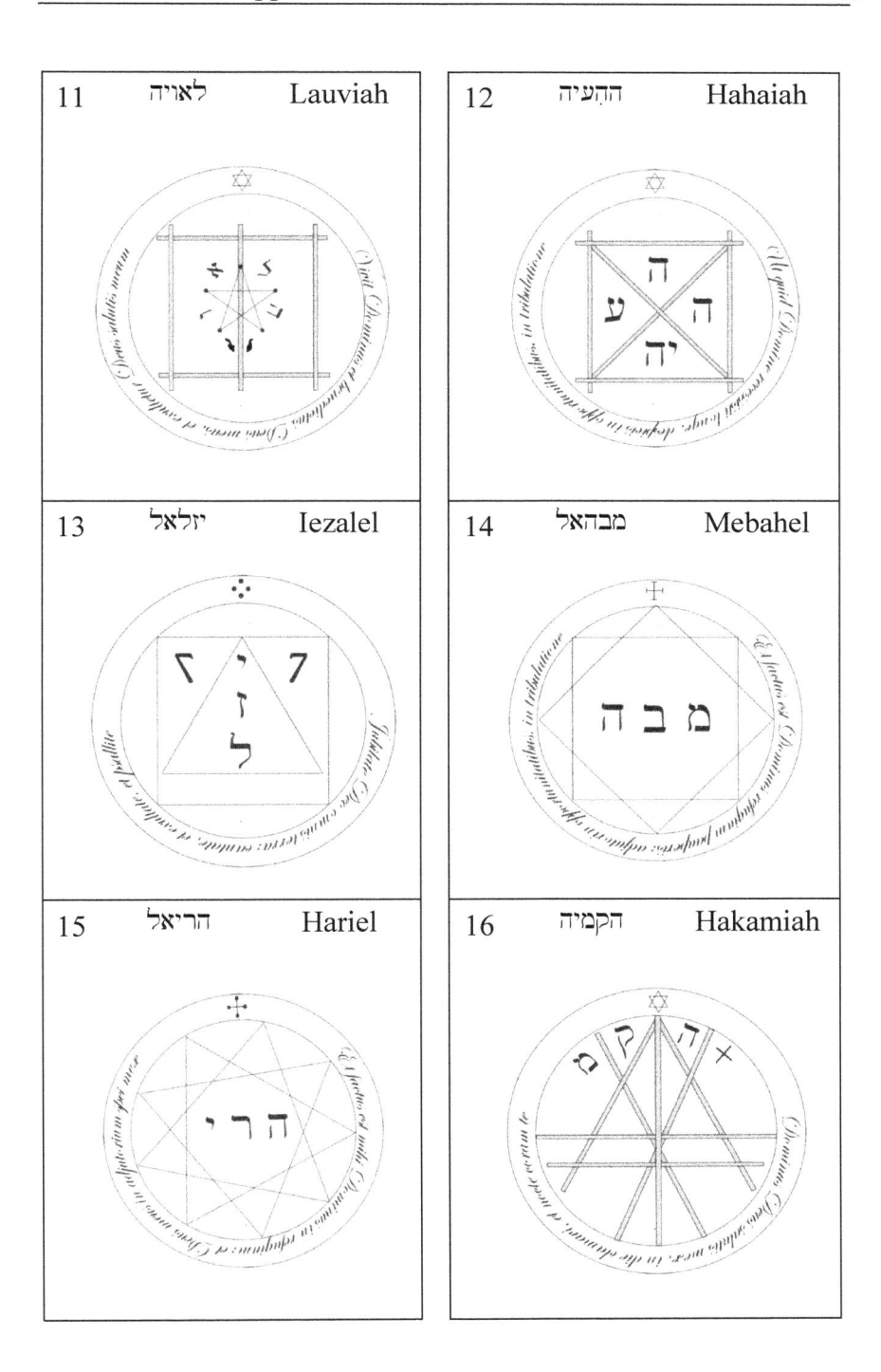

11	לאויה	Lauviah	12	הההעיה	Hahaiah
13	יזלאל	Iezalel	14	מבהאל	Mebahel
15	הריאל	Hariel	16	הקמיה	Hakamiah

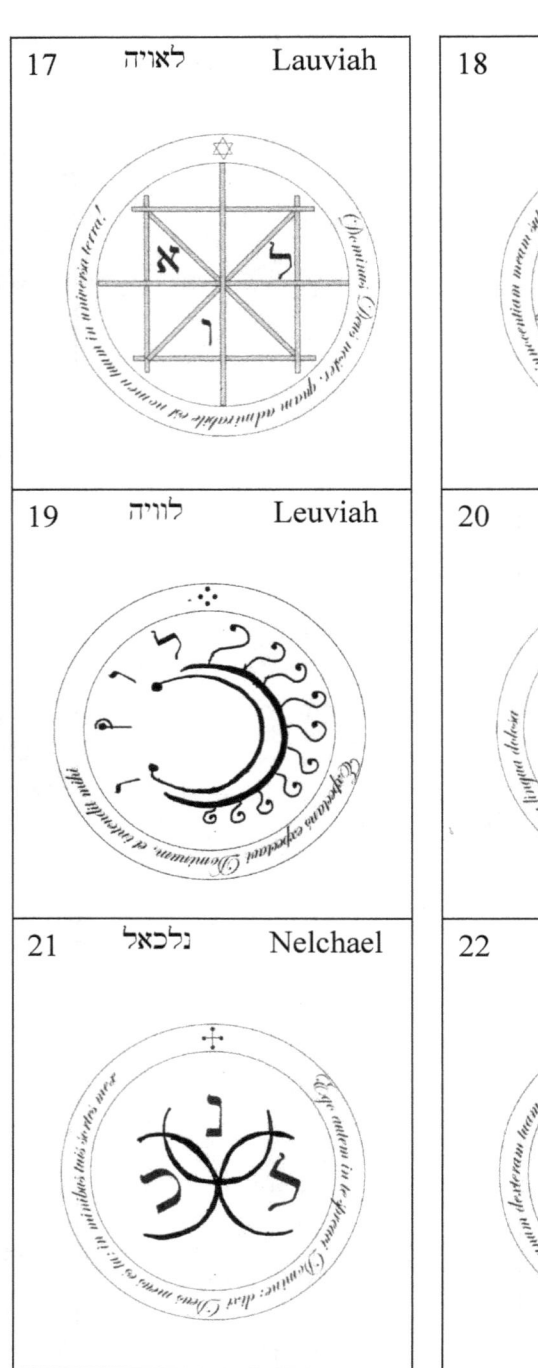

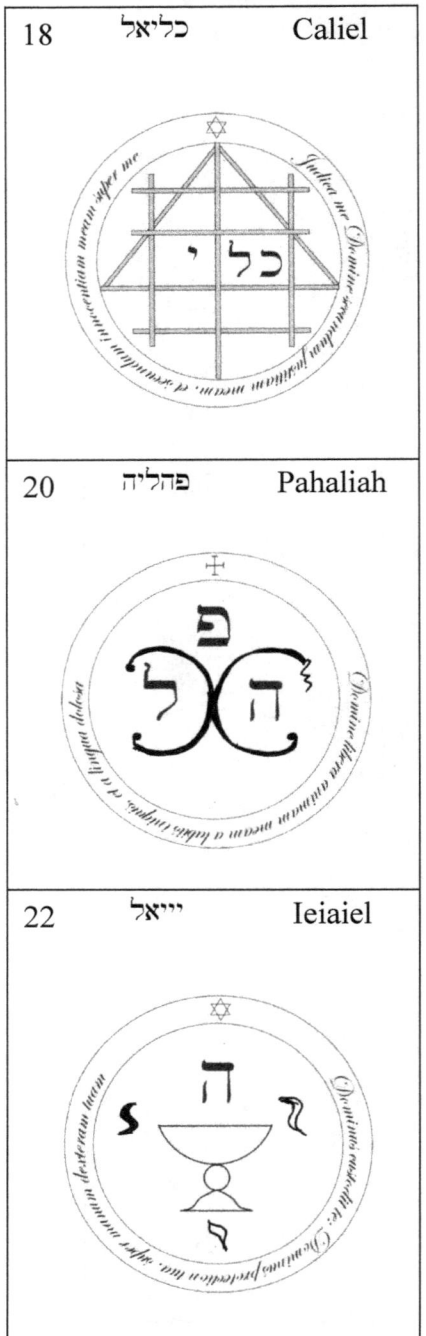

17	לאויה	Lauviah
18	כליאל	Caliel
19	לוויה	Leuviah
20	פהליה	Pahaliah
21	נלכאל	Nelchael
22	ייאל	Ieiaiel

Appendix F: Lévi's Seals of the 72 Geniuses 177

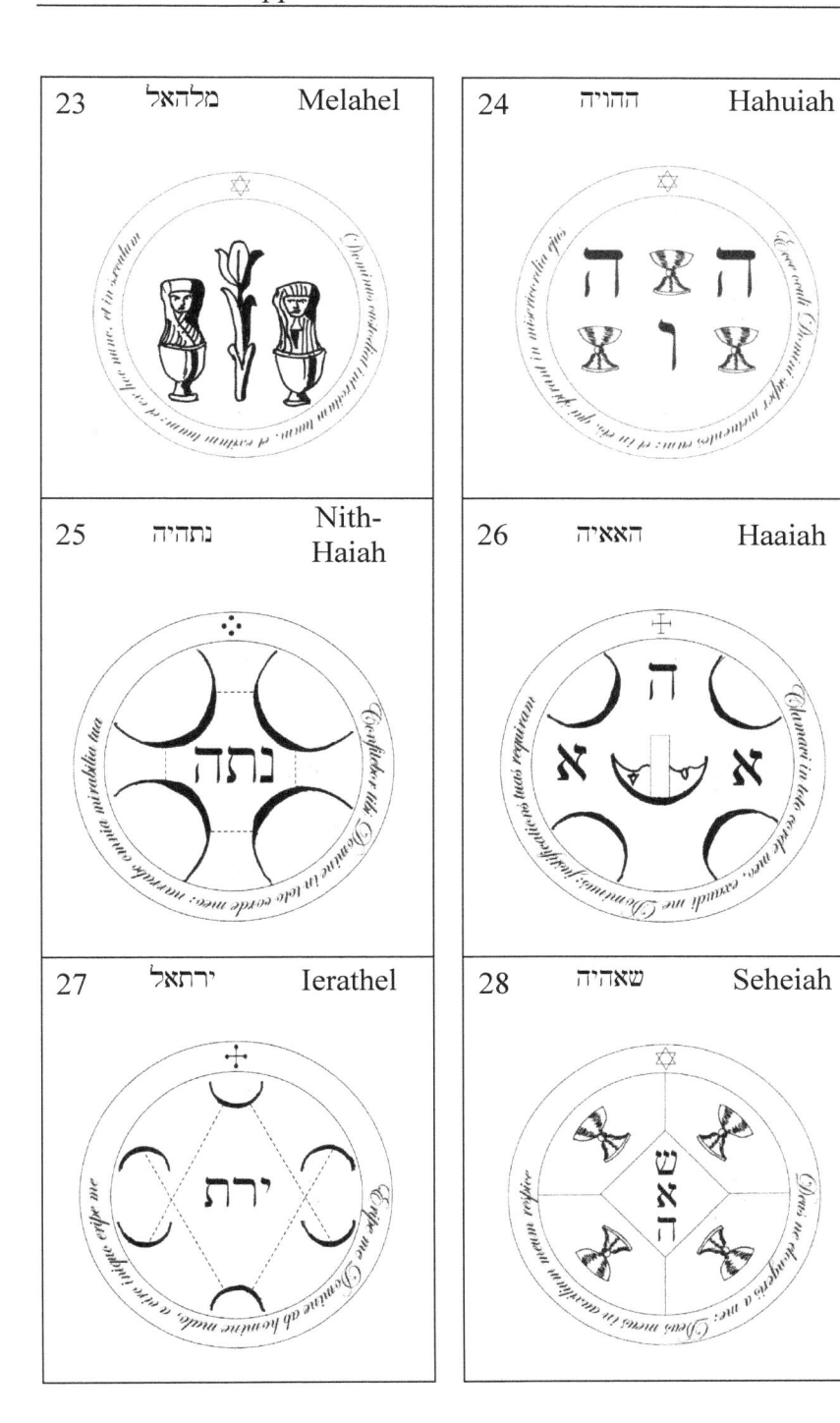

23	מלהאל	Melahel	24	ההויה	Hahuiah
25	נתהיה	Nith-Haiah	26	האאיה	Haaiah
27	ירתאל	Ierathel	28	שאהיה	Seheiah

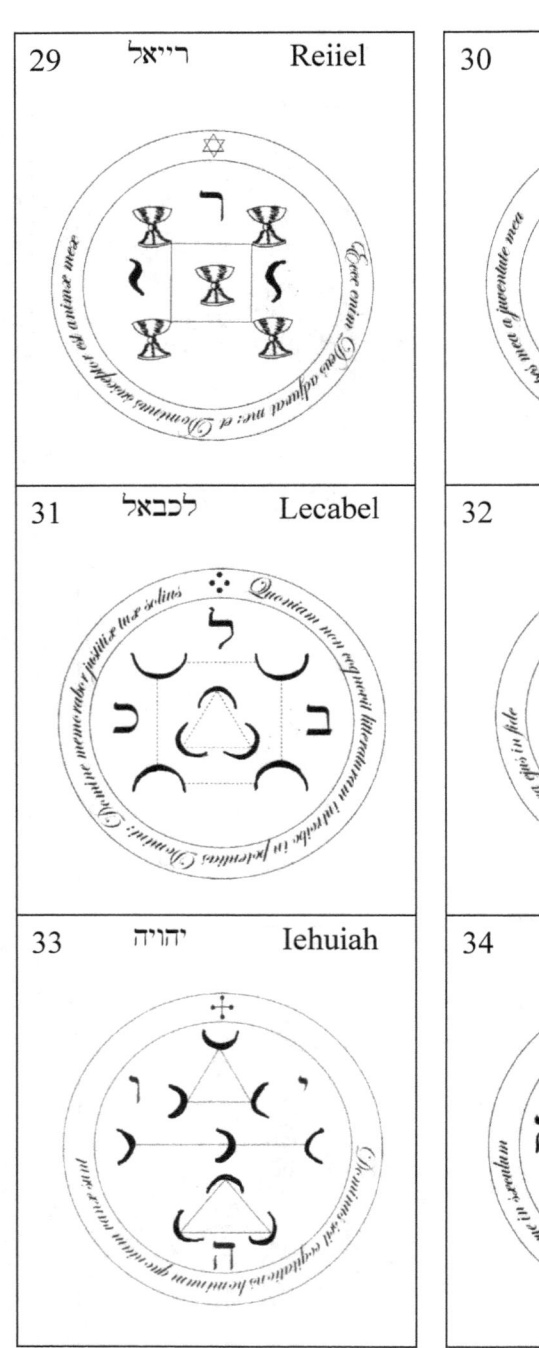

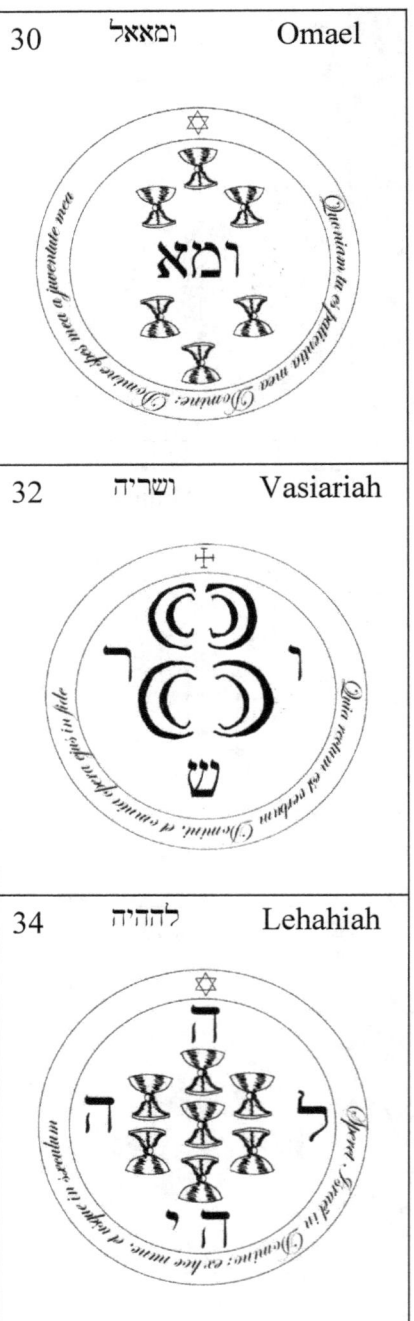

29	רייאל	Reiiel	30	ומאאל	Omael
31	לכבאל	Lecabel	32	ושריה	Vasiariah
33	יהויה	Iehuiah	34	לההיה	Lehahiah

Appendix F: Lévi's Seals of the 72 Geniuses

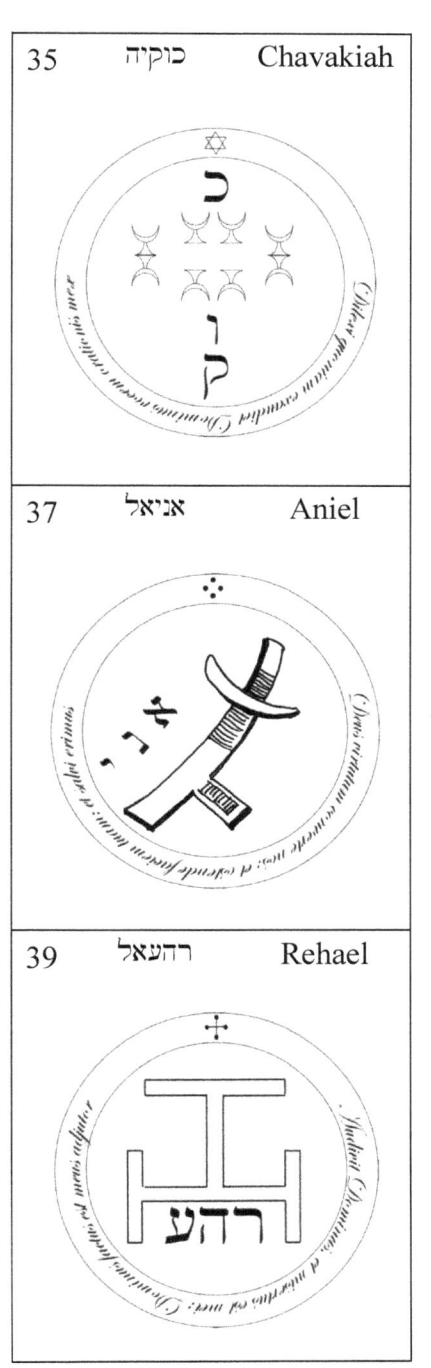

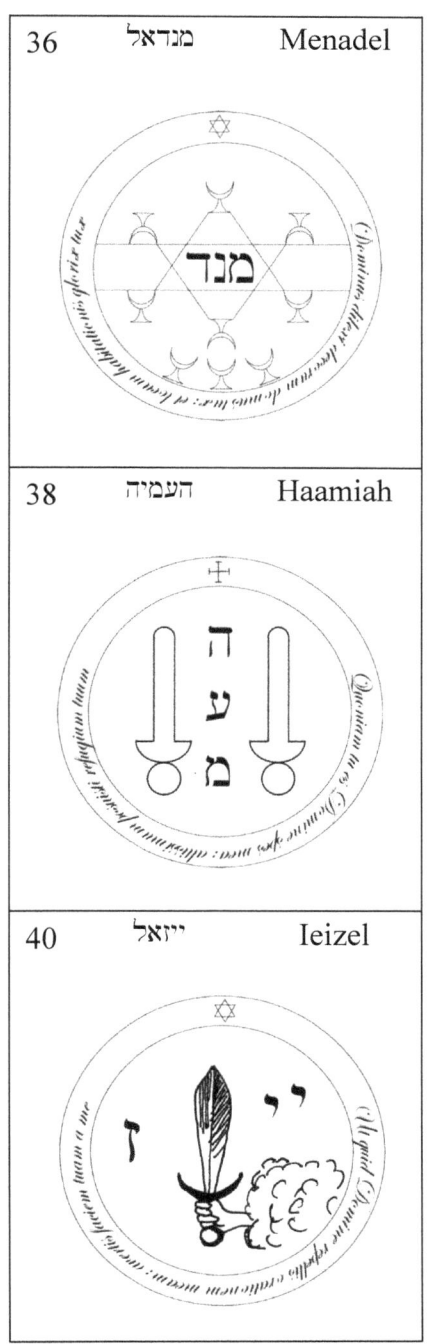

35	חוקיה	Chavakiah	36	מנדאל	Menadel
37	אניאל	Aniel	38	העמיה	Haamiah
39	רהעאל	Rehael	40	ייזאל	Ieizel

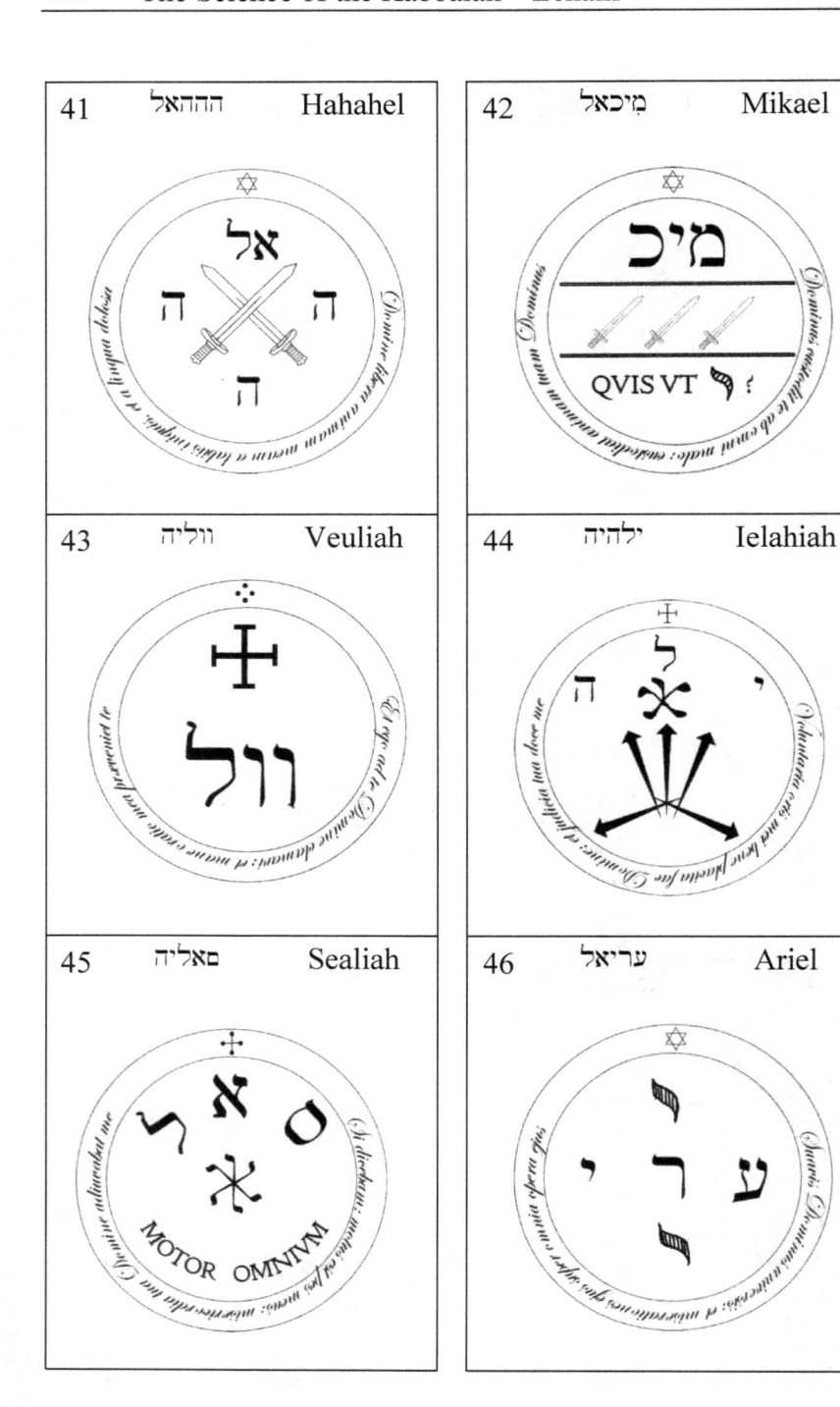

41 Hahahel הההאל	42 Mikael מִיכאל
43 Veuliah וליה	44 Ielahiah ילהיה
45 Sealiah סאליה	46 Ariel עריאל

Appendix F: Lévi's Seals of the 72 Geniuses

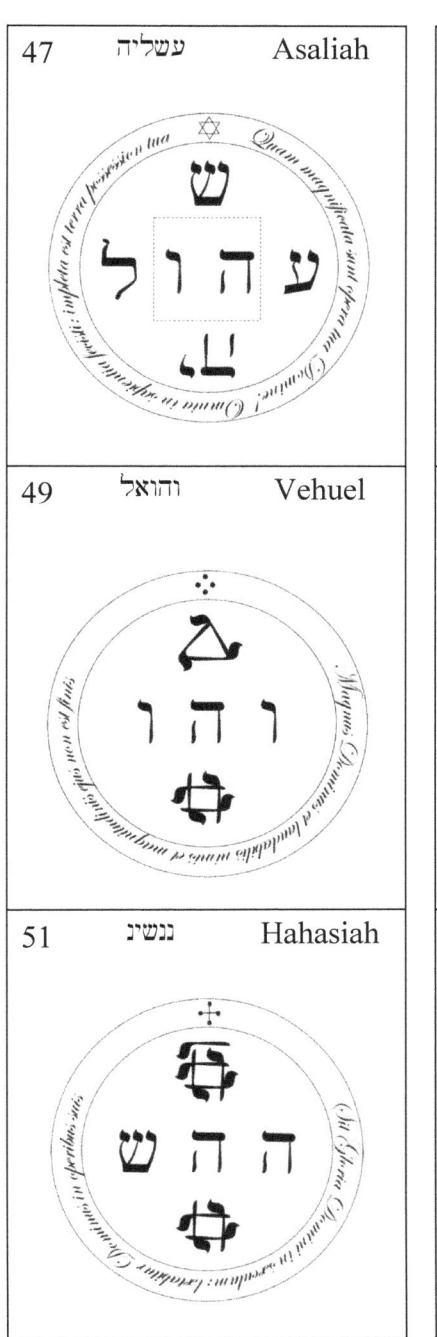

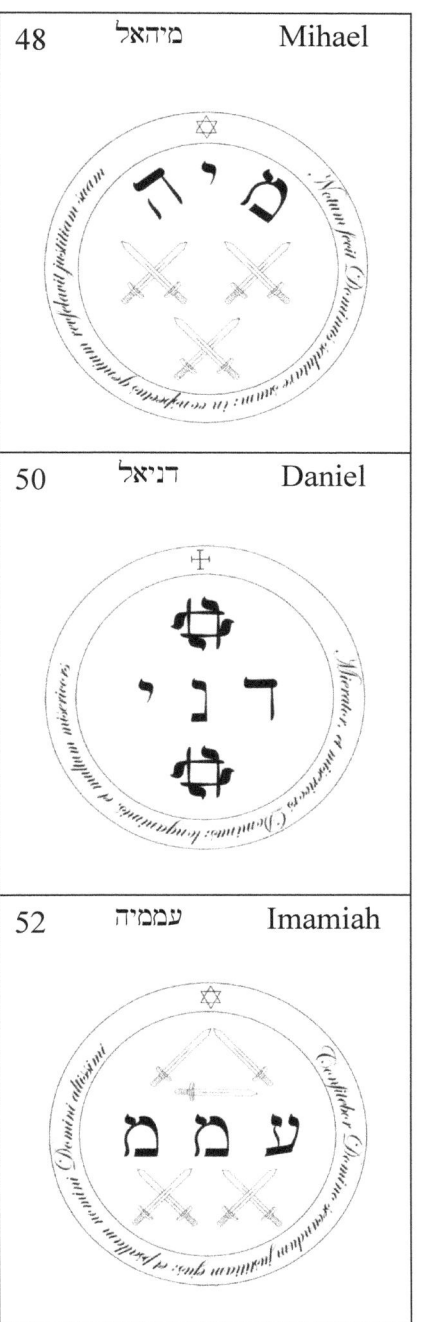

47	עשליה	Asaliah	48	מיהאל	Mihael
49	והואל	Vehuel	50	דניאל	Daniel
51	ננשין	Hahasiah	52	עממיה	Imamiah

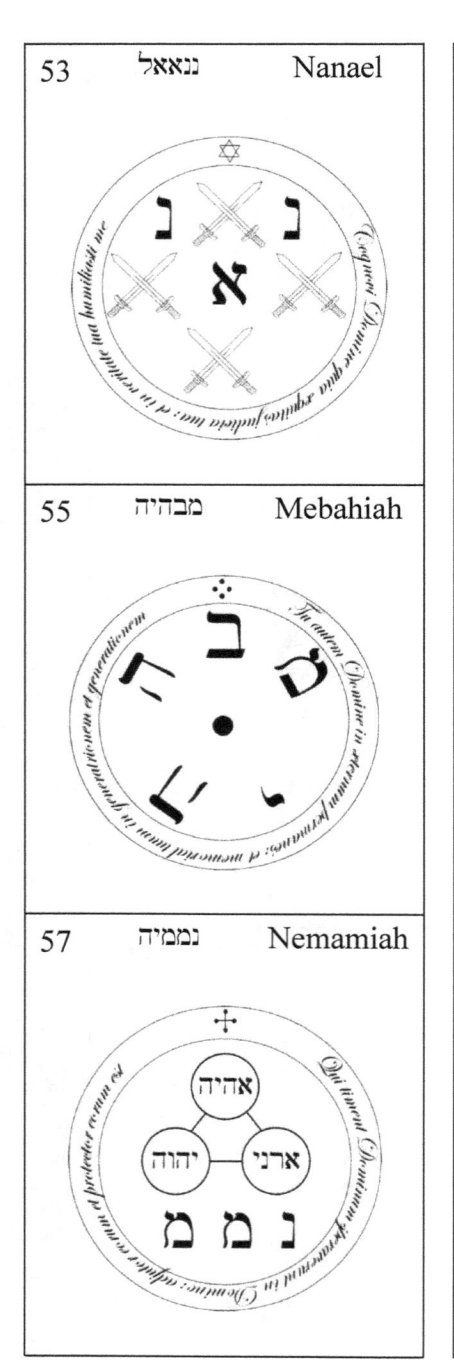

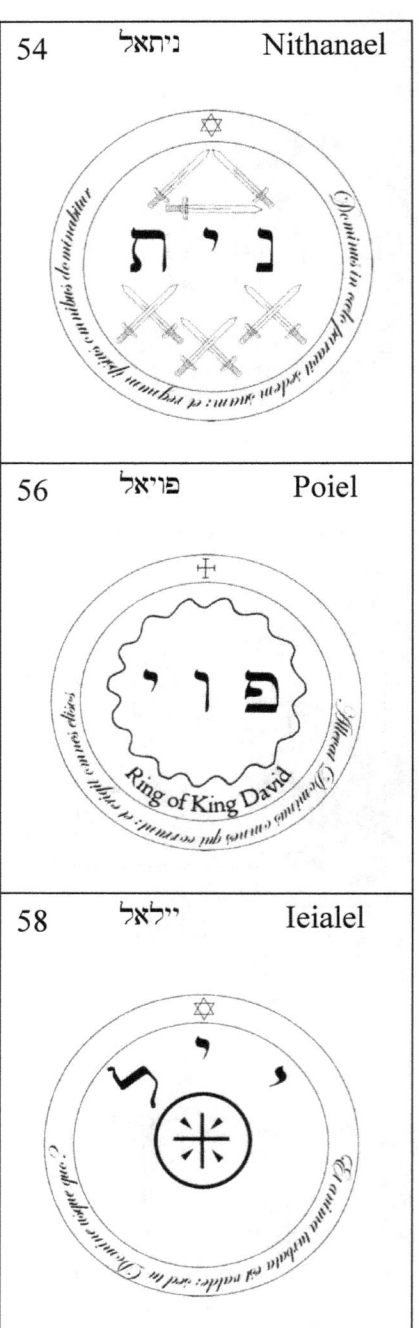

53	ננאל	Nanael	54	ניתאל	Nithanael
55	מבהיה	Mebahiah	56	פויאל	Poiel
57	נממיה	Nemamiah	58	ייאלל	Ieialel

Appendix F: Lévi's Seals of the 72 Geniuses

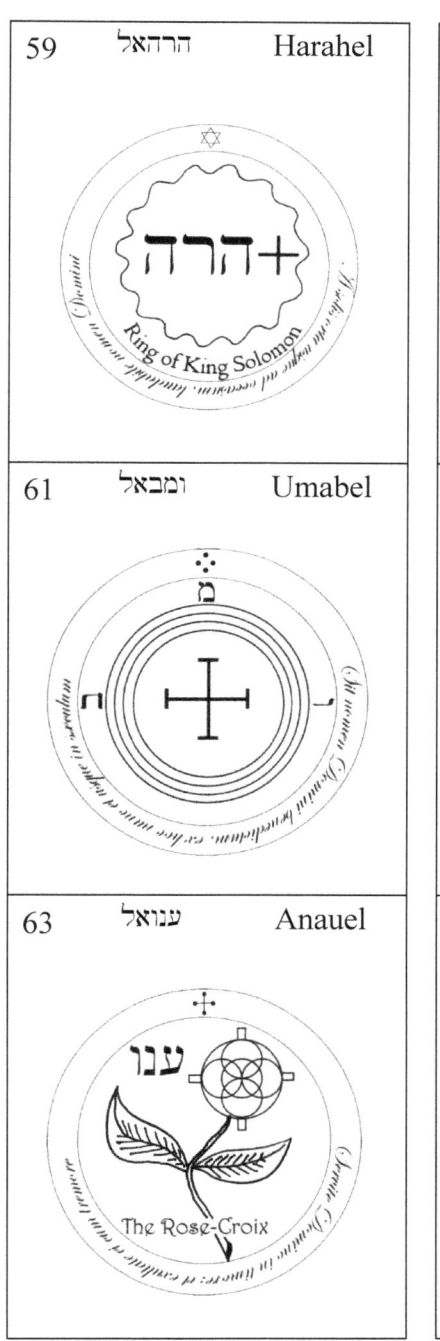

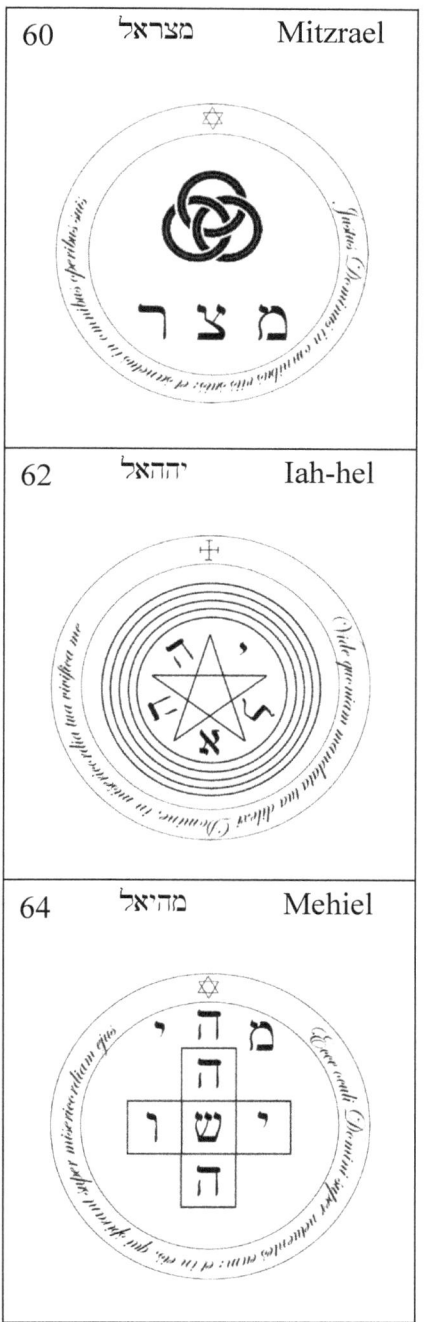

59	הרהאל	Harahel	60	מצראל	Mitzrael
61	ומבאל	Umabel	62	יההאל	Iah-hel
63	ענואל	Anauel	64	מהיאל	Mehiel

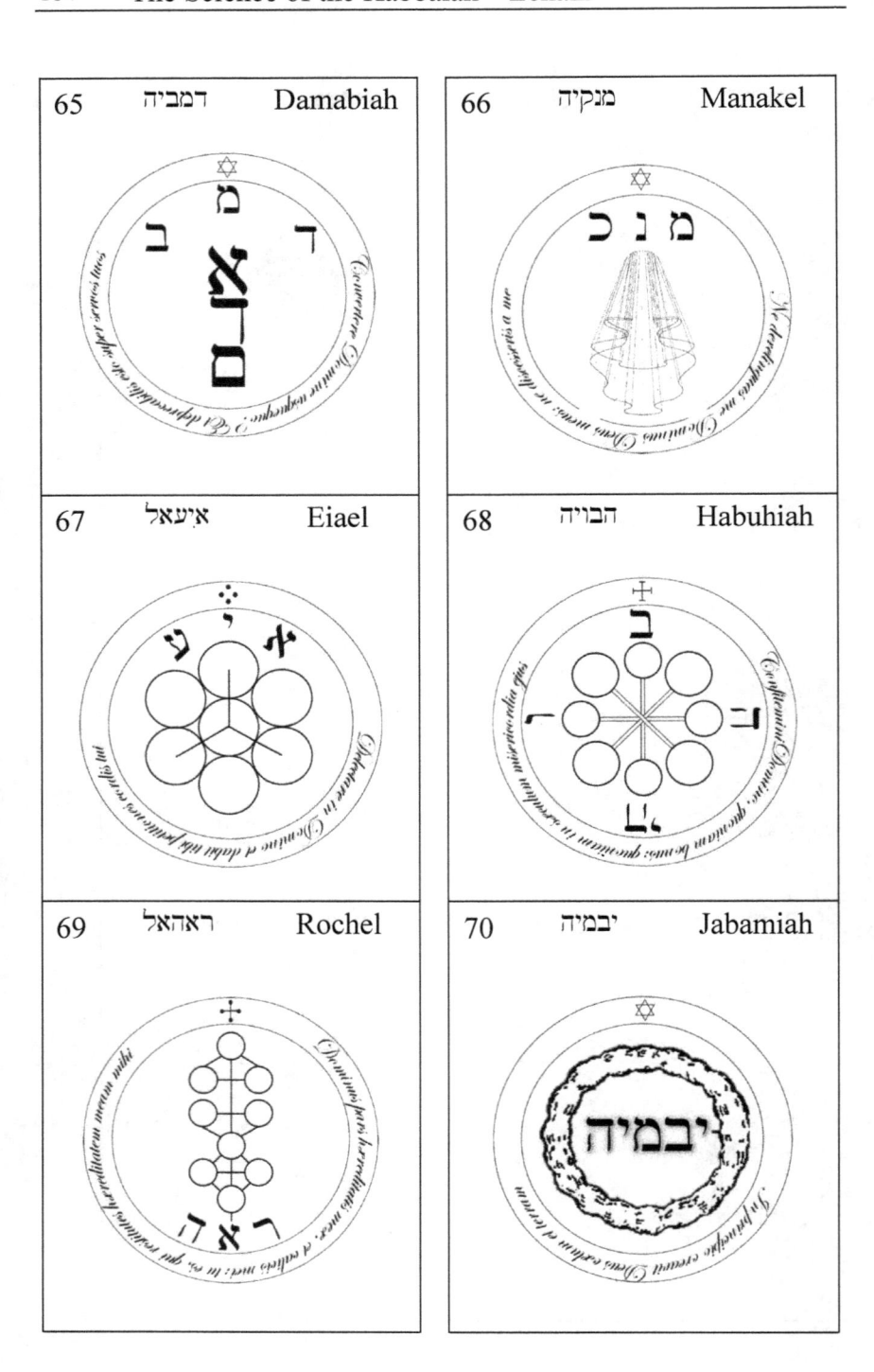

65	דמביה Damabiah	66	מנקיה Manakel
67	איעאל Eiael	68	הבויה Habuhiah
69	ראהאל Rochel	70	יבמיה Jabamiah

| 71 Haiaiel היאל | 72 Mumiah מומיה |

Appendix G: Lévi's Notes on the Composition and Use of the Clavicles[136]

These Clavicles, recreated in their original purity and designed for the first time by me, Eliphas Lévi, in 1860, are executed in their purity and without any mixing with Samaritan or Egyptian images, solely with the aid of figures, hieroglyphic signs and numbers.

The Hebrews had a horor of using figures in sacred images, and it's for that reason that the figures of the Zohar are almost all drawn solely with letters.

The complement of this book is the Italian game of Tarot, which Solomon's talismans explain and summarize.

One should note that the Tens found in the Tarot don't appear in the talismans; this is because the number 'ten', being the synthesis of unity, is virtually contained in the unity of each number.

The images of the talismans can be engraved on the seven metals or drawn on virgin parchment; then consecrated and magnetized with a clear intention. They can be used as focuses of magnetic light. They are censed with ritual incense and kept in silk or in glass boxes so that they don't lose their powers.

They should neither be lent not given away, unless they are created with the intention of being given to another person and created in their presence.

They are used to repel illusions and prestiges. Erring spirit tremble at their approach, because they are fixed symbols, and letters of the Word which is entire in itself and which victorious commands all spirits.

But to use these keys properly, one must maintain great lucidity of mind and great purity of heart; otherwise these figures will become instruments of evil to which the imprudent or sinful Operator will become the first victim.

---

[136] Taken from the *Clefs Majeures et Clavicules de Salomon* by Eliphas Lévi, Paris, 1860.